Form and Fabric in Landscape Architecture

Form and Fabric in Landscape Architecture provides an original, visual approach to the study of landscape architecture by creating a spatial morphology based on use and experience of landscapes. It explores aesthetic, spatial and experiential concepts by providing a structure through which landscapes can be understood and conceived in design. 'Fabric' is the integrated structure of whole landscapes, while 'form' refers to the components that make up this fabric. Together form and fabric create a morphology of landscape useful for the development of visual–spatial design thinking and awareness.

This book is intended as both an introduction to the discipline for students of landscape architecture, architecture and planning, and a source of continuing interest for more experienced environmental designers.

Catherine Dee is Senior Lecturer in Landscape Design, Department of Landscape, University of Sheffield, UK.

Form and Fabric in Landscape Architecture

A visual introduction

Catherine Dee

Routledge
Taylor & Francis Group

LONDON AND NEW YORK

For John and Will

First published 2001 by Spon Press

This edition published 2013 by Routledge

2 Park Square, Milton Park, Abingdon, Oxon OX14 4RN

711 Third Avenue, New York, NY 10017

*Routledge is an imprint of the Taylor & Francis Group,
an informa business*

Typeset in Gill Sans by Bookcraft Ltd, Stroud, Gloucestershire

British Library Cataloguing in Publication Data
A catalogue record for this book is available from the British Library

Library of Congress Cataloging in Publication Data
Dee, Catherine, 1958–
    Form and fabric in landscape architecture: a visual introduction/
    Catherine Dee
        p. cm.
    Includes bibliographical references (p.)
    1 Landscape architecture 2 Landscape design I Title
SB472.D44 2001
712–dc21   2001020788

ISBN 0–415–24638–5 (pbk)
ISBN 0–415–24637–7 (hbk)

I would like to thank past and present students of the Department of
Landscape, University of Sheffield from whom I have learned ways of
understanding landscape architecture.

For their critical observations I thank Prue Chiles, Andy
Clayden, Ralph Johns, Anna Jorgensen, Ruth Lockley and Claire
Rishbeth.

Particular thanks go to past teachers and colleagues Anne Beer
and Owen Manning who inspired me to make this book and who
provided detailed critical advice and the seeds of ideas.

Contents

Contents

Contents

Introduction

About this book

Landscape architecture involves the spatial organisation of outdoor places to meet human needs and desires while protecting or enhancing natural environments and processes. Landscapes usually need to function in diverse ways for different people. The designer aims to create places that meet social, environmental, cultural, aesthetic and practical requirements.

This book is intended both as an introduction to the discipline of landscape architecture and also a source of continuing interest for more experienced environmental designers.

A morphological approach to design

While landscapes are living, dynamic, 'bio-cultural' systems, they can also be thought of as complex, spatial 'structures'. The aim of this book is to promote the development of a three-dimensional design sensibility by exploring and defining the physical form of landscape as 'material' for design. 'Fabric' refers to the integrated spatial structure of whole landscapes (as well as the context for design), while 'form' refers to the components or parts that make up this fabric. Together form and fabric create a morphology of landscape that is useful for visual–spatial design thinking and awareness.

The morphology is organised into seven parts. The first of these parts, landscape fabric, considers landscapes as integrated wholes and defines qualities considered desirable in design. The next five parts illustrate spaces, paths, edges, foci and thresholds. These five parts have been conceived by identifying forms in landscapes that are used and experienced by people in distinct ways and for particular purposes and therefore require specific consideration by designers. The final part, detail, refers to 'close up', sensory and tactile landscape components. Although divided into these sections, this is essentially a book about relationships, wholes and the integration of these parts.

An experiential approach to design

The book proposes an 'experiential' approach to design. This means that human experience of landscape helps to shape both the concepts in the book and an understanding of design. It also means that annotated images communicate not only landscape morphology but also the experience of this morphology. The intention is to

1

encourage designers to make connections between experience and design. The spatial and physical ideas in the book are based on my experience of teaching landscape architecture and my own experiences of landscape: moving through it, stopping, looking, feeling, touching, talking, eating, sheltering, remembering. They are also strongly informed by a wide range of design theorists and writers concerned with human experience and the use of places. The bibliography and further reading sections at the end of the book identify some primary influences.

A visual approach to design

Landscape architects learn to design primarily through visual–spatial information. This is therefore a visual manual. It explores conceptual and physical dimensions of landscapes and design through drawings. It does not describe or define a design process. Instead it provides an annotated visual narrative and structure through which landscapes can be interpreted, understood and conceived in design. The value of the drawings comes also from their ability to describe image making which is (still) useful in landscape architectural practice (in addition to other visual media, including digital images). Handwritten annotations add layers of meaning to the drawings, frequently articulating activities and feelings associated with the landscape forms illustrated. This is intended to reinforce the concept of experiential landscape architecture.

Landscape elements and the morphology

The landscape elements of 'landform' or 'topography', 'vegetation', 'water' and 'structures' are conceived and illustrated as being the primary physical material with which designers create landscape form and fabric. Each of the morphological sections incorporates examples of how these elements create landscape forms. While in design the subtle integration of topography, vegetation, water and structures is paramount, they have been artificially separated to enable exploration of their design potential.

Using this book

Primary uses

The book can be used in several different ways. Its main uses are:

- to provide a conceptual framework (the seven-part morphology) for understanding the experience, use and structure of landscapes for design
- as a reference book for design considerations relevant to the creation and integration of spaces, paths, edges, thresholds, foci and detail
- to provide examples and sources of inspiration for ways in which the elements of topography, vegetation, structures and water may be used in design.

The parts

The purpose, content and structure of the seven morphological parts are briefly summarised here. Each section in the book begins with an introduction and a series of definitions of the landscape form explored in that part.

Landscape fabric

This part of the book provides an overview of the broader landscape and landscape processes as a context for design. It defines and describes a range of qualities that are considered desirable in landscapes such as robustness, mystery and diversity. It then illustrates – through a range of different kinds of designed landscapes – the holistic integration of spaces, paths, edges, foci and thresholds and the integration of landform, vegetation, structures and water to make places.

Spaces

The section on spaces explores the enclosure and definition of distinct areas of land for human activities. Spaces are considered the primary means by which landscapes are organised, understood, used and experienced. Design considerations in the creation of spaces are described. This section then illustrates diverse examples of how the landscape elements may be used to create spaces in landscapes.

Paths

The paths section explores the design of linear places of movement in the landscape. The emphasis here is on pedestrian environments. Like spaces, paths are also considered primary design forms that influence the use and experience of landscapes. Design considerations for paths are defined, followed by a more detailed exploration of the design potential of landscape elements in the creation of paths.

Edges

This section explores transitional linear places where one space or landscape part becomes another. Often neglected in design, edges are considered primary structural components of landscapes because of their integrative and social functions. Design considerations are again identified, together with examples of the use of landscape elements in the design of edges.

Foci

'Foci' refers to differentiated, contrasting or isolated forms or places in the landscape that possess cultural, social, practical and orientation functions because of their visual distinction. Design functions and qualities of foci are considered and examples are given of the use of landscape elements as foci.

Thresholds

Thresholds are identified as distinct small spaces or forms in the landscape that, like edges, have transitional and integrative functions. Unlike edges, thresholds have 'focused' rather than linear spatial form and support distinct and wide-ranging social and cultural uses and experiences. Design considerations related to these uses are identified, followed by examples of thresholds created by landscape elements.

Detail

Detail explores the 'close-up' 'tactile' or 'immediate' scale of landscape, its experience and the design considerations for this scale. The section briefly explores the sensory potential of earth and rock, vegetation, structures and water as design elements.

The drawings and their interpretation

Annotated drawings have equal status with the text throughout the book and should not be considered purely as 'supporting' illustrations. The drawings illustrate actual and imaginary places, together with illustrations of the work of artists. Some have been drawn to illustrate an idea formed during the process of writing, while at other times the need to write has emerged from the making of drawings. The important factor in interpreting the drawings is that they are intended to be used in diverse ways and should enable the designer to 'learn what they wish' from the images. The drawings mainly (although not exclusively) illustrate 'western', temperate and urban landscapes. They show places of personal value and significance, but the reader is invited to question assumptions and values that are inevitably implicit in the imagery and to develop their own understandings.

Book structure

The book structure can be used in a linear or non-linear way. It can be 'dipped into' to refer to specific aspects, or studied in its entirety as a conceptual framework.

1 Landscape fabric

'Landscape fabric' has been chosen as a term to represent whole and integrated landscapes at various scales. 'Fabric' is used because it suggests interconnected wholes made of parts which are created through process. It also suggests cohesion and robustness, which are considered to be positive qualities of designed landscapes.

The 'fabric' section of this book has two main purposes. First, it aims to introduce some of the broader physical, environmental and social contexts in which the design of places by professional landscape architects takes place.

In the second part, the fabric of individual places at 'design scales' is explored. The purpose is to identify qualities considered desirable in designed places and also to illustrate how spaces, paths, edges, foci and thresholds make up the 'fabric' of landscapes. In addition, the illustration of 'whole' places aims to reinforce the concept that integration of landform, vegetation, structures and water is paramount in design.

Contexts for the
design of landscapes

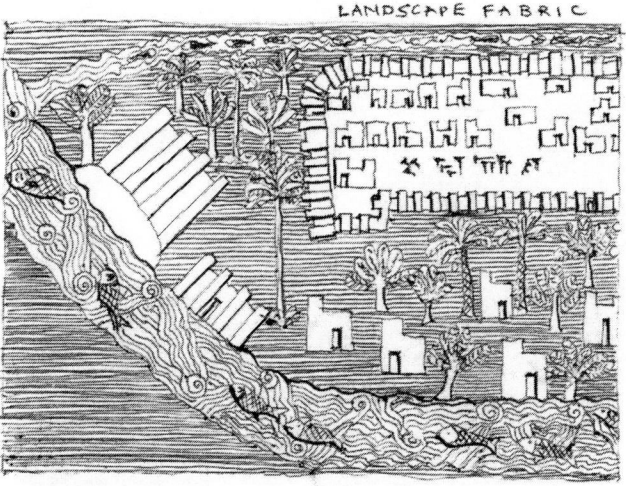

LANDSCAPE FABRIC

DRAWING OF A BAS-RELIEF OF AN ANCIENT MESOPOTAMIAN
SETTLEMENT
IMAGE SHOWS INTERACTION OF NATURAL LANDSCAPE,
BUILDINGS/SETTLEMENT AND AGRICULTURE; CULTURE
AND NATURE.

The following pages summarise some important
contexts for landscape architecture. These include
physical contexts such as the natural environmental
context for design, as well as social and cultural contexts.

ABSTRACT DRAWING FROM REMOTELY SENSED PHOTOGRAPH OF WEATHER SYSTEM OVER GREENLAND

Global landscape

The design of local landscapes should always be considered in the context of the global environment. This is of particular importance in relation to sustainability and the need to protect natural places, systems and resources. Landscapes are part of natural systems which support life. Design can contribute to or detract from these systems.

Choices in design affect the global landscape. For example, energy can be conserved by improving microclimates through design or by using local building materials to avoid transportation. Biodiversity can be increased or reduced.

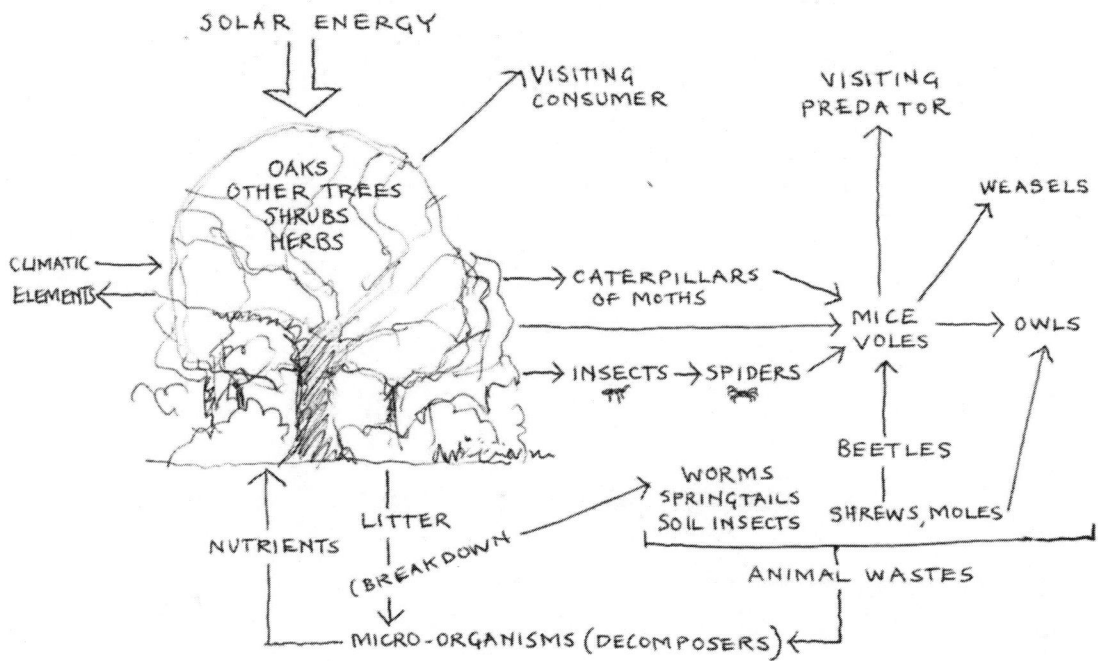

FOOD WEB OF AN ENGLISH OAKWOOD

Landscape processes and systems

It is essential for designers to have an understanding of the natural processes that make and influence the landscape. It is also important to understand how people have changed and continue to alter landscapes through agriculture, industry and settlement. Landscape architecture modifies or harnesses natural processes (for example, the growth of plants, rainfall) for human purposes through construction and management. The aims of design are often to conserve, protect or enhance natural environments or to regenerate natural systems in places which have been contaminated or laid waste. The primary natural systems and elements that form the context for, and may be altered in, landscape design are briefly:

- local climate
- local hydrology
- local geology and geomorphology
- local soils
- local vegetation
- local air
- local fauna
- local ecosystems (the interaction of all of the above).

All of these aspects need to be surveyed and evaluated before landscapes can be changed in design. The 'natural' elements of water, topography and vegetation are the 'material' of design along with processed substances.

SUSTAINABLE APPROACHES TO DESIGN COULD TRANSFORM CITIES FOR PEOPLE AND WILDLIFE

DRAWING WITH ADDED VEGETATION AFTER DAUMIER'S "THE LAUNDRESS"

Landscapes and people

Landscapes are for people. The design of landscape takes place in the context of people's cultural, social, political, economic and environmental needs. Landscape design is considered to be a holistic activity which attempts to integrate concerns for all of these human aspects. This book seeks to link morphology of landscape to human experience and use, but it does this within particular social, cultural and environmental contexts. The physical and social contexts illustrated are primarily relatively affluent (in global terms), northern, temperate urban landscapes. Some ideas, principles and assertions have broader relevance to the design of landscapes beyond this context. Others are specific to this context.

A SWALEDALE LANDSCAPE, YORKSHIRE UK.
LANDSCAPE REGION FORMED BY AGRICULTURE, SETTLEMENT, TOPOGRAPHY, VEGETATION
MANAGEMENT

Regional landscapes

Natural and semi-natural systems, agriculture, settlement, transport, climate and culture affect the form and fabric of regional landscapes. Landscape and environmental planning of regions is beyond the scope of this book but designed landscapes should always be considered in a regional context. Many regions have positive economic, social, cultural and environmental functions into which

new designed landscape should 'fit' or enhance and contribute to. Other regional landscapes may be degraded economically, socially, environmentally or aesthetically. In these contexts, landscape design contributes to and is carried out within the context of a broader economic, social and environmental strategy for a region's 'regeneration'.

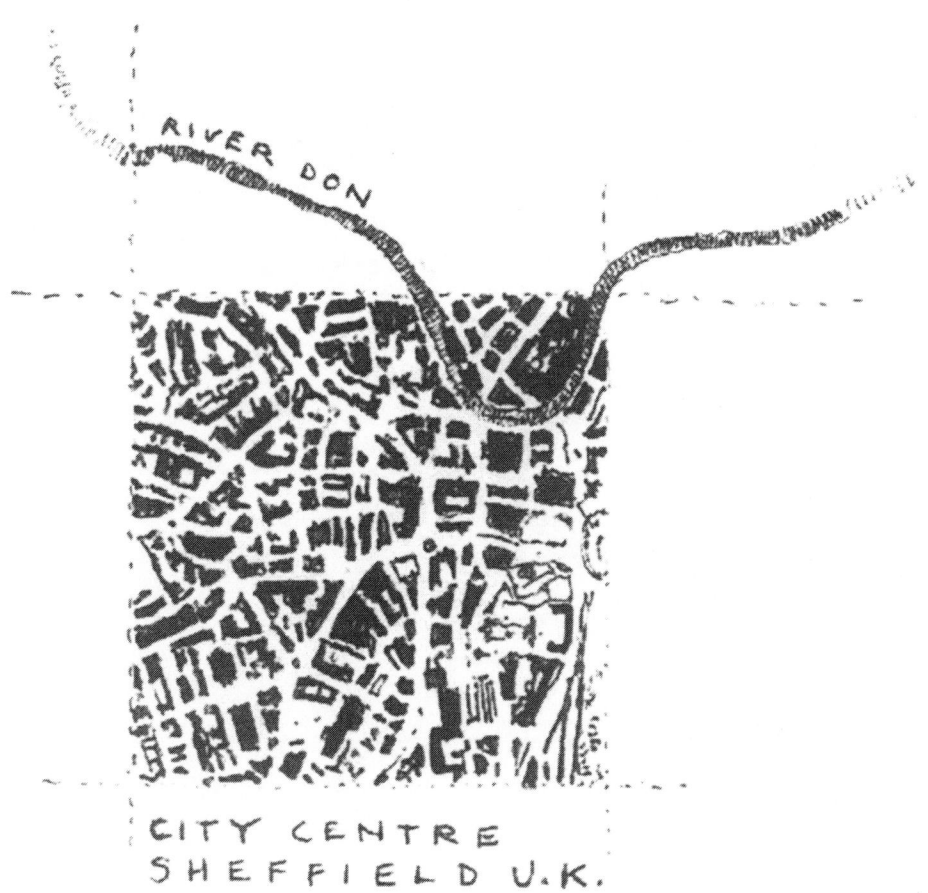

RIVER DON

CITY CENTRE
SHEFFIELD U.K.

Towns and cities

Cities and towns continue to be dominant 'landscapes' for human dwelling. Cities in particular can take many different forms and are dynamic 'systems' rather than fixed structures. Most landscape design takes place within cities and towns and potentially contributes to their success as liveable places by influencing forms and functions. The landscapes considered and illustrated in this book are primarily urban landscapes.

City districts

Cities often have distinct (though changing) districts influenced by history, landuses communications and architecture as well as climate, topography, water and vegetation. Landscape design takes place within these district settings as well as the city-wide context.

11

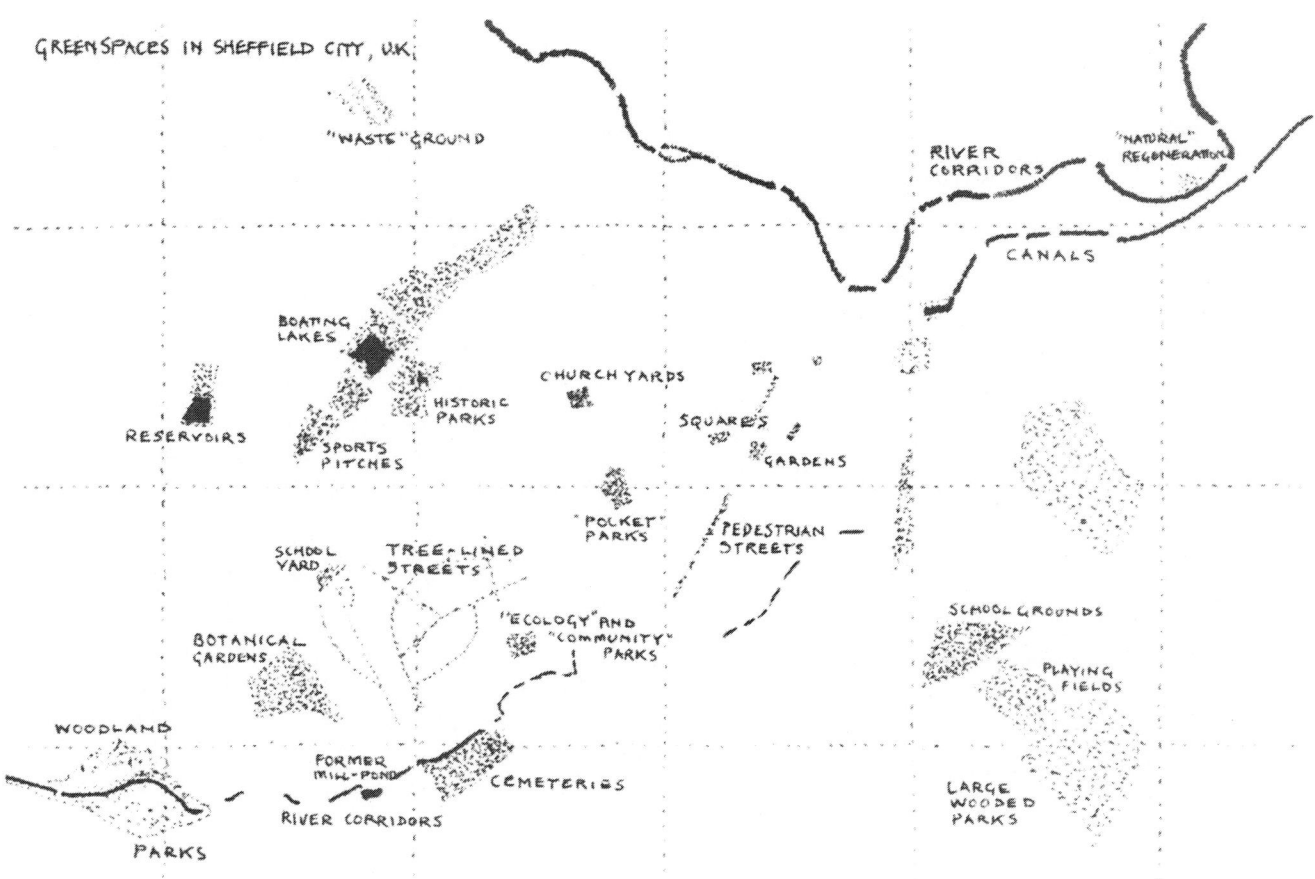

GREENSPACES IN SHEFFIELD CITY, UK.
"WASTE" GROUND
RIVER CORRIDORS
"NATURAL" REGENERATION
CANALS
BOATING LAKES
CHURCH YARDS
SQUARES
GARDENS
RESERVOIRS
HISTORIC PARKS
SPORTS PITCHES
"POCKET" PARKS
"PEDESTRIAN STREETS"
SCHOOL YARD
TREE-LINED STREETS
SCHOOL GROUNDS
BOTANICAL GARDENS
"ECOLOGY" AND "COMMUNITY" PARKS
PLAYING FIELDS
WOODLAND
FORMER MILL-POND
CEMETERIES
LARGE WOODED PARKS
RIVER CORRIDORS
PARKS

Urban greenspace and communications

Landscape design takes place within the context of urban greenspace planning and transport networks. In this book the term 'greenspace' is to a certain degree interchangeable with 'landscape at design scales' and is used to describe all (not just 'green') outdoor places that offer recreational, social, cultural and environmental benefits to city dwellers. Landscape architecture involves the design of all types of outdoor places to provide these benefits. The planning and design of 'greenspace' and

transport networks and routes (paths) are also the concern of landscape architects as well as urban designers, transport planners and engineers. The designed landscapes that this book deals with are typically urban greenspaces. They include public parks of different scales and types, and public gardens, squares and streets.

Models of design and qualities of place

In designing new places or regenerating old places, landscape architects follow philosophical, aesthetic, social, ecological and ethical 'models'. The following pages define and describe a series of qualities which contribute to my own model of design. These qualities are derived from diverse sources including personal experience, but in particular they are strongly influenced by 'social' and 'environmental psychological' research as well as 'aesthetic' theories of design. Some of this work is referred to in this section and in the introduction, and is listed in the further reading section at the end of this book. These qualities are further illustrated throughout the book.

Responsiveness

Responsiveness can be regarded as one of the most desirable qualities of a designed place. This means responsiveness to people, to nature and to place. Designers need to be informed about people's uses and experience of landscape and then respond to this in design. At the same time they need to understand natural processes and systems and respond by protecting, enhancing, adapting or restoring these. Being responsive to place means developing a sensitivity to landscapes and their specific character or distinctiveness before changing them. Change is inherent in design but landscape architects need to respect existing qualities and context.

Originality

While responsiveness is paramount in design, simply being responsive does not amount to design. Landscape architects need to develop ideas about what places might be as well as understand what they are or have been. Designers need to be original. What originality means in any given context can vary, and newness in landscapes has always been contentious. 'Avant-garde' approaches to landscape (newness or difference for its own sake) are limited because they often fail to address sufficiently people's use of places (and natural processes). At the other extreme, designing purely on the basis of social functions or seeing design as the result simply of analytical and scientific activity, or fearing newness in design, are also inadequate. The challenge and attraction of landscape architecture is the need for integrated, original ideas for people, place and nature. This is especially important in the context of sustainability.

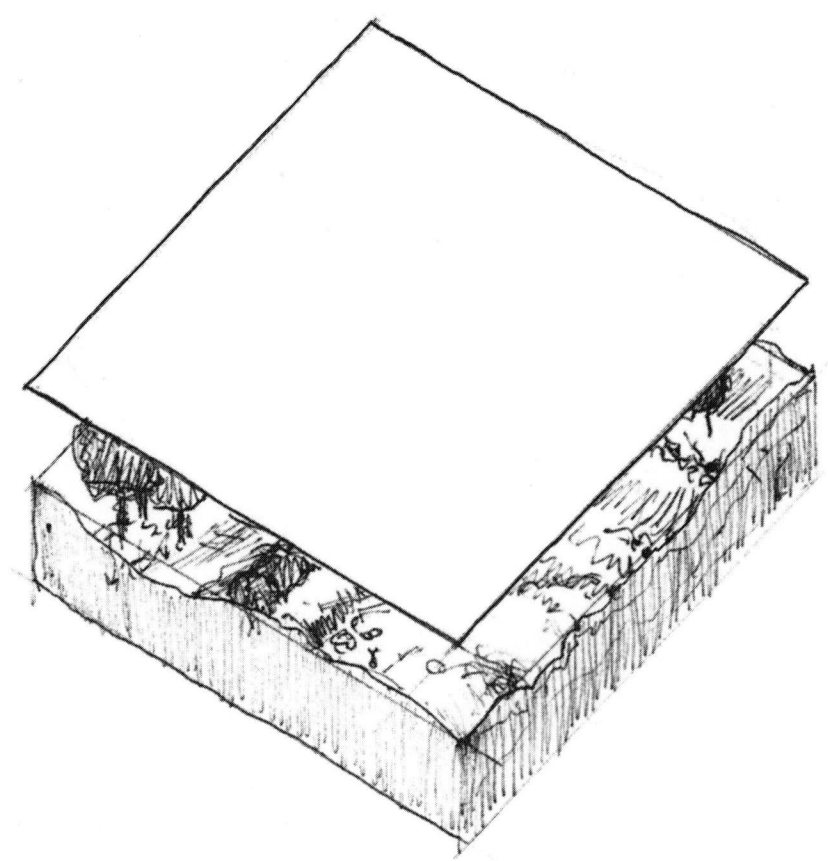

Recycling versus *tabula rasa*

Sweeping away old landscape for new is sometimes confused with creativity and originality in design. A *tabula rasa* approach to landscape architecture, where existing site conditions and landscape elements are cleared or ignored, is inappropriate in nearly all contexts for several reasons. First, recycling and conservation of materials, structures and vegetation is desirable for sustainability reasons. Second, landscapes accrue meanings and distinctive qualities over time and through use. Landscape design can be seen as a process of adding other layers of form and meaning that integrate or juxtapose to older layers and meanings. Third, vegetation (particularly trees) takes many years to mature and to offer environmental and aesthetic benefits so, wherever possible, trees and vegetation of ecological value should be conserved. Fourth, landscapes – however degraded – often have uses and meanings for local people. The landscape architect must always seek to find out about and understand site uses before developing proposals for a site.

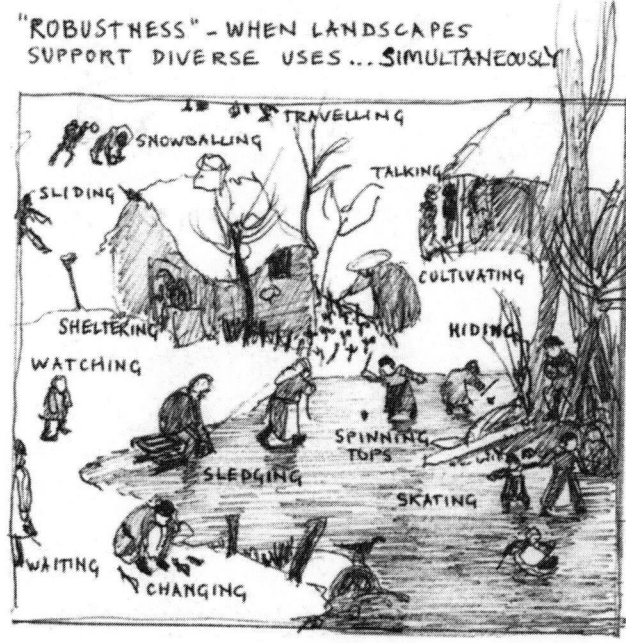

"ROBUSTNESS" - WHEN LANDSCAPES SUPPORT DIVERSE USES ... SIMULTANEOUSLY

TRAVELLING

SNOWBALLING

SLIDING

TALKING

CULTIVATING

SHELTERING

HIDING

WATCHING

SPINNING TOPS

SLEDGING

SKATING

WAITING

CHANGING

DRAWING AFTER DETAIL FROM "THE CENSUS AT BETHLEHEM" 1566 PIETER BRUEGEL THE ELDER

Robustness and inclusiveness

The very public nature of landscapes means that they are used by and must therefore be designed for a very wide range of people and activities. The quality that a landscape has when it provides simultaneously for diversity of use and experience can be defined as 'robustness' (Bentley *et al.* 1984). Robust landscapes are accommodating, flexible and inclusive. They 'stand up to' and 'support' different interpretations and use. A frequent aim of design is to achieve robustness by creatively accommodating and reconciling different uses.

DRAWING OF GIORGIO DE CHIRICO'S "MELANCHOLY AND MYSTERY OF A STREET" 1914 OIL ON CANVAS

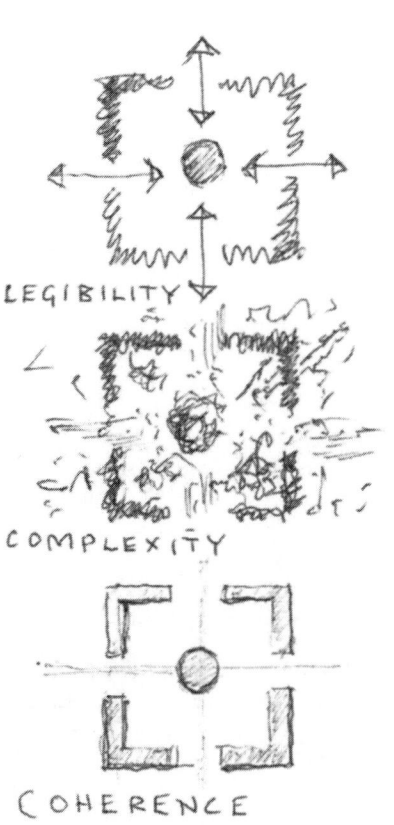

Mystery, legibility, complexity and coherence

Through their environmental behaviour research, Rachel and Stephen Kaplan (1989) developed four complementary qualities that influence people's experience of and preference for landscapes. Legibility refers to how easily an environment can be 'read' or 'made sense of' to enable people to predict in landscapes. Mystery describes the quality of an environment that encourages us to discover more about a place; to 'engage with it'. Coherence refers to the order of a place; how well it 'fits together'. Complexity refers to the diversity and richness of elements within a place. The work of the Kaplans suggests that all of these qualities are simultaneously required in order for people to enjoy and respond fully to places. Landscape architecture should aim to achieve these qualities in designed places as a dominance or exclusion of one or more can lead to places that are disliked and unused by people.

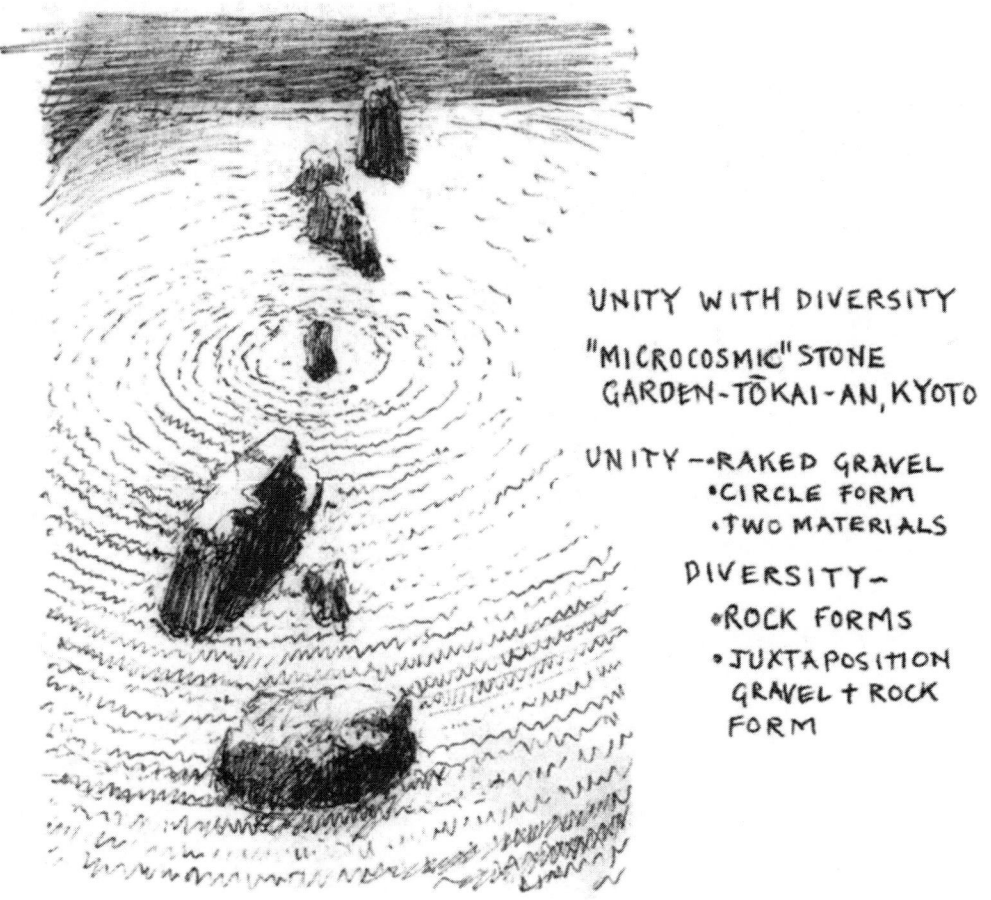

UNITY WITH DIVERSITY

"MICROCOSMIC" STONE
GARDEN-TŌKAI-AN, KYOTO

UNITY→•RAKED GRAVEL
•CIRCLE FORM
•TWO MATERIALS

DIVERSITY→
•ROCK FORMS
•JUXTAPOSITION
GRAVEL + ROCK
FORM

Unity with diversity

The principle of unity with diversity in the form and detail of landscape is similar to the Kaplans' 'complexity and coherence', but is worth considering separately as a visual characteristic of designed places. The need for people to make sense of the order of places requires a certain degree of unity of form, elements and detail. Unity can be achieved for example through repetition or use of specific geometry, or through a limited 'palette' of materials. A landscape that is unified but lacks diversity can be considered monotonous. Diversity in landscape architecture refers to difference in form, elements and detail. A diverse landscape that lacks any unifying characteristics may be perceived as chaotic and therefore disorienting and alienating. Depending on the context, landscape architecture will seek to balance unity and diversity within a place or emphasise either characteristic which may be lacking in surrounding landscapes.

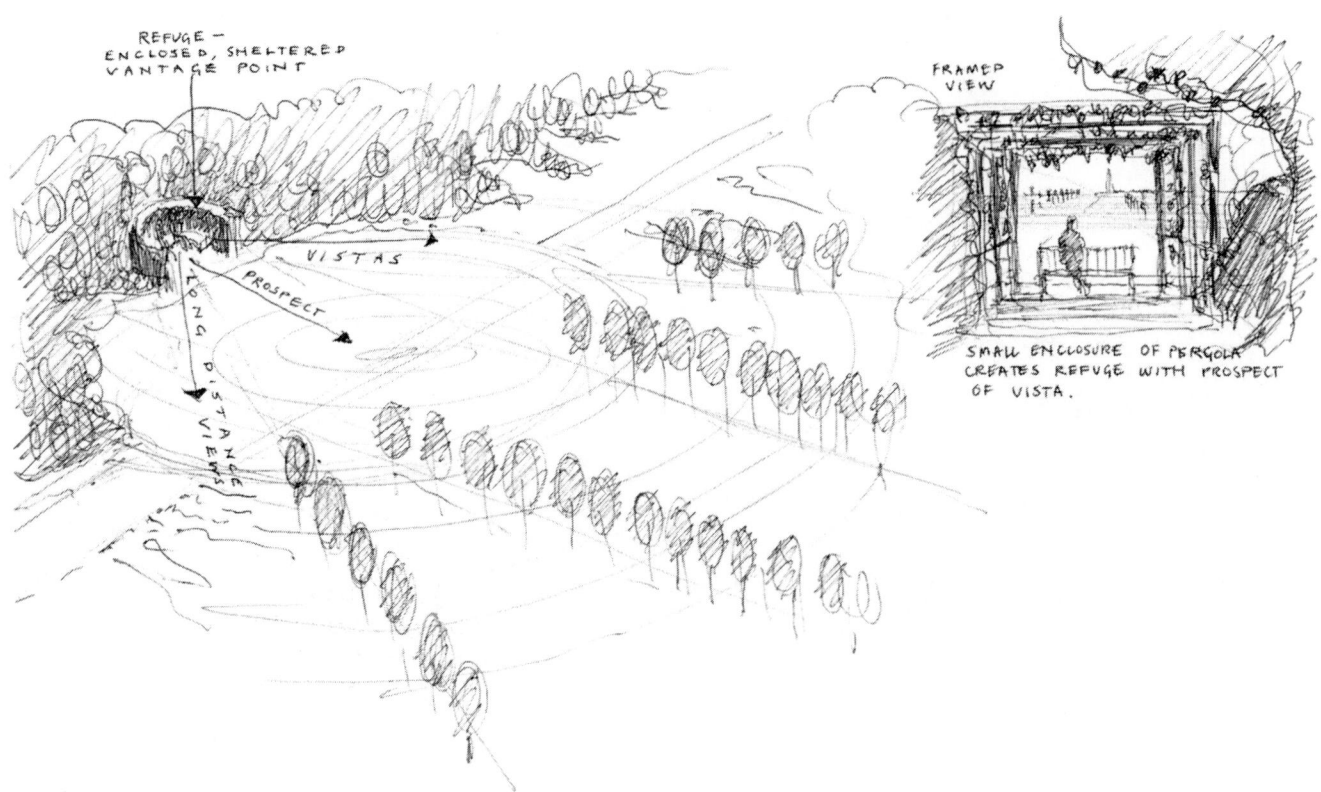

REFUGE —
ENCLOSED, SHELTERED
VANTAGE POINT

VISTAS

PROSPECT

LONG DISTANCE VIEWS

FRAMED
VIEW

SMALL ENCLOSURE OF PERGOLA
CREATES REFUGE WITH PROSPECT
OF VISTA.

Prospect and refuge theory

Appleton's (1996) prospect–refuge theory has been very influential in the development of understanding landscape experience. It informs many aspects of this book, including concepts about edges, foci and thresholds. Landscapes that enable prospect while providing refuge are considered so important in providing pleasurable landscapes that prospect–refuge is included here as a desirable quality of design landscapes in a wide range of contexts.

MANY JAPANESE GARDENS ACHIEVE WHOLENESS -
METICULOUS AND SUBTLE INTEGRATION AND
JUXTAPOSITION OF ELEMENTS. EACH ELEMENT
PLAYS A ROLE IN WHOLENESS OR IS ABSENT.

Wholeness and integration

Wholeness refers to qualities of integration and completeness in a designed place. Integration is absolutely fundamental to successful design and an overriding principle. The designer has to consider how to bring together the forms of vegetation, topography, structures and water in integrated ways and how to integrate spaces, paths, edges, thresholds and foci. A whole design has all parts of the design 'working' to enhance by complementing or juxtaposing all other parts. In wholeness, the sum of the landscape forms and elements is greater than the parts.

The integrated design of places

In the following pages that complete this section, examples of integrated design are illustrated and explored with the aim of demonstrating how spaces, paths, edges, thresholds and foci form whole places and how design elements may be combined. Examples of integrated landscapes occur throughout the book, but this section aims to emphasise integration and to counteract the notion that the elements and forms in design as organised in the remaining parts of this book can be considered separately when designing.

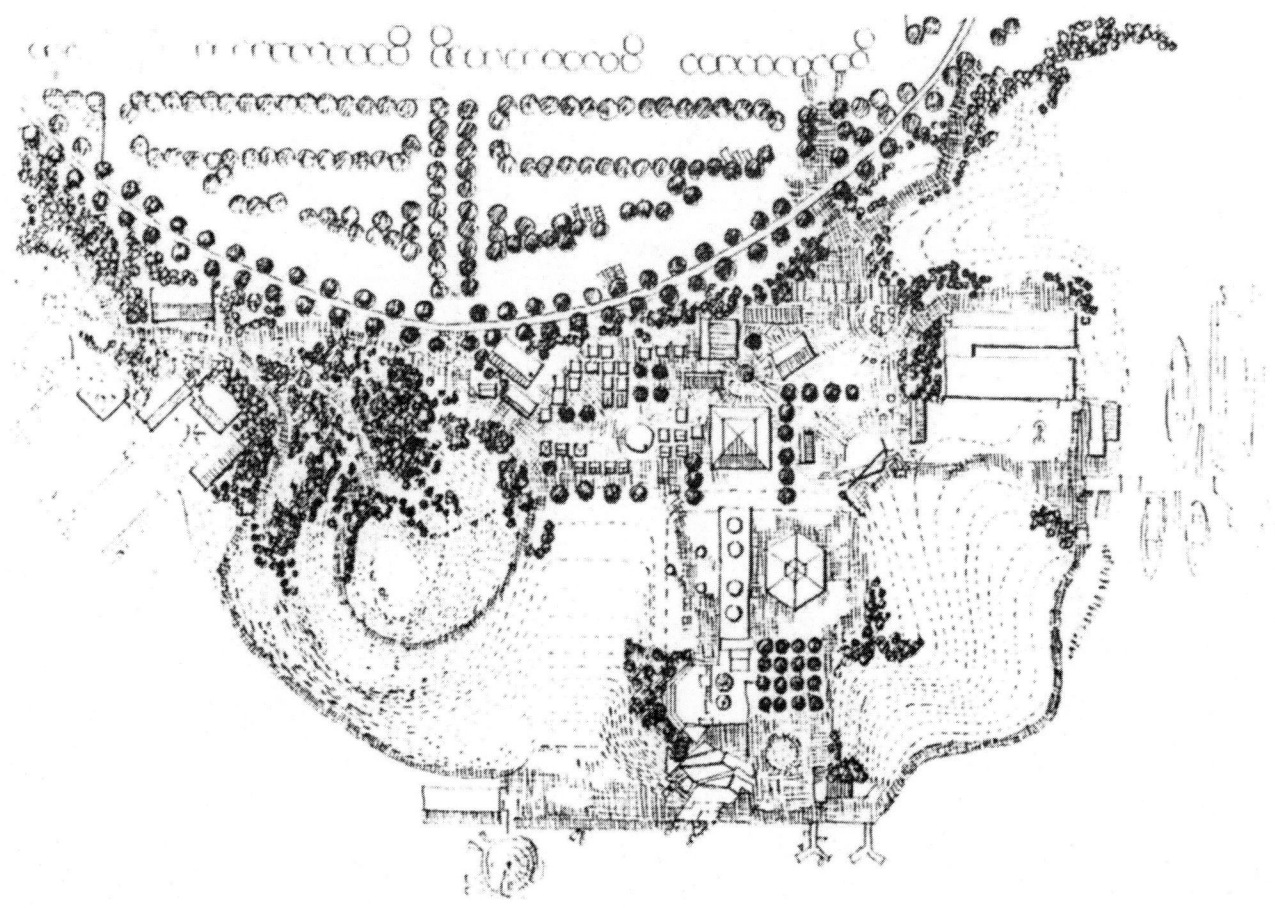

Integrated design – an example

Gasworks Park, Seattle, Richard Haag Associates

The landscape illustrated on this and the following pages is Gasworks Park in Seattle. It was designed by Richard Haag Associates with the first phase completed in 1975. It has been chosen as an example of an urban park that displays many of the qualities considered important in design which are identified on previous pages in this section. The images aim to 'deconstruct' the layers, characteristics and forms of the park to illustrate their integration. The drawings and information are based on Haag Associates' own drawings and other published sources.

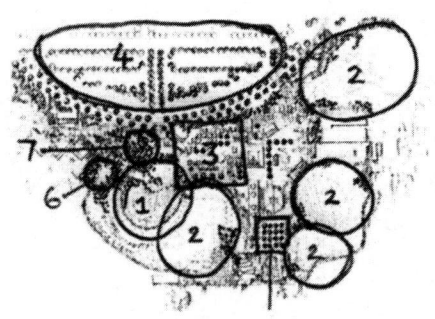

1. **GREAT MOUND SPACE** + FOCUS
   TREE EDGE, SPIRALLING PATH
   PROSPECT, GAMES, WALKING RESTING

2. **BOWL SPACES** - CONTRAST WITH
   MOUND, ENCLOSURE LEAD TO
   WATER'S EDGE, DRAMATISE TOWERS

3. **MARKET SPACE** - DEFINED BY
   PAVING & FORMAL TREE LINES

4. **CAR PARK SPACE** - DEFINED /
   ENCLOSED FORMAL TREE LINES
   AXIAL PATH THROUGH TO PARK

5. **TREE-SPACE - "FORMALISED FOREST"**
   TREE-GRID DEFINES + ENCLOSES
   CONTRAST TO NATURALISTIC TOPOGRAPHY

6. **GLADE SPACE** - "CUT OUT OF"
   WOODLAND PLANTING. PATH
   MOVES THROUGH. CONTRAST TO OPENNESS

7. **FOREST SPACE** - DENSITY AND
   ENCLOSURE CONTRASTS WITH
   OPENNESS - SECLUSION INFORMALITY

SPACES OF GAS WORKS PARK

2. BOWL SPACE
   TOPOGRAPHY - KEY SPACE FORMING ELEMENT

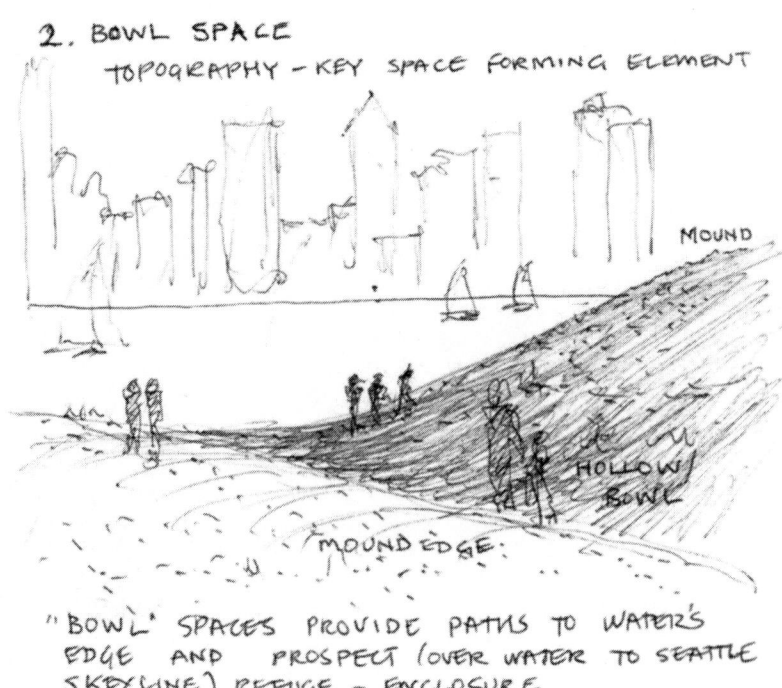

MOUND

MOUND EDGE

HOLLOW/ BOWL

"BOWL" SPACES PROVIDE PATHS TO WATER'S
EDGE AND PROSPECT (OVER WATER TO SEATTLE
SKEYLINE) REFUGE - ENCLOSURE

23

GAS WORKS PARK......

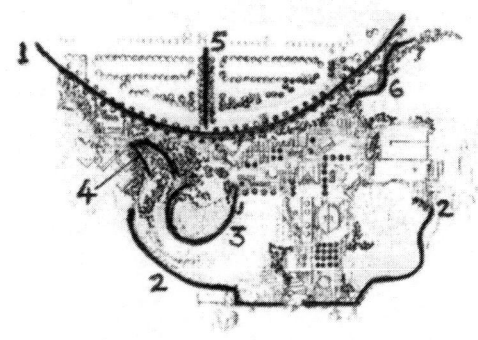
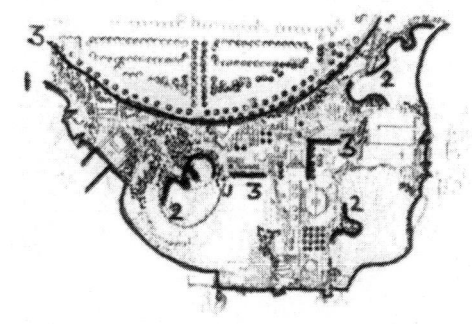

PATHS

1. ACCESS ROAD – AVENUE. ·SWEEPS ALONG EDGE OF PARK · AVENUE ORIENTATES
2. WATER'S EDGE PATH CATERS FOR MOVEMENT ALONG EDGE
3. MOUND SPIRAL PATH DRAWS PEOPLE UP... CHANGING PROSPECTS
4. FOREST PATHS – ENCLOSED SECLUDED – CONTRAST TO OPEN PATHS
5. AXIAL AVENUE PATH CHANNELS PEOPLE TO ENTRANCE PARK
6. MEANDERING PATH

EDGE   GROUPED FOCI
                       FORM EDGE

COMPLEX HORIZON OF GAS WORKS TOWERS PROVIDE DISTINCT EDGE GWING IDENTITY TO PARK.

EDGES

1. WATER'S EDGE – VARIED AND DYNAMIC
2. WOODLAND EDGE – DEFINES EDGE OF TOPOGRAPHIC SPACES
3. AVENUE EDGES – DEFINE SPACES AND MARK TRANSITIONS

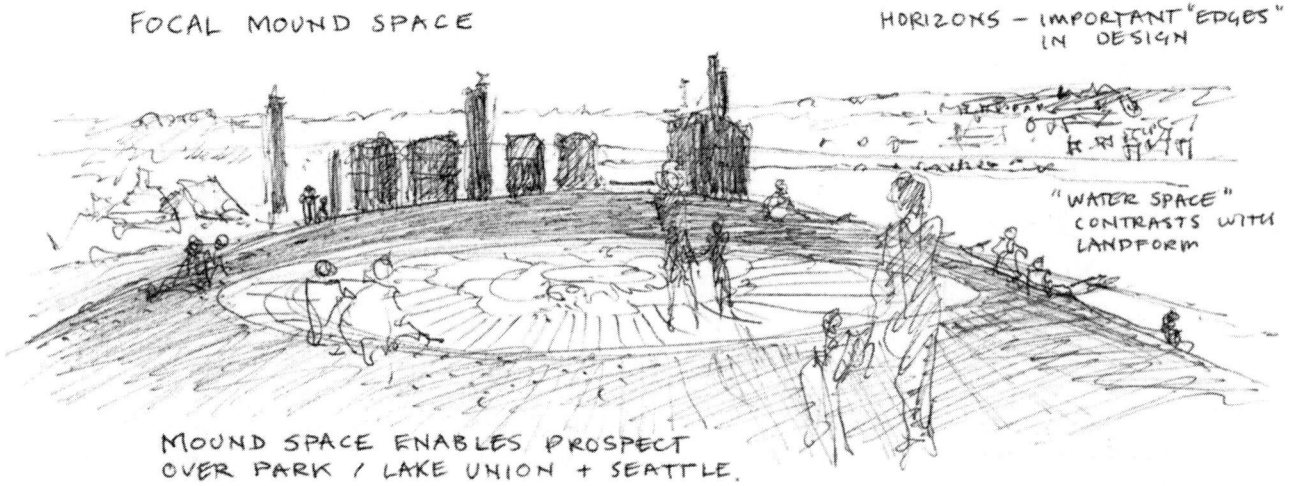

FOCAL MOUND SPACE

HORIZONS – IMPORTANT "EDGES" IN DESIGN

"WATER SPACE" CONTRASTS WITH LANDFORM

MOUND SPACE ENABLES PROSPECT OVER PARK / LAKE UNION + SEATTLE.

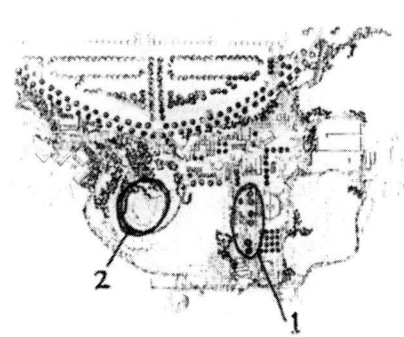

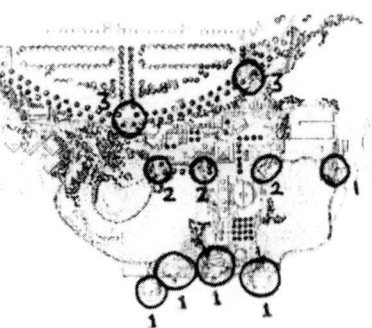

FOCI

1. GAS WORKS TOWERS RETAINED AS MONUMENTAL FOCI/FOLLIES
2. MOUND - FOCUS DRAWING PEOPLE TO THE TOP

THRESHOLDS

1. WATER/LAND THRESHOLDS
2. "HARD" TO "SOFT" LANDSCAPE THRESHOLDS
3. GATEWAY THRESHOLDS/ PARK ENTRANCE PLACES

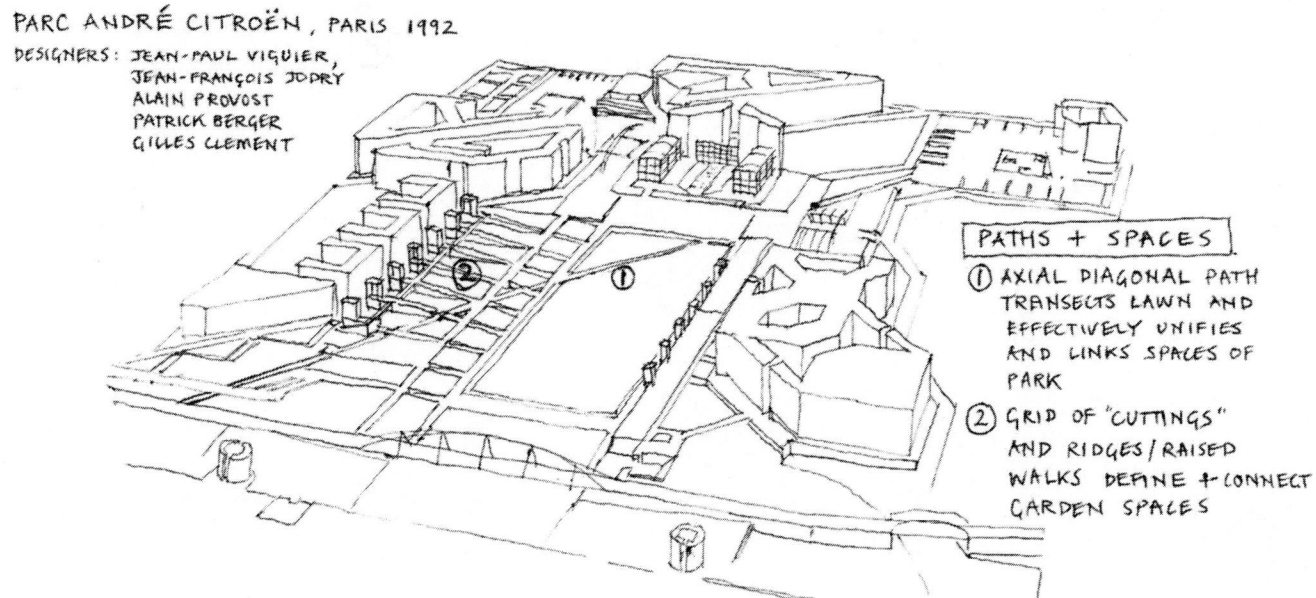

PARC ANDRÉ CITROËN, PARIS 1992
DESIGNERS: JEAN-PAUL VIGUIER,
JEAN-FRANÇOIS JODRY
ALAIN PROVOST
PATRICK BERGER
GILLES CLEMENT

PATHS + SPACES
① AXIAL DIAGONAL PATH
TRANSECTS LAWN AND
EFFECTIVELY UNIFIES
AND LINKS SPACES OF
PARK
② GRID OF "CUTTINGS"
AND RIDGES/RAISED
WALKS DEFINE + CONNECT
GARDEN SPACES

Integration of spaces and paths

Examples on these pages illustrate inventive integration
of spaces and paths.

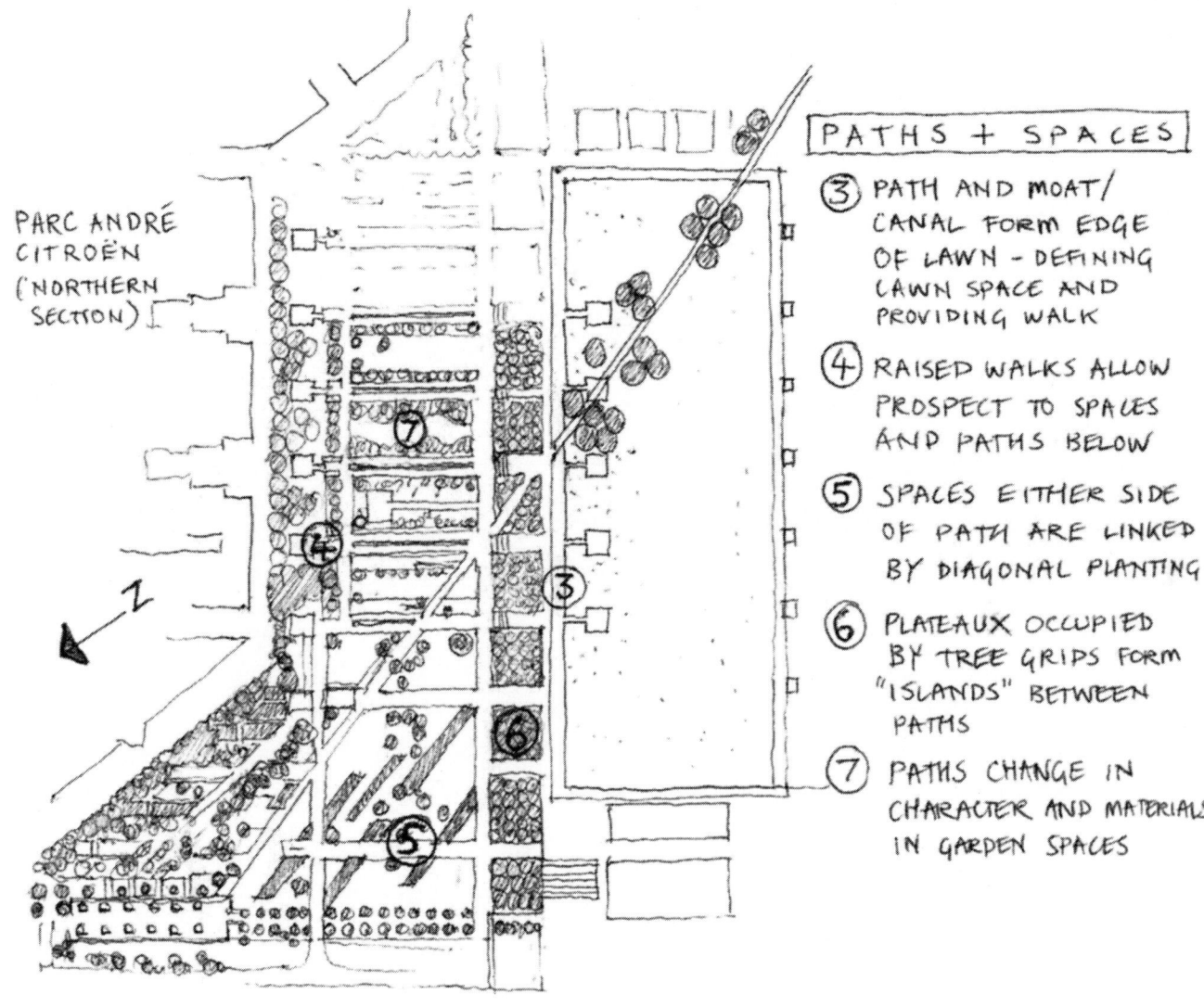

PARC ANDRÉ CITROËN (NORTHERN SECTION)

PATHS + SPACES

③ PATH AND MOAT/ CANAL FORM EDGE OF LAWN - DEFINING LAWN SPACE AND PROVIDING WALK

④ RAISED WALKS ALLOW PROSPECT TO SPACES AND PATHS BELOW

⑤ SPACES EITHER SIDE OF PATH ARE LINKED BY DIAGONAL PLANTING

⑥ PLATEAUX OCCUPIED BY TREE GRIDS FORM "ISLANDS" BETWEEN PATHS

⑦ PATHS CHANGE IN CHARACTER AND MATERIALS IN GARDEN SPACES

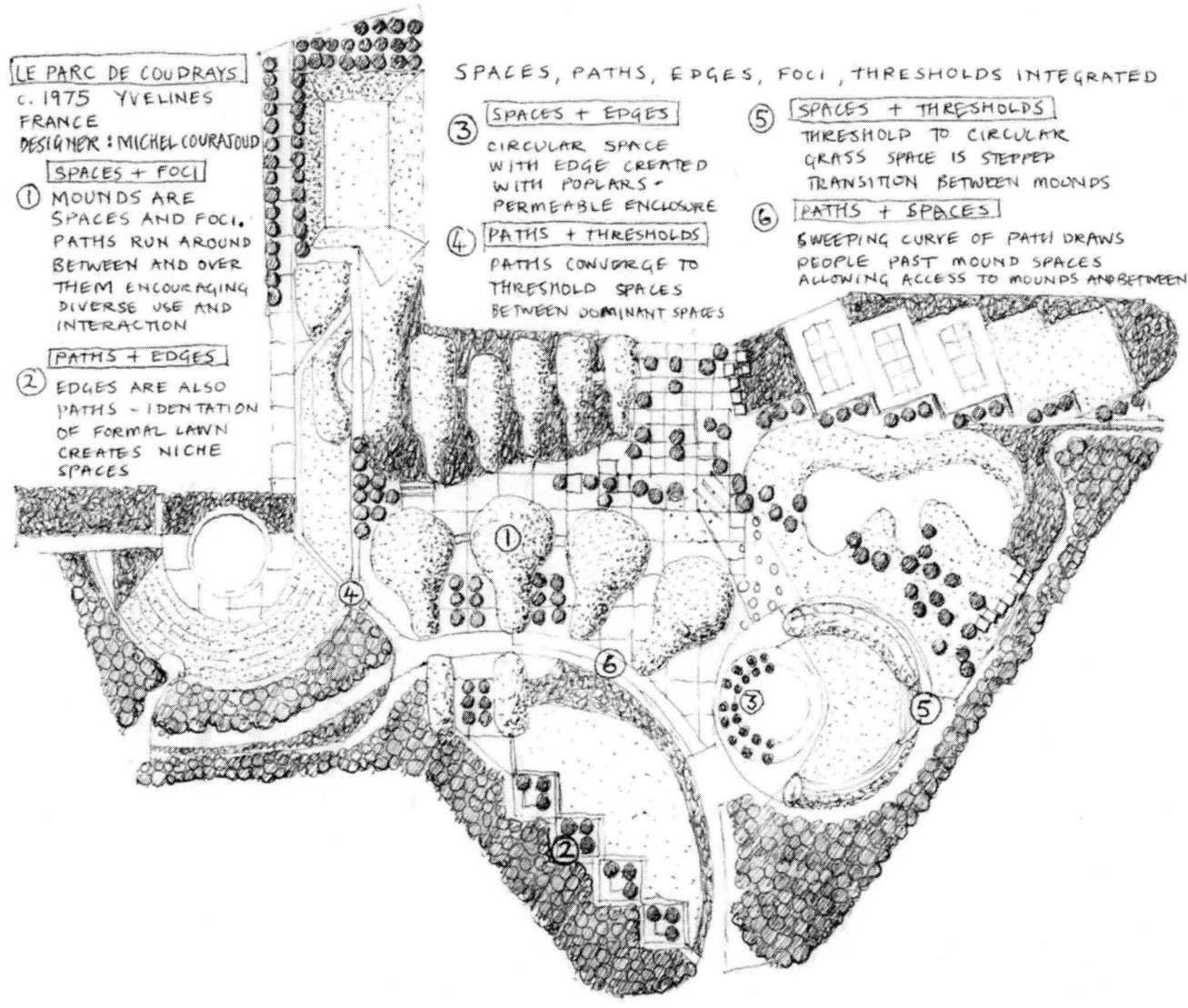

LE PARC DE COUDRAYS
c. 1975 YVELINES
FRANCE
DESIGNER : MICHEL COURAJOUD

SPACES + FOCI
① MOUNDS ARE
SPACES AND FOCI.
PATHS RUN AROUND
BETWEEN AND OVER
THEM ENCOURAGING
DIVERSE USE AND
INTERACTION

PATHS + EDGES
② EDGES ARE ALSO
PATHS - IDENTATION
OF FORMAL LAWN
CREATES NICHE
SPACES

SPACES, PATHS, EDGES, FOCI, THRESHOLDS INTEGRATED

SPACES + EDGES
③ CIRCULAR SPACE
WITH EDGE CREATED
WITH POPLARS -
PERMEABLE ENCLOSURE

PATHS + THRESHOLDS
④ PATHS CONVERGE TO
THRESHOLD SPACES
BETWEEN DOMINANT SPACES

SPACES + THRESHOLDS
⑤ THRESHOLD TO CIRCULAR
GRASS SPACE IS STEPPED
TRANSITION BETWEEN MOUNDS

PATHS + SPACES
⑥ SWEEPING CURVE OF PATH DRAWS
PEOPLE PAST MOUND SPACES
ALLOWING ACCESS TO MOUNDS AND BETWEEN

Integration of spaces, paths, edges, thresholds and foci

Examples on these pages illustrate inventive integration
of landscape forms.

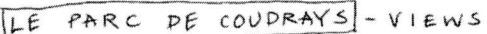

LE PARC DE COUDRAYS - VIEWS

● WHALE LIKE SMOOTH GRASS MOUNDS ARE
BOTH SPACES AND FOCI ATTRACTING PEOPLE
TO WALK ON AND BETWEEN THEM

● POPLARS PROVIDE CONTRASTING
VERTICAL EMPHASIS AS
DEFINING EDGE OF CIRCULAR
SPACE

● INDENTED / ZIG-ZAG EDGE TO FORMAL
LAWN PROVIDES NICHE SPACES AND
INTEGRATES SPACE OF LAWN AND PATH

ROTUNDA GARDENS AT HAFENINSEL
SAARBRÜCKEN, GERMANY
DESIGNER: PETER LATZ + PARTNER

TOPOGRAPHY + VEGETATION
A FORMAL HEDGE ACCENTUATES
THE TOPOGRAPHIC ENCLOSURE OF
THE "BOWL" SPACE

TOPOGRAPHY + WATER
THE TOPOGRAPHIC "BOWL" IS BOTH
A SETTING FOR THE CIRCULAR
POOL AND A STEPPED ACCESS
TO WATER

TOPOGRAPHY + STRUCTURES
THE TOPOGRAPHIC "BOWL" SPACE IS
A BUILT STRUCTURE - AMPHITHEATRE
RETAINING WALLS DEFINE SPACE
STAIRCASES LINK AXES.

VEGETATION + WATER
FORMAL VEGETATION ECHOES POOL
FORM. DARKNESS OF VEGETATION
CONTRASTS WITH LIGHT OF WATER

VEGETATION + STRUCTURES
VEGETATION CLOTHES STRUCTURES WITH
CLIMBING PLANTS. FORMAL HEDGES
ECHO STRUCTURES

WATER + STRUCTURES
STRUCTURES IN WATER SUGGEST INDUSTRIAL
PIERS AND TOWERS. STRUCTURE PROVIDES
FOCUS IN WATER SPACE

Integration of topography, vegetation, structures and water

Examples on these pages illustrate inventive approaches
to the integration of landscape elements.

STOURHEAD GARDENS,
WILTSHIRE UK 1740's
HENRY HOARE

TOPOGRAPHY + VEGETATION
SMOOTH LAWN ACCENTUATES
TOPOGRAPHIC SWEEPS WHICH
ARE FRAMED AND ARTICULATED
BY TREES.

TOPOGRAPHY + WATER
ROLLING TOPOGRAPHY COMPL-
EMENTS STILL MIRRORED SURFACE
OF WATER AND SINUOUS CURVES
OF WATER'S EDGE.

AFTER F.M. PIPER'S PLAN 1779

TOPOGRAPHY + STRUCTURES
STRUCTURES SIT ON RAISED GROUND ALLOWING
PROSPECT TO AND FROM THEM

VEGETATION + WATER
WATER REFLECTS MASS OF TREES AND
CONTRASTS TO THEIR TEXTURE WITH A SMOOTH
PLANE. WATER PROVIDES LIGHT-TREES
DARKNESS. WATER CREATES SPACE TREES
ENCLOSE.

VEGETATION + STRUCTURES
TREES CONTRAST IN TONE AND TEXTURE WITH
STRUCTURES. VEGETATION IS CLEARED TO
ALLOW VISTAS FROM ONE STRUCTURE TO
ANOTHER.

WATER + STRUCTURES
STILL WATER REFLECTS STRUCTURES. WATER
PROVIDES SMOOTH OPEN *PLANE* OVER WHICH
STRUCTURES ARE VIEWED

2 Spaces

Landscape architecture essentially involves organising and dividing land. Spaces are the result of this division and thus the primary medium of design. Spaces provide for different human uses and enjoyment of the landscape.

In this chapter, a series of conceptual frameworks for designing space are defined. The organisation of space is described as a process of manipulating ground, 'wall' and 'sky' planes. Types of enclosure and their characteristics and issues affecting the design of spaces including social, aesthetic and environmental aspects are explored and illustrated.

Examples of the use of topography, vegetation, structures and water in the formation of spaces are illustrated.

SPACES ARE ENCLOSED AND DEFINED BY LANDFORM, VEGETATION, WATER + STRUCTURES FOR HUMAN ACTIVITY..

DETAIL FROM GUISTO UTENS' "VILLA MEDICI _ PRATOLINO" 1599

Definitions

Space can be defined as ...

- an area of land enclosed, defined or adopted by people for human purposes
- a medium and concept of landscape architecture
- a place for outdoor activities
- an enclosure
- the 'opposite' of form or mass.

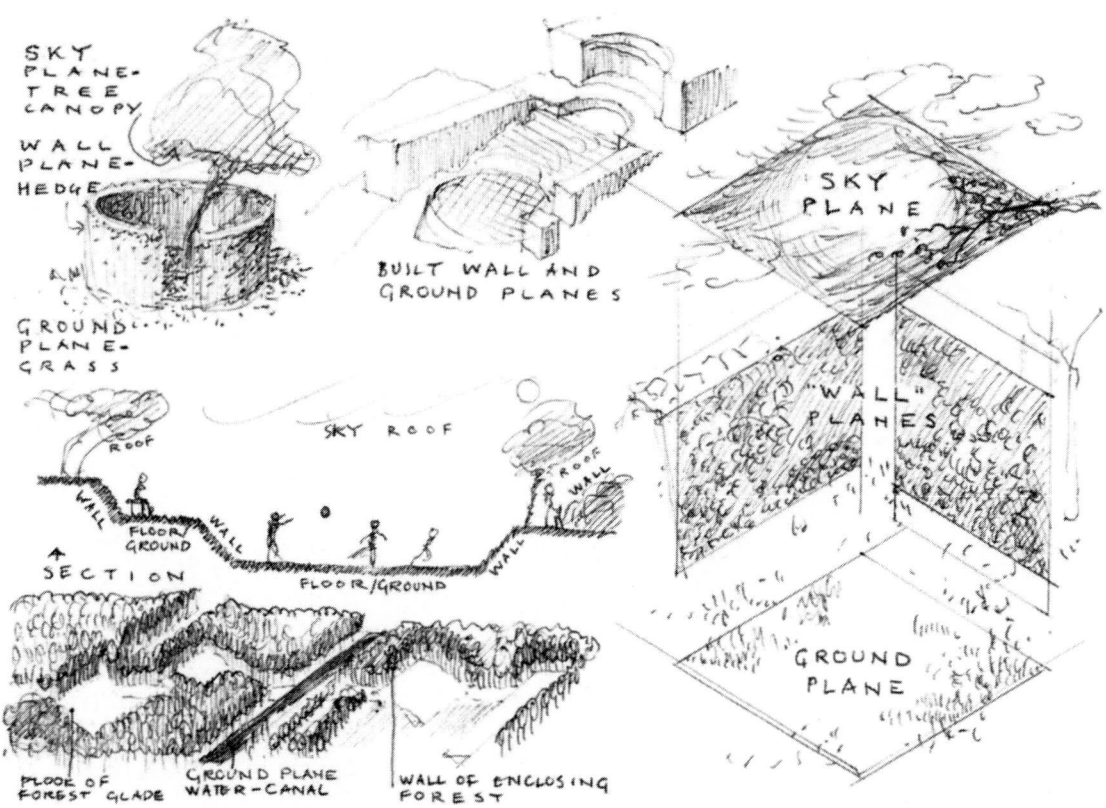

Ground, 'wall' and 'sky' planes

For design purposes a space can be thought of as an area defined in three dimensions by:

- the ground plane,
- 'wall' or vertical planes,
- the 'sky' plane.

The design of outdoor spaces can be conceived of as a process of manipulating mainly the first two planes and occasionally the third. To think of places as being composed of abstract planes which make three dimensional forms helps the designer to develop spatial awareness and the ability to 'create with space'. Differing somewhat from the planes of most buildings, landscape planes are often relatively complex, rugged and varied with a great deal of variation in horizontal and vertical surfaces. In topographic design, the ground plane may unobtrusively and subtly merge with a wall plane. 'Wall' planes may consist of vegetation that is coarsely textured and merges from the ground to an overhead 'sky' plane. Consequently, landscape design planes are often fluid, translucent, rich, complex, ambiguous and thick. It is some of these qualities that can make wall planes places in their own right. These are referred to as 'edges' and have a separate section later in this book devoted to exploring their potential in design.

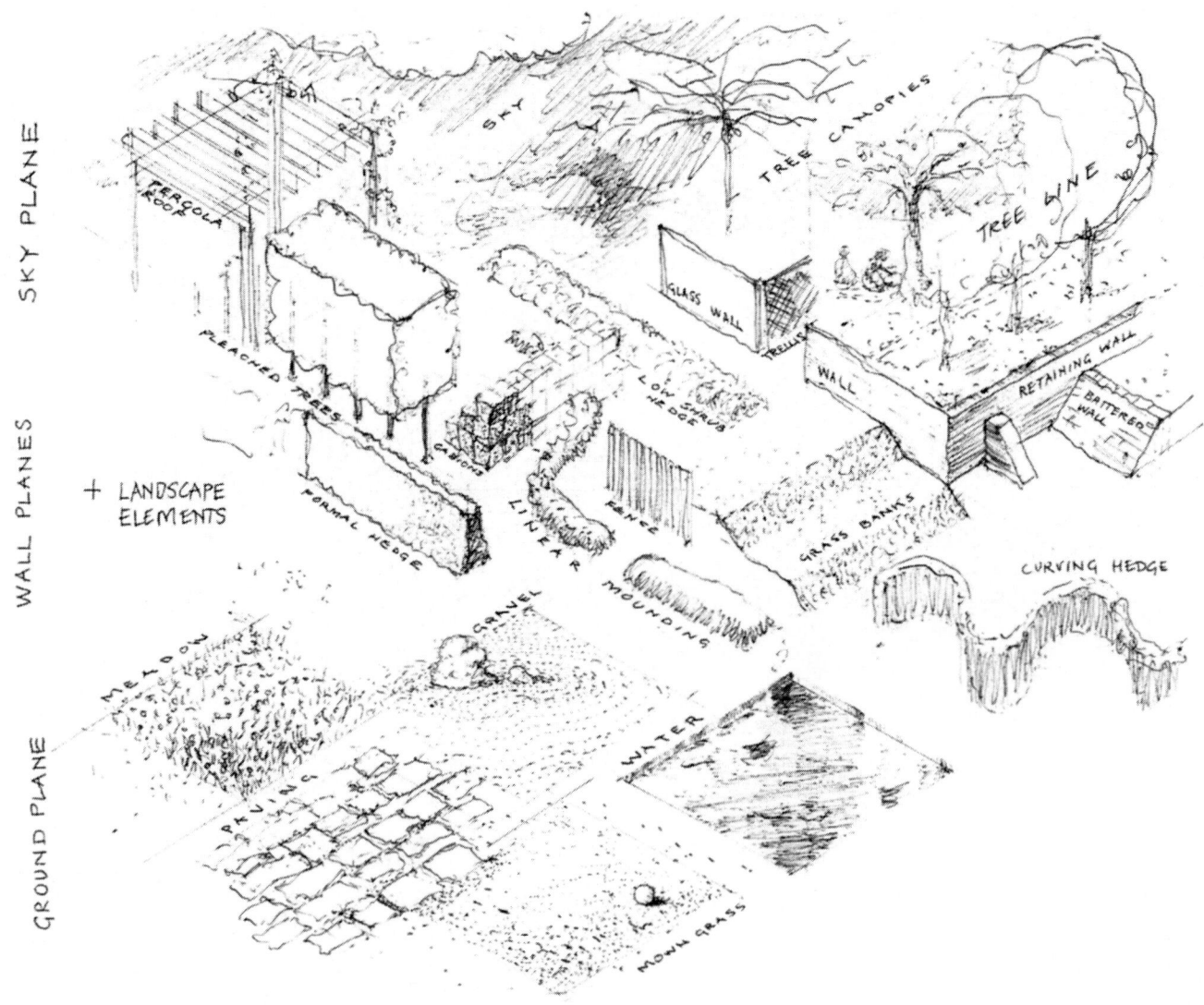

Design planes and landscape elements

Within each plane the landscape architect inventively uses and integrates the elements of landform, vegetation, structures, and water – singly or in any combination. These elements can be thought of as a basic palette of spatial design. The design of spaces is not simply a process of organising planes and elements in abstract ways, but to enable places to function for people and nature.

35

DRAWING OF "THE UPS AND DOWNS" BY JEAN DUBUFFET . 1977.

PUBLIC SPACES NEED TO FUNCTION FOR MANY DIFFERENT USES AND USERS

People's use and experience of spaces

A wide range of factors influence people's use and experience of spaces and therefore determine how they might be designed. Children, adults, elderly people, different ethnic groups and cultures, men and women – all experience and use places in different and distinct ways, as well as in similar ways. The design of spaces should always be informed and underpinned by an understanding of different people's needs and activities and experiences of landscapes.

Public spaces need to function for an extremely wide range of uses including:

- social and recreational purposes, for example, gathering, eating, dancing

- work, for example, buying, selling, mending, studying
- health and fitness
- aesthetic and cultural purposes (linked to social and recreational)
- ecological and environmental purposes.

A frequent aim in the design of spaces is thus to achieve 'robustness' (see p. 16) in spaces by accommodating and reconciling different landuses.

The form, character, proportion, scale and microclimate of spaces, and their relationship to other spaces all affect human use and experience, and are considered in the following pages.

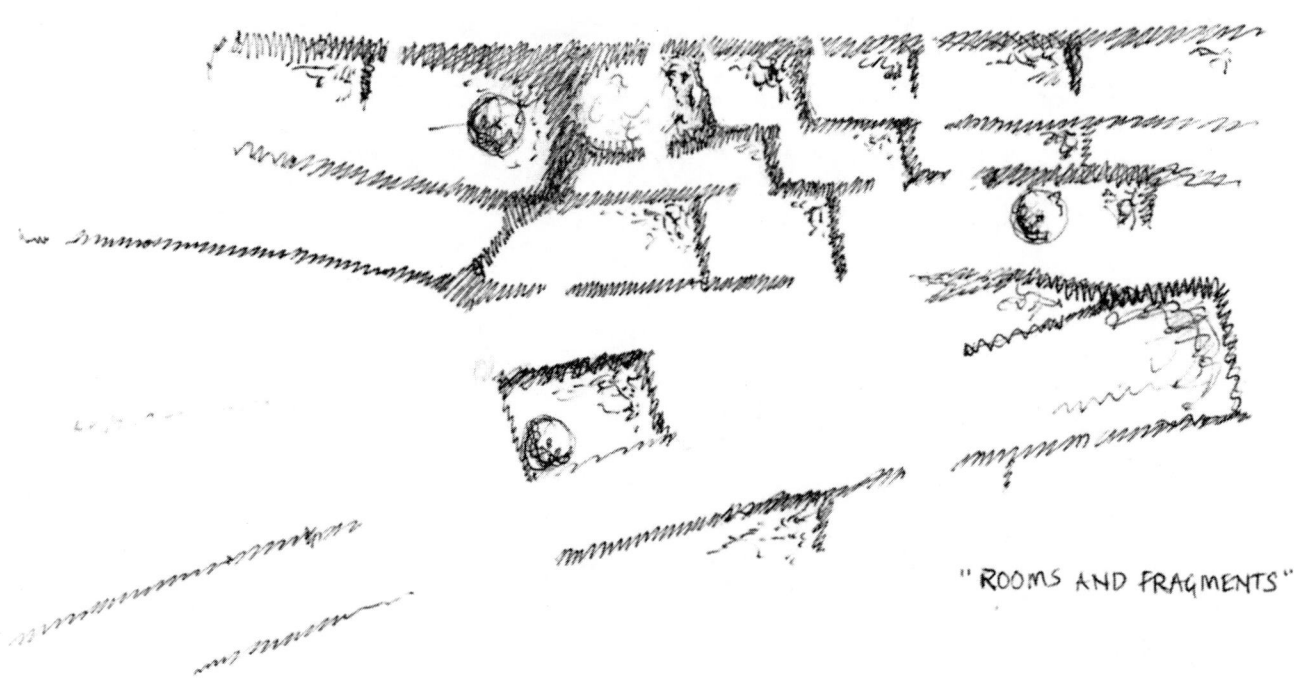

"ROOMS AND FRAGMENTS"

Form of spaces

Space design involves the generation of specific forms or shapes for places. There are many ways of doing this, but some common methods by which designers create and articulate form are through the use of:

- interpretation of existing site forms
- geometry
- metaphor
- symbolism
- abstraction and use of natural forms
- archetypes
- vernacular
- historic paradigms.

Experienced and effective designers combine several of these ways of thinking about a design. Forms developed for spaces may be limited if only one approach is used to generate a design. 'Layered' concepts are often what is required.

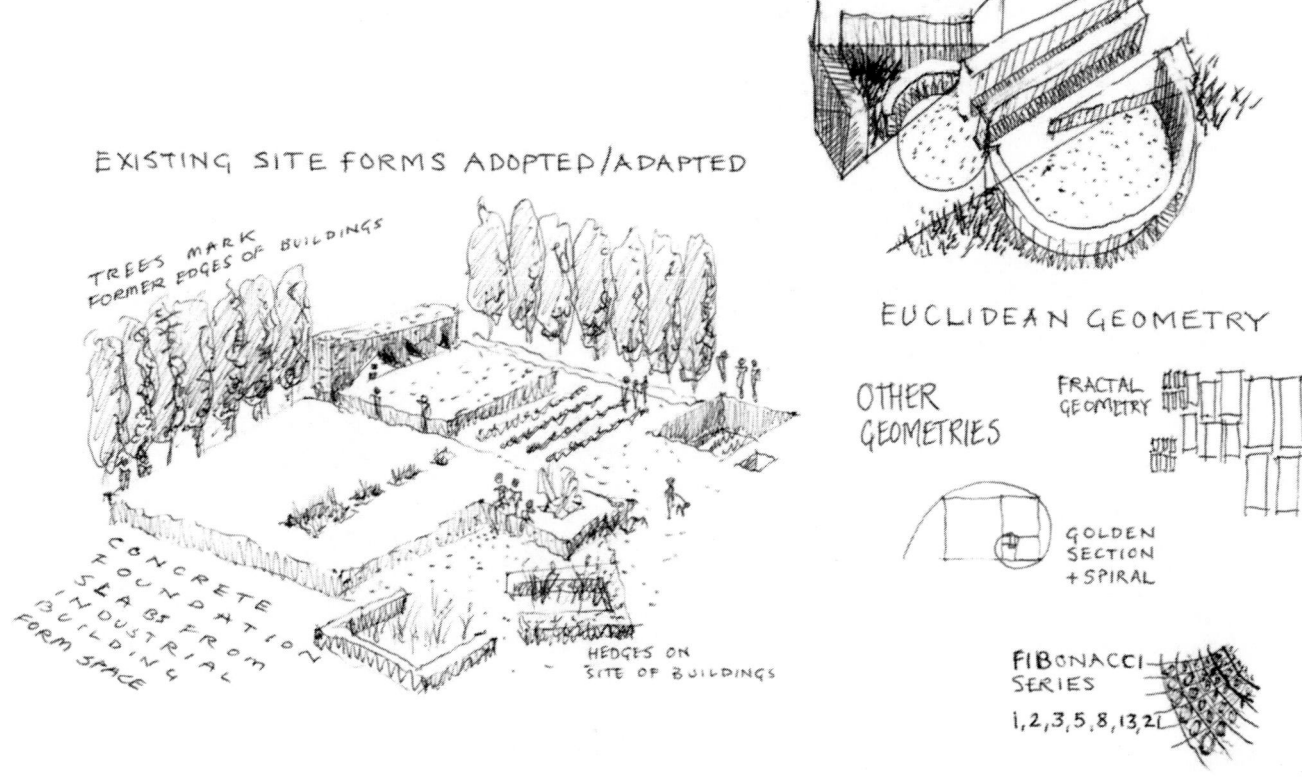

EXISTING SITE FORMS ADOPTED/ADAPTED

TREES MARK FORMER EDGES OF BUILDINGS

CONCRETE FOUNDATION SLABS FROM INDUSTRIAL BUILDINGS FORM SPACE

HEDGES ON SITE OF BUILDINGS

EUCLIDEAN GEOMETRY

OTHER GEOMETRIES

FRACTAL GEOMETRY

GOLDEN SECTION + SPIRAL

FIBONACCI SERIES
1,2,3,5,8,13,21

Interpretation of existing site forms

Design frequently involves the creation of spaces to provide for changed landuse such as former industrial sites to new recreational facilities. Design of these spaces may involve modification and recycling of existing site forms rather than developing completely new ones. Existing site characteristics are often a source of design inspiration. See 'Recycling versus *tabula rasa*' (p. 15) for more about this.

Geometry

The use of geometry by designers includes both simple geometries (for example, circular forms, rectangular forms) and more complex geometries such as fractal geometry (where forms and proportions of a 'macro' structure are repeated in the 'micro' structure of that form). Geometry and the science of mathematics have exerted and continue to exert a powerful influence on the forms created by landscape architects.

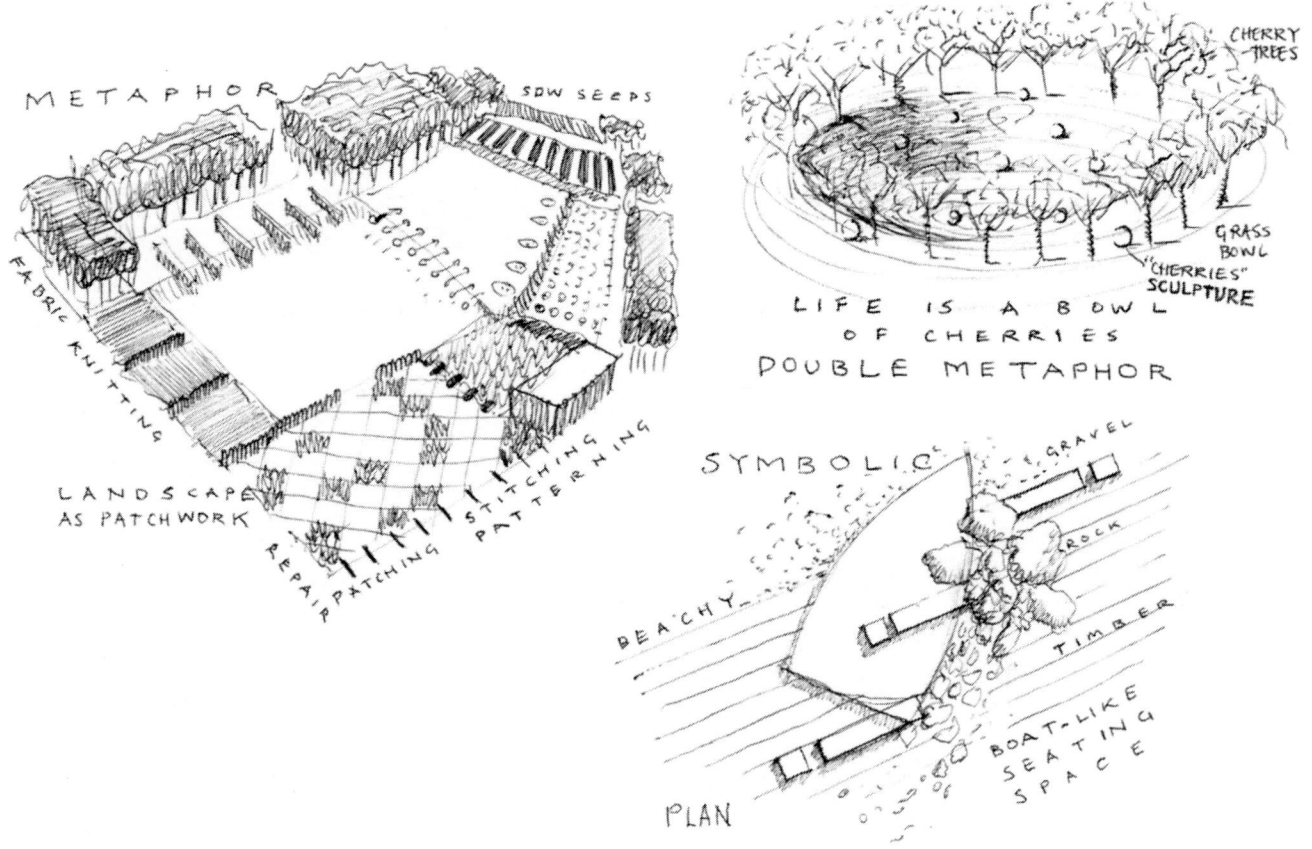

Metaphor

The use of metaphor to generate form involves conceiving of or describing the landscape as another (normally) unrelated thing or action in a non-literal way. 'Dead space', or 'Space is flowing' are examples of landscape metaphor. Designers challenge and create metaphors as well as exploit existing ones. Popular metaphors may include, for example, 'mother nature', 'whispering wind', 'lazy river'. Using popular metaphors can result in clichéd design. The benefit of using a new metaphor is that it can enable fresh ways of thinking about landscape, thereby allowing original forms and meanings to emerge.

Symbolism

Symbolism possesses similarities to the use of metaphor for generating form but with a fundamental difference. Unlike metaphor, symbolism involves the conscious and careful abstraction of a form which is directly and literally relevant to a place and its function or history. Symbolism is used in design with the intention that users of the landscape should understand and respond to the meaning(s) of the symbol(s). Problems with the use of symbolism by designers include a tendency towards literalness, obviousness and cliché which leave no room for viewers' (users') interpretations.

39

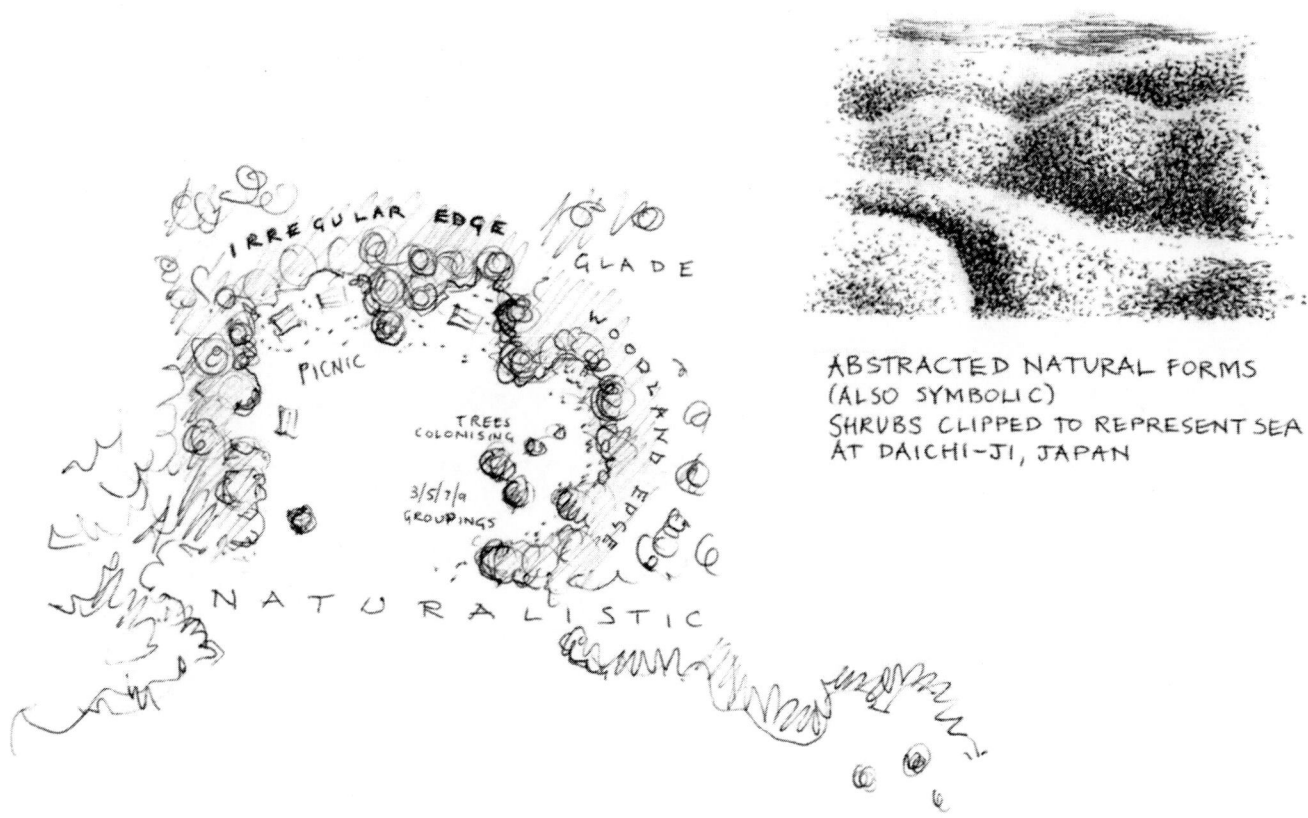

ABSTRACTED NATURAL FORMS
(ALSO SYMBOLIC)
SHRUBS CLIPPED TO REPRESENT SEA
AT DAICHI-JI, JAPAN

Abstraction and use of natural forms

Related to geometry, metaphor and symbolism, the abstraction and use of natural forms is a rich source for generating design. Spaces can be given form through the abstraction of naturally occurring forms and patterns of vegetation, rock, waterbodies and landscape processes at both macro and micro scales. Alternatively, natural processes such as plant colonisation can be allowed to 'shape' space or natural features can be retained to structure places.

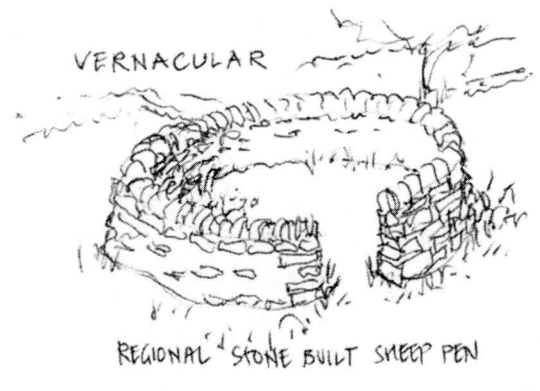

VERNACULAR

REGIONAL STONE BUILT SHEEP PEN

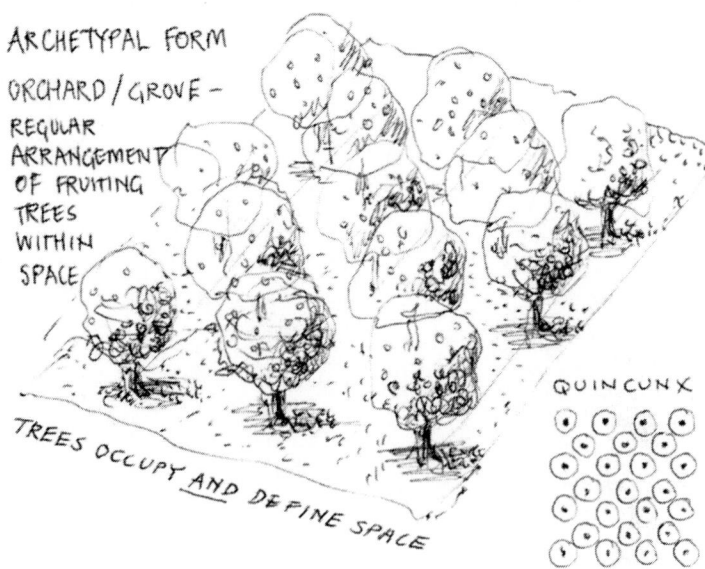

ARCHETYPAL FORM

ORCHARD / GROVE –
REGULAR
ARRANGEMENT
OF FRUITING
TREES
WITHIN
SPACE

TREES OCCUPY AND DEFINE SPACE

QUINCUNX

Archetypes

Archetypes can be described as similar forms or physical arrangements of human environments which have been repeated or copied over long periods of time and continue to perform the same types of functions. They are considered to be universal. For example, the amphitheatre may be described as an archetypal form because it has been consistently used for similar purposes over time in different contexts.

Vernacular

Vernacular refers to regionally distinct landscapes and landscape forms created by people who were not usually professional designers. Understanding and using vernacular can help landscape architects to interpret existing landscapes and to relate new spaces to site history for continuity and unity in regional landscapes.

Historic paradigms

Precedent and paradigms from historic landscapes can also be a source of or influence on generation of form in design. Studying past landscapes is a primary way to learn about the discipline of landscape architecture and the context of contemporary concepts and approaches to design.

41

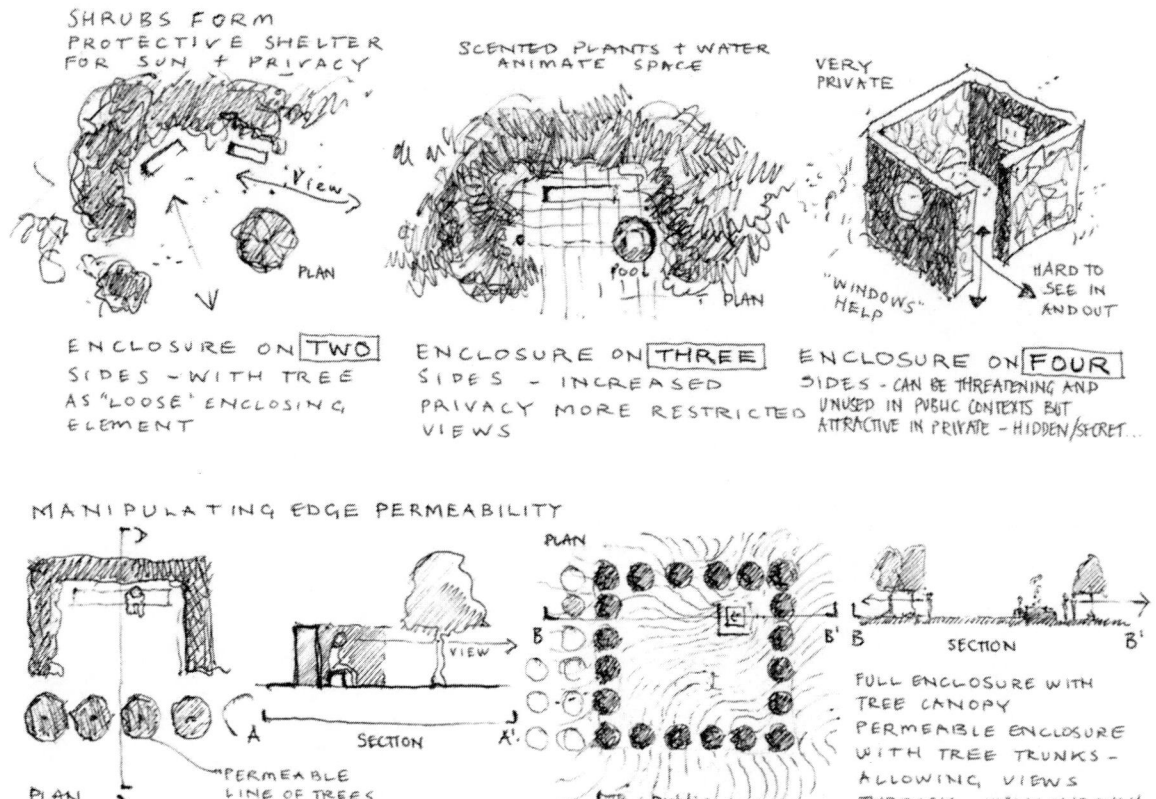

SHRUBS FORM PROTECTIVE SHELTER FOR SUN + PRIVACY

SCENTED PLANTS + WATER ANIMATE SPACE

VERY PRIVATE

ENCLOSURE ON TWO SIDES - WITH TREE AS "LOOSE" ENCLOSING ELEMENT

ENCLOSURE ON THREE SIDES - INCREASED PRIVACY MORE RESTRICTED VIEWS

ENCLOSURE ON FOUR SIDES - CAN BE THREATENING AND UNUSED IN PUBLIC CONTEXTS BUT ATTRACTIVE IN PRIVATE - HIDDEN/SECRET...

MANIPULATING EDGE PERMEABILITY

"PERMEABLE LINE OF TREES"

- Public square

FULL ENCLOSURE WITH TREE CANOPY PERMEABLE ENCLOSURE WITH TREE TRUNKS - ALLOWING VIEWS THROUGH - WALK THROUGH

Space enclosure

In design, enclosure by vegetation, landform, structures or water in wall planes enables the definition and separation of spaces and their related human activities.

The type and degree of enclosure affects human experience and use, microclimate and character.

Degrees and permeability of enclosure

The landscape architect must decide how enclosed or 'open' a space should be – ranging from entirely open with space defined only on the ground plane, to fully enclosed in wall planes.

Full enclosure suggests and provides security and privacy, but can be experienced as threatening and unsafe in a public urban environment. Enclosure on two or three sides provides refuge but allows prospect.

The height of an enclosure affects scale. There is a tendency among inexperienced designers to make enclosing planes too high and dense, thereby creating claustrophobic and intimidating places. Conversely, too little structure or enclosure can result in a monotonous and bleak landscape. Visual and physical permeability of enclosing planes is an extremely important concept in landscape architecture and is one that the designer can use with subtle variation.

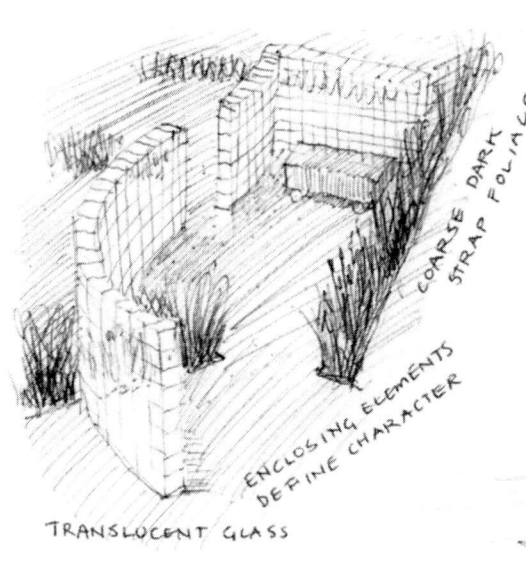

COARSE DARK STRAP FOLIAGE

ENCLOSING ELEMENTS DEFINE CHARACTER

TRANSLUCENT GLASS

TREES, GRANITE, HEATHER DEFINE CHARACTER

BLACK + WHITE

SHINE + SPECKLE

POLISHED BLACK GRANITE + SILVER BIRCH ENCLOSE

Enclosure and character of spaces

The nature of enclosing elements contributes largely to defining the character of a space. A solid smooth concrete wall, roughly textured hedge, billowing trees, dry-stone wall, translucent glass, or meadowed bank all have very different character, texture, qualities and associations which influence how a place is experienced.

ENCLOSURE - TRAPPING SUN

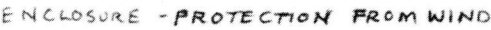

ENCLOSURE - PROTECTION FROM WIND

ENCLOSURE - COOLING SHADE

Enclosure and microclimate

Enclosure substantially affects microclimate and therefore human comfort and use. In temperate climates, warm south-facing walls ripen fruit and enable tender plants to be grown. A south-facing bank is good for basking in the sun. Broad trees provide dappled shade, cooling the air and making sitting spaces. Pines and dunes protect places from coastal winds. Open valleys channel cooling winds into hot cities. Climate is fundamental to landscape architecture and the designer always considers and works with it.

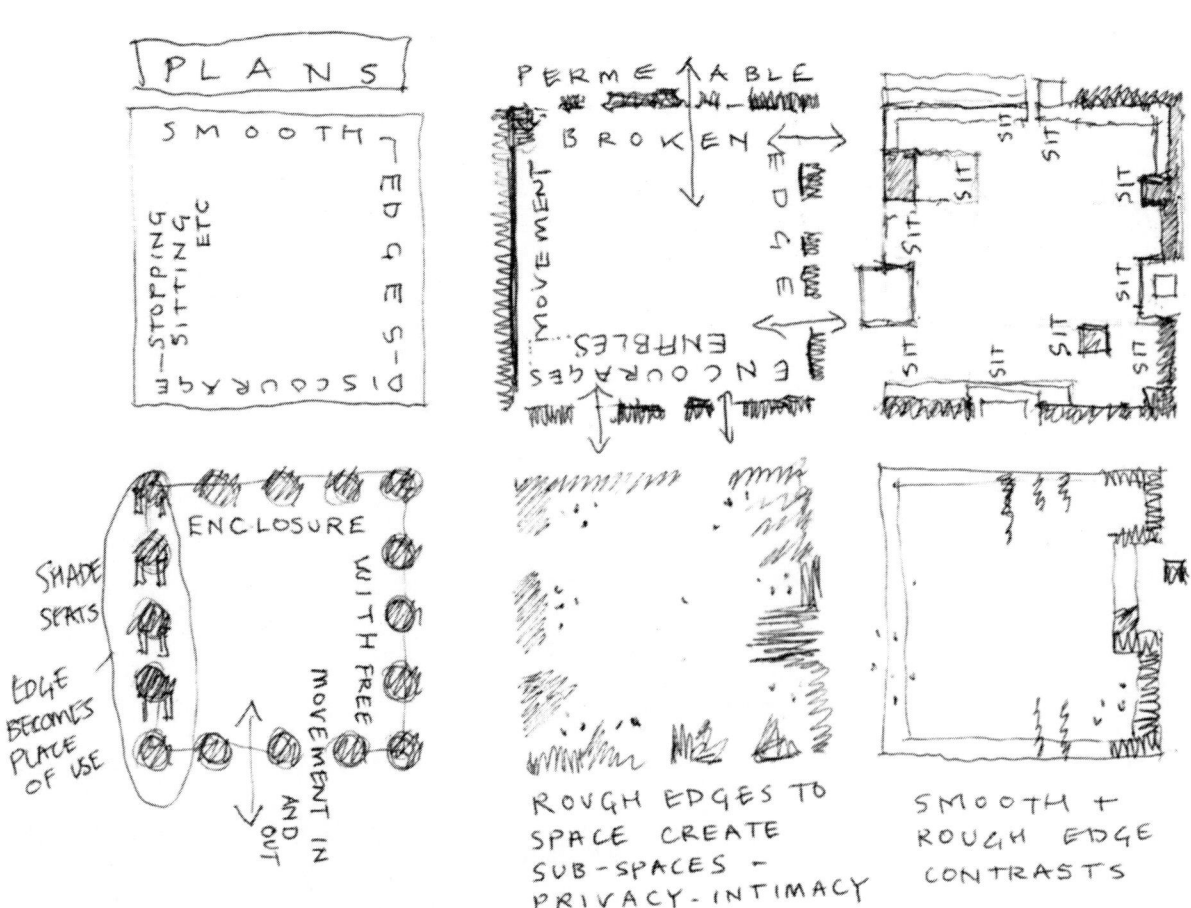

ROUGH EDGES TO SPACE CREATE SUB-SPACES - PRIVACY-INTIMACY

SMOOTH + ROUGH EDGE CONTRASTS

Spaces and edges

An edge occurs at the place where openness (space) transforms into the solidity of enclosing elements. In landscape architecture, harsh and immediate transitions from space to solid are often neither desirable nor feasible. This is due, in part, to the nature of landscape elements particularly vegetation. Plants 'mesh' space within their form. Sudden transitions in designed space ignore the potential of spatial subtleties and the social and ecological opportunities that transitional places offer. The enclosing edge of a space is often a well-used place. This is considered so important to spatial thinking in landscape architecture that a part of this book is devoted to the design and consideration of edges both as enclosing elements of space and as places in their own right (see p. 115).

45

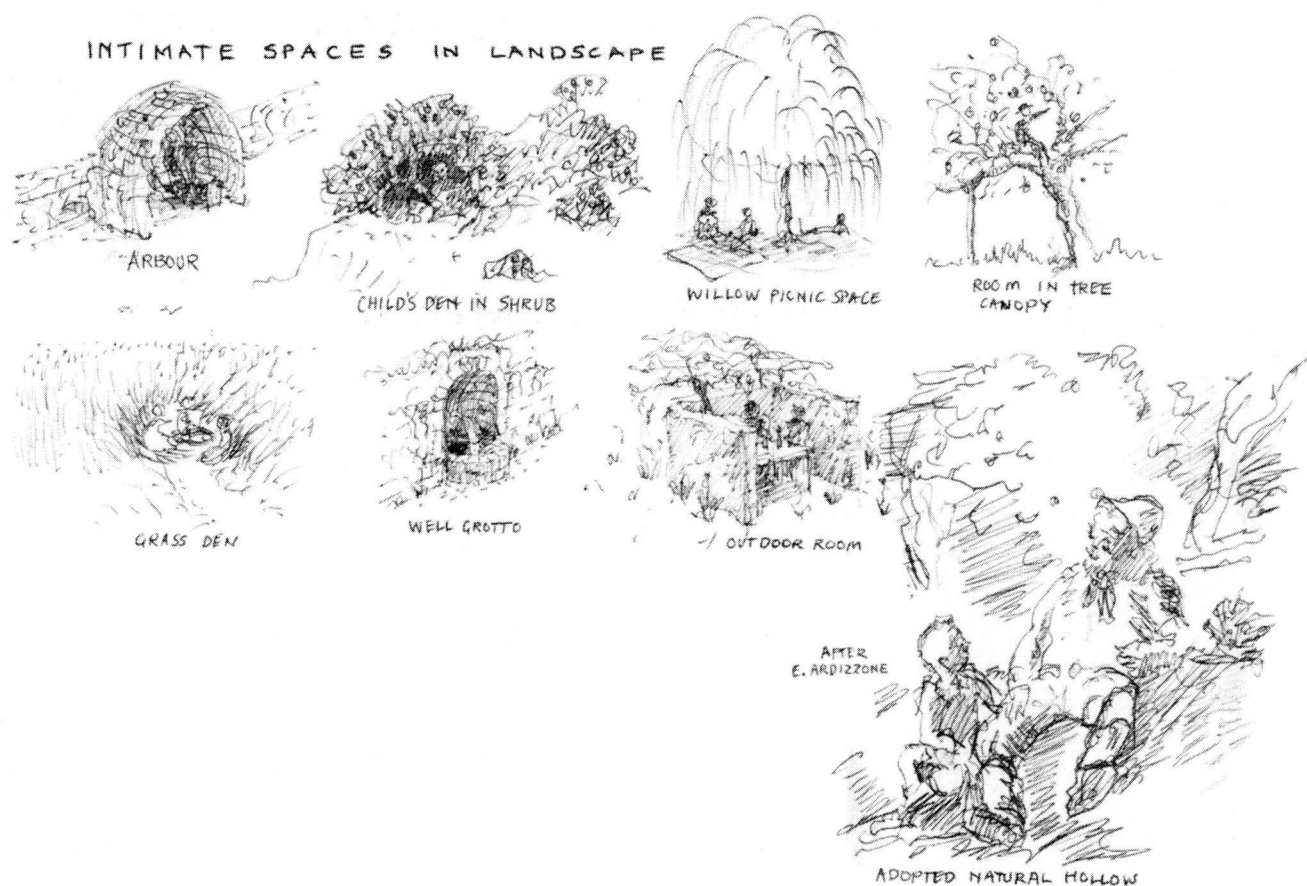

INTIMATE SPACES IN LANDSCAPE

ARBOUR

CHILD'S DEN IN SHRUB

WILLOW PICNIC SPACE

ROOM IN TREE CANOPY

GRASS DEN

WELL GROTTO

OUTDOOR ROOM

AFTER E. ARDIZZONE

ADOPTED NATURAL HOLLOW

Scale of spaces

Scale refers to the perceived relative size of parts of the landscape to each other, to human size and to the emotional effect of this relative size. Hence, judgements can be made about scale. 'Too large or small in scale' can refer to relationships of parts of a landscape or to the size a person feels in relation to a landscape. Scale can also refer to size in relation to human activity, for example: 'this space is too small in scale for public events'.

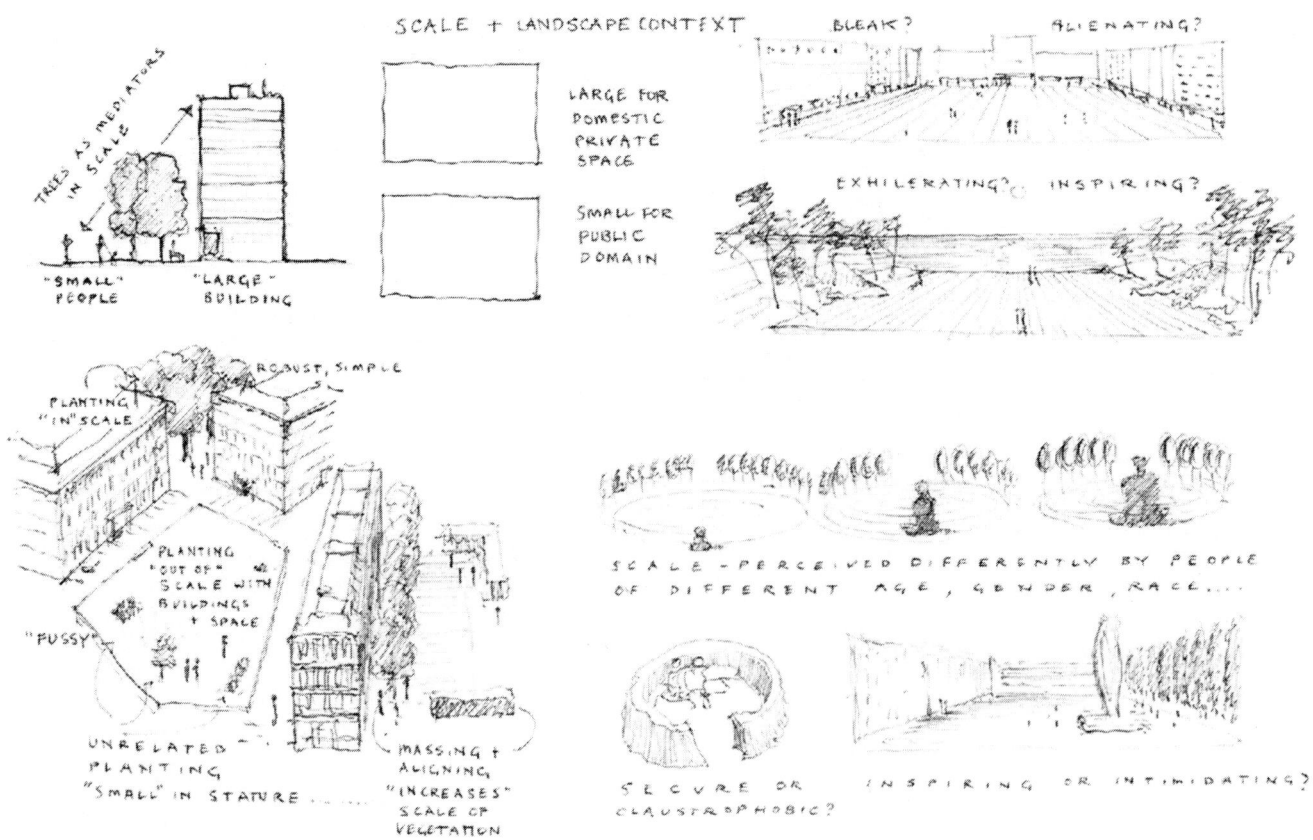

Human scale

Human scale has a range of meanings but generally refers to the size of an environment or parts of an environment that engender positive feelings by being 'close in size' to the human body. These feelings may include comfort, security, reassurance, orientation, friendliness and a feeling of being able to 'relate to one's surroundings'. Human-scale spaces do not intimidate or alienate by the largeness of their size. However, human scale is, like scale in general, a relative term. For example, a child will experience space as different in scale to an adult (hence the term 'child-scale').

Scale and context

Scale is also a relative concept depending on the context of a landscape space. Public and domestic landscapes require and are experienced at different scales. Indoor and outdoor scales differ. The size of natural or rural spaces engenders different human responses to similarly-sized urban places.

VASTNESS AFTER JOHN CONSTABLE'S "SEASCAPE STUDY WITH RAIN CLOUDS" 1824-1825

Vastness to intimacy

The designer can manipulate scale to engender emotional responses, from the comfort and the intimacy of small-scale places to the exhilaration of openness where sky and wind dominate. As scale is relative, effects of scale are achieved by juxtaposition and an understanding of the relationship of parts to whole. The landscape architect can deliberately contrast scales for dramatic impact or unify spaces by using similar scales.

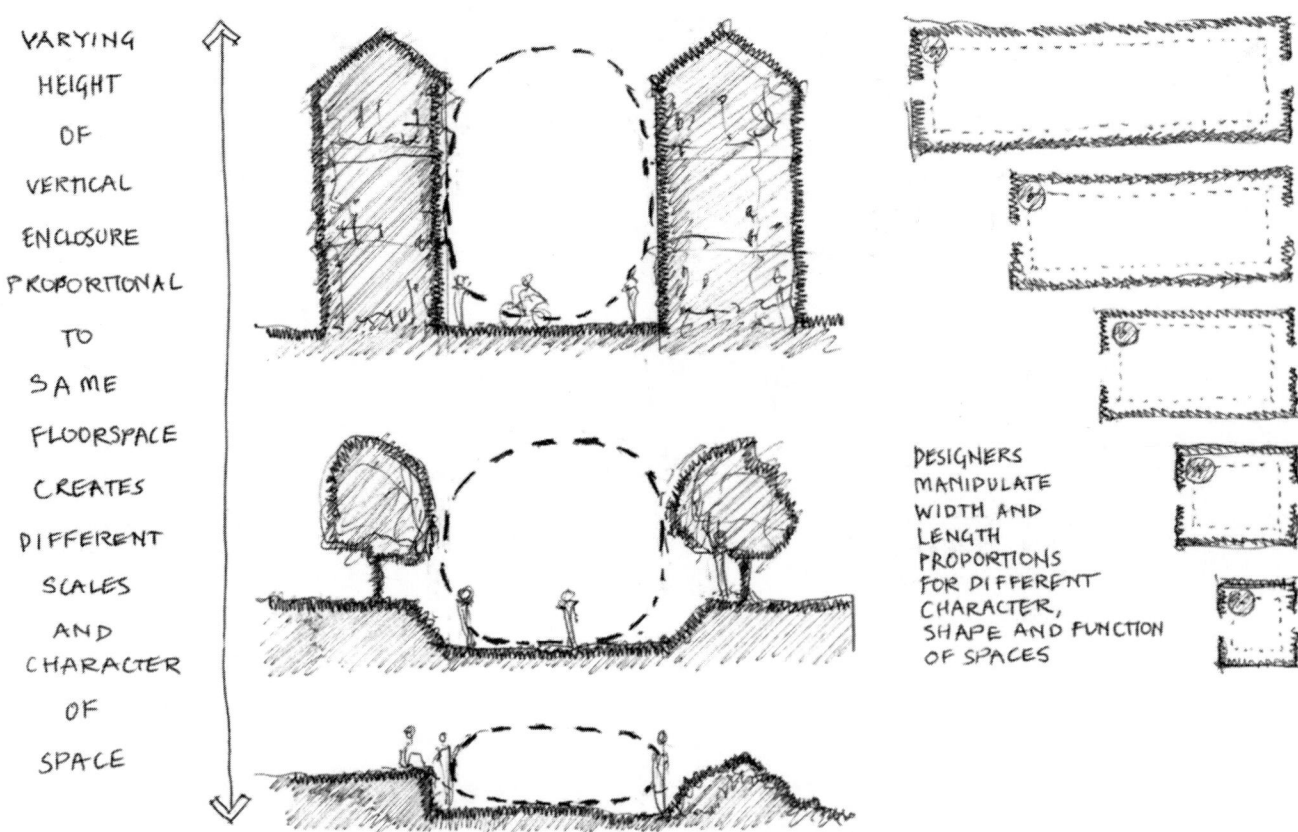

VARYING HEIGHT OF VERTICAL ENCLOSURE PROPORTIONAL TO SAME FLOORSPACE CREATES DIFFERENT SCALES AND CHARACTER OF SPACE

DESIGNERS MANIPULATE WIDTH AND LENGTH PROPORTIONS FOR DIFFERENT CHARACTER, SHAPE AND FUNCTION OF SPACES

Proportion of spaces

Proportion refers to the relative dimensions of parts of a three-dimensional form or space. The designer adapts and composes the relative length, width and height of a space or series of spaces and so decides on proportions.

Satisfying proportions

It is claimed that certain length, width and height ratios provide greater aesthetic satisfaction than others. For example, the 'golden section' is said to provide rectangular forms and relationships which are more pleasing than other rectangular forms and organisations. Others suggest that building heights and street or square widths have optimum ratios for pleasing proportions (Greenbie 1981). A good way to understand proportion and its effects is to experience, study and measure in the landscape.

EXPOSURE?

ENCLOSURE LOW IN PROPORTION TO SPACE FLOOR (FOR ADULTS NOT CHILDREN)

CLAUSTRAPHOBIC?

TALL SIDES OF SPACE IN PROPORTION TO FLOOR WIDTH

HIGH SIDED SUNKEN SPACE - PROPORTIONS CAN INTIMIDATE

Over-vertical and under-vertical enclosure

As previously suggested, if the height of enclosing vertical planes appears too great in proportion to the width and length of the ground plane, a space can be experienced as claustrophobic and threatening. Equally, a lack of vertical height in enclosure can also be intimidating and exposing.

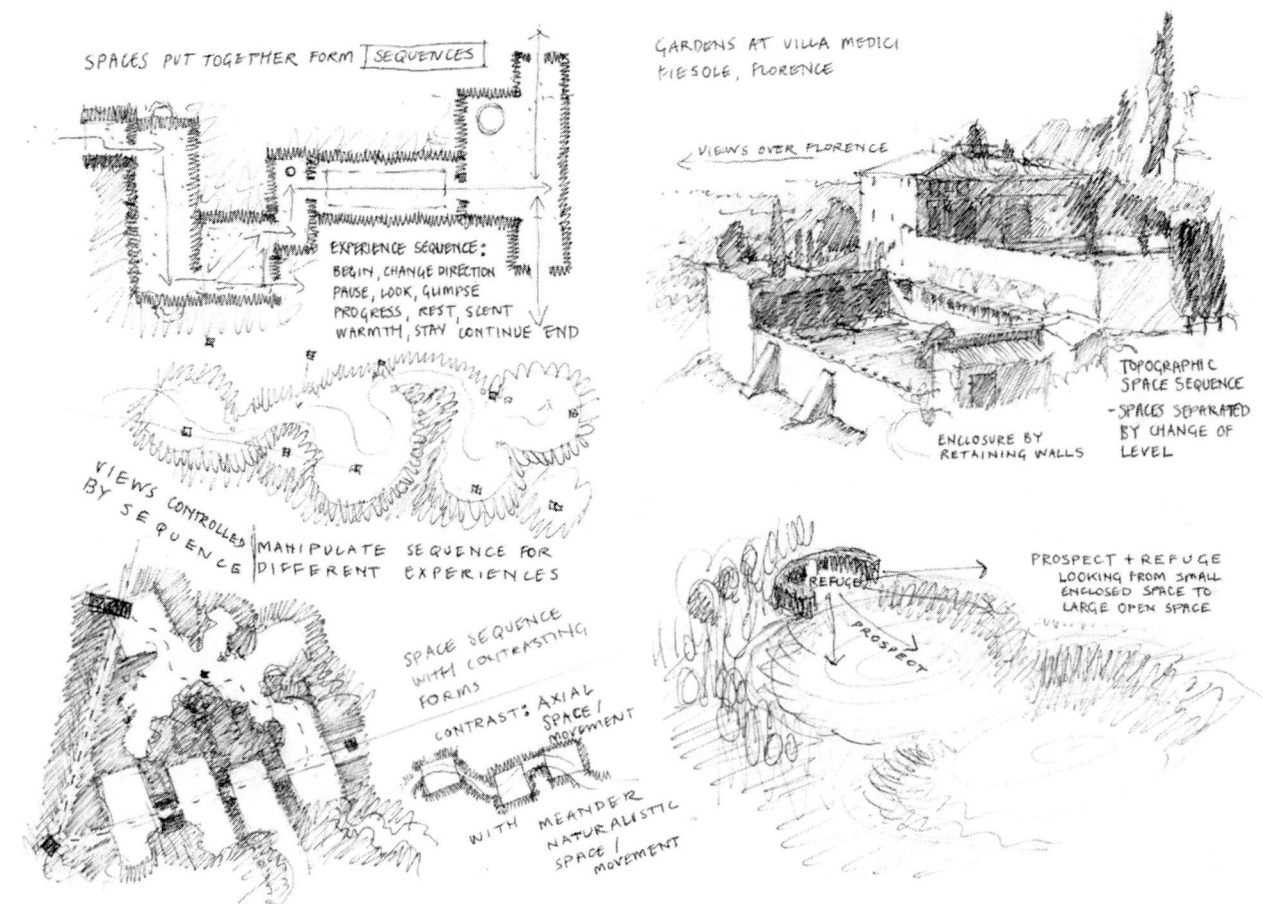

Space relationships

The design of landscapes involves not only the design of single spaces but deciding how different spaces should be related to each other. The designer can organise space relationships by thinking about how places might be experienced and used.

Sequence of spaces

Landscapes are places of movement. Therefore, a central consideration for landscape architects is to consider the sequential experience of moving from one space to another. Sequential experience and space relationships are also explored in the sections on Paths (see pp. 83 and 85) and Thresholds (p. 171).

Topographic space relationships

Landscapes are rarely flat, and the design of topographic space relationships is one of the biggest challenges in landscape architecture in addition to providing creative opportunity. The topographic spaces section explores some of this potential.

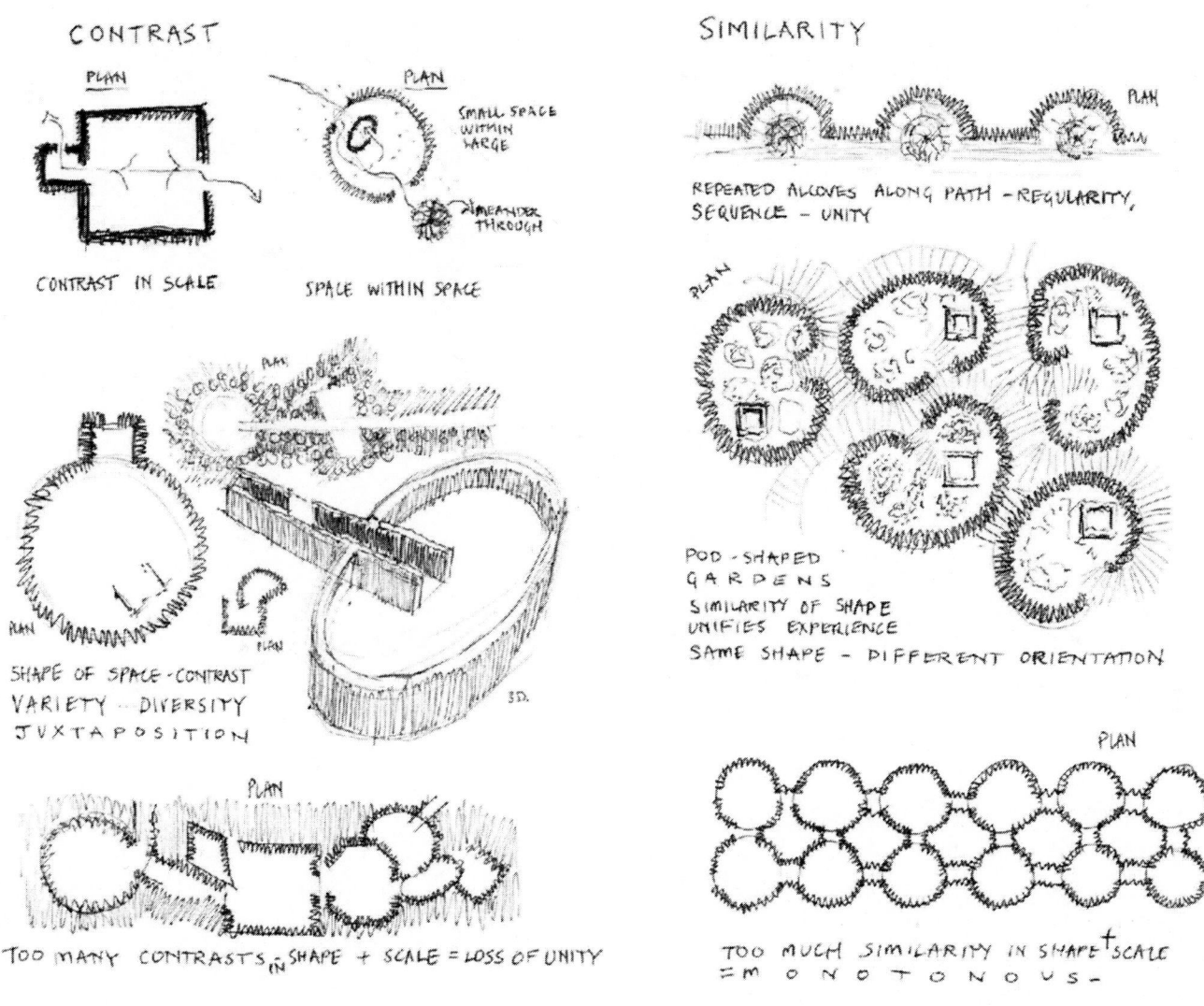

CONTRAST

SIMILARITY

PLAN

PLAN

SMALL SPACE
WITHIN
LARGE

MEANDER
THROUGH

CONTRAST IN SCALE

SPACE WITHIN SPACE

REPEATED ALCOVES ALONG PATH - REGULARITY,
SEQUENCE - UNITY

PLAN

PLAN

3D.

POD - SHAPED
G A R D E N S
SIMILARITY OF SHAPE
UNIFIES EXPERIENCE
SAME SHAPE - DIFFERENT ORIENTATION

SHAPE OF SPACE - CONTRAST
VARIETY - DIVERSITY
J U X T A P O S I T I O N

PLAN

PLAN

TOO MANY CONTRASTS IN SHAPE + SCALE = LOSS OF UNITY

TOO MUCH SIMILARITY IN SHAPE + SCALE
= M O N O T O N O U S -

Contrast and similarity of spaces

A landscape can be unified by repeating spaces of similar shape or size. Likewise, diversity in landscapes can be achieved through varying size or shape of spaces. The designer must make judgements about how much diversity and unity are required and may seek to balance the two to avoid monotony or chaos.

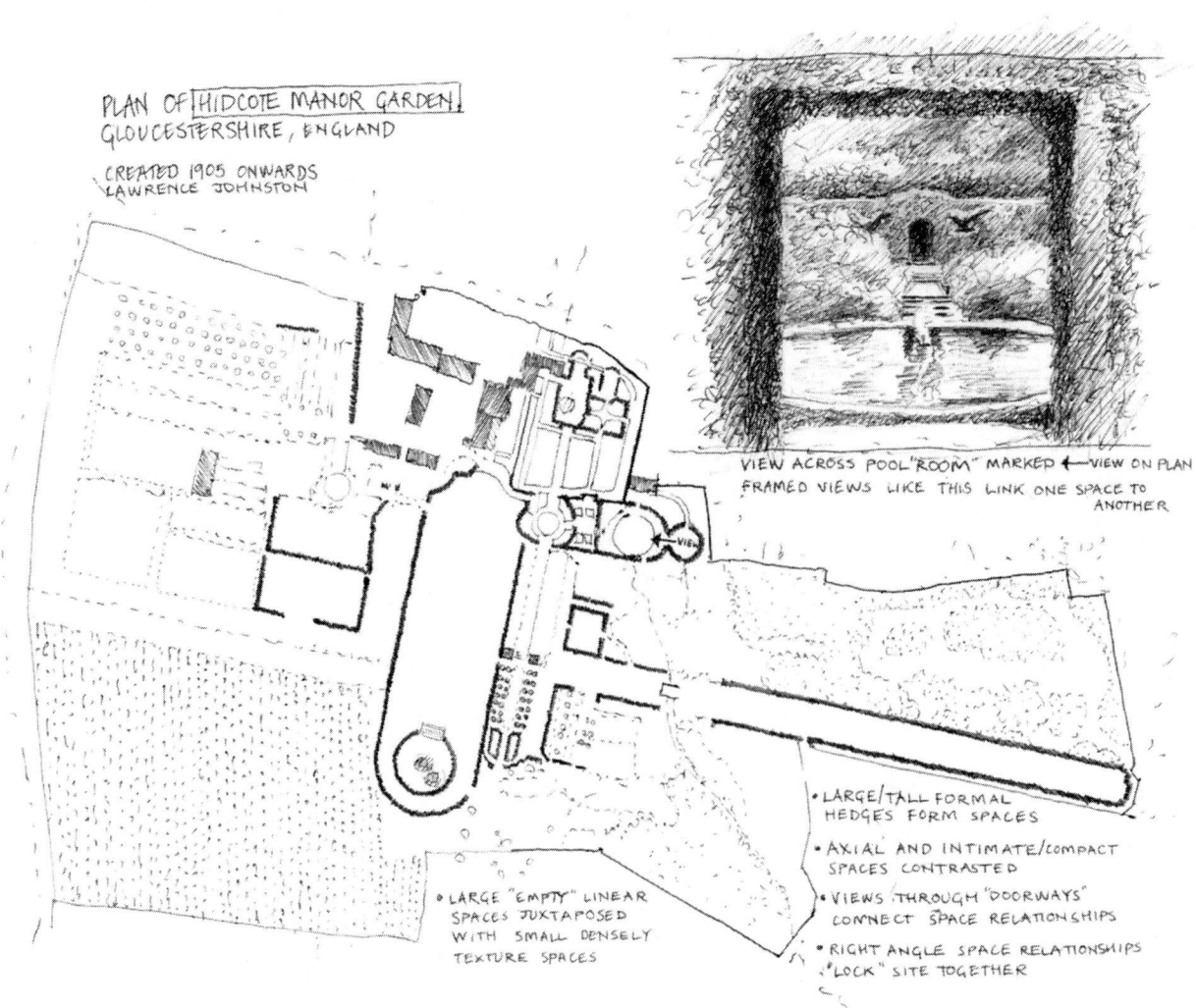

PLAN OF HIDCOTE MANOR GARDEN,
GLOUCESTERSHIRE, ENGLAND

CREATED 1905 ONWARDS
LAWRENCE JOHNSTON

VIEW ACROSS POOL "ROOM" MARKED ← VIEW ON PLAN
FRAMED VIEWS LIKE THIS LINK ONE SPACE TO
ANOTHER

• LARGE/TALL FORMAL
HEDGES FORM SPACES

• AXIAL AND INTIMATE/COMPACT
SPACES CONTRASTED

• VIEWS THROUGH "DOORWAYS"
CONNECT SPACE RELATIONSHIPS

• RIGHT ANGLE SPACE RELATIONSHIPS
"LOCK" SITE TOGETHER

• LARGE "EMPTY" LINEAR
SPACES JUXTAPOSED
WITH SMALL DENSELY
TEXTURE SPACES

Space relationships – an example

Hidcote Manor gardens provide a good example of effective spatial sequences using contrast and similarity of scale and proportion, axiality and perpendicular spatial arrangements. The garden is often described as a series of outdoor rooms. Each room has distinct characteristics, colours and purpose but each forms part of a whole sequence. Pleasure is derived from sequential movement through the spaces. The high hedges enclose spaces and frame views and vistas of spaces within the garden and the landscape beyond simultaneously providing a sense of unity, continuity, mystery, anticipation and containment.

Topographic spaces

DRAWING OF: ISAMU NOGUCHI'S "CONTOURED PLAYGROUND"
1941, NEW YORK, PLASTER

The following pages explore the use of topography to create spaces.

Topographic design

Landform is perhaps the most fundamental element in landscape architectural design. Natural and artificial topography can be manipulated, modified, or conserved to fully or partially enclose space. Learning to do this with subtlety, sensitivity and originality is an essential design skill.

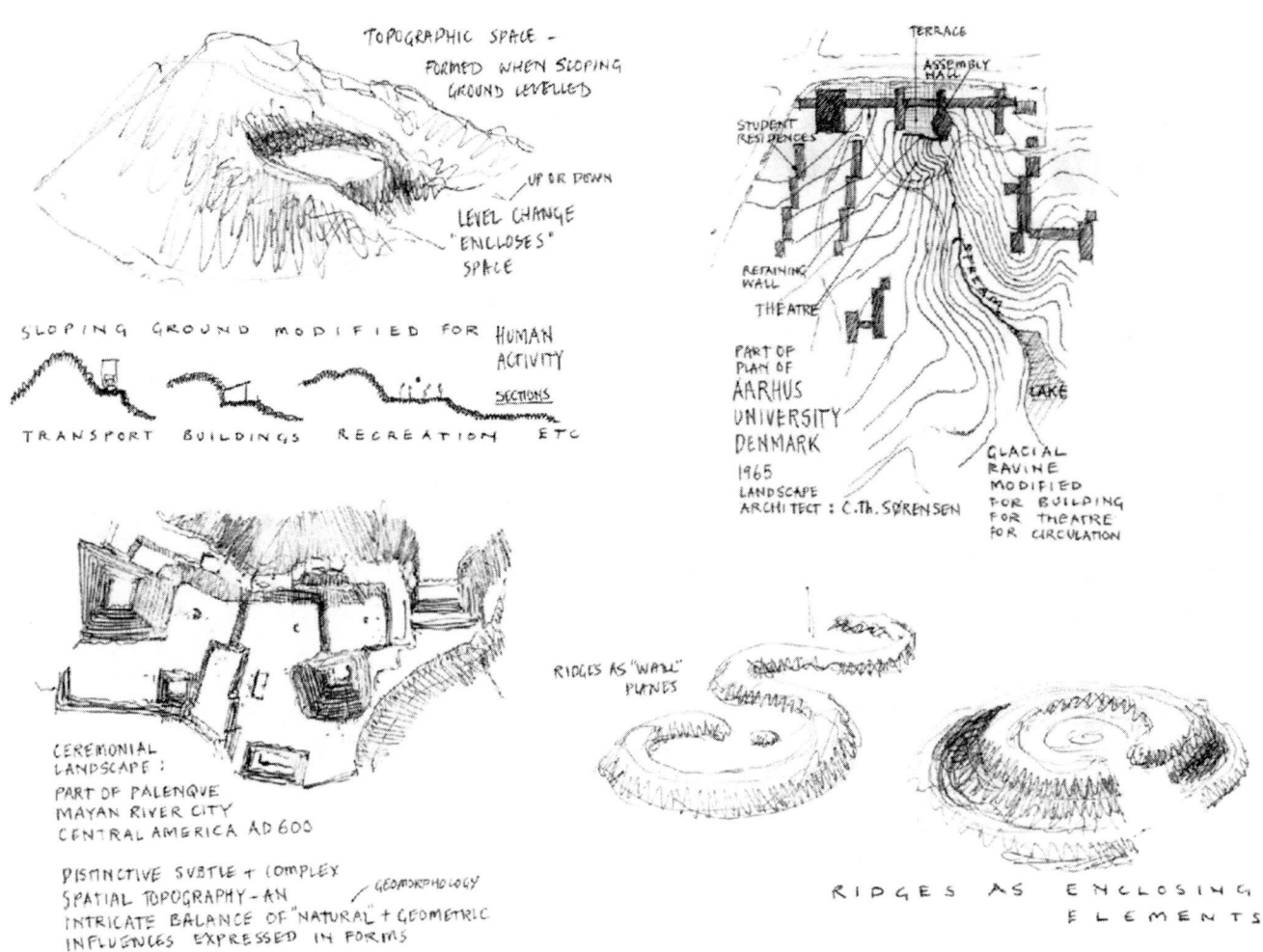

TOPOGRAPHIC SPACE - FORMED WHEN SLOPING GROUND LEVELLED

UP OR DOWN

LEVEL CHANGE "ENCLOSES" SPACE

SLOPING GROUND MODIFIED FOR HUMAN ACTIVITY

SECTIONS

TRANSPORT   BUILDINGS   RECREATION   ETC

TERRACE

ASSEMBLY HALL

STUDENT RESIDENCES

RETAINING WALL

THEATRE

PART OF PLAN OF AARHUS UNIVERSITY DENMARK 1965 LANDSCAPE ARCHITECT : C.Th. SØRENSEN

STREAM

LAKE

GLACIAL RAVINE MODIFIED FOR BUILDING FOR THEATRE FOR CIRCULATION

CEREMONIAL LANDSCAPE : PART OF PALENQUE MAYAN RIVER CITY CENTRAL AMERICA AD 600

DISTINCTIVE SUBTLE + COMPLEX SPATIAL TOPOGRAPHY - AN INTRICATE BALANCE OF NATURAL + GEOMETRIC INFLUENCES EXPRESSED IN FORMS

GEOMORPHOLOGY

RIDGES AS "WALL" PLANES

RIDGES AS ENCLOSING ELEMENTS

Flatness and degrees of intervention

The effect of gravity means that human beings consistently seek to create flat or horizontal spaces for many activities, including building, dwelling and a wide range of social, cultural and recreational activities. The designer must often decide how much intervention there should be to alter the natural or existing topography. Thus existing topography exerts a powerful influence on design forms and solutions.

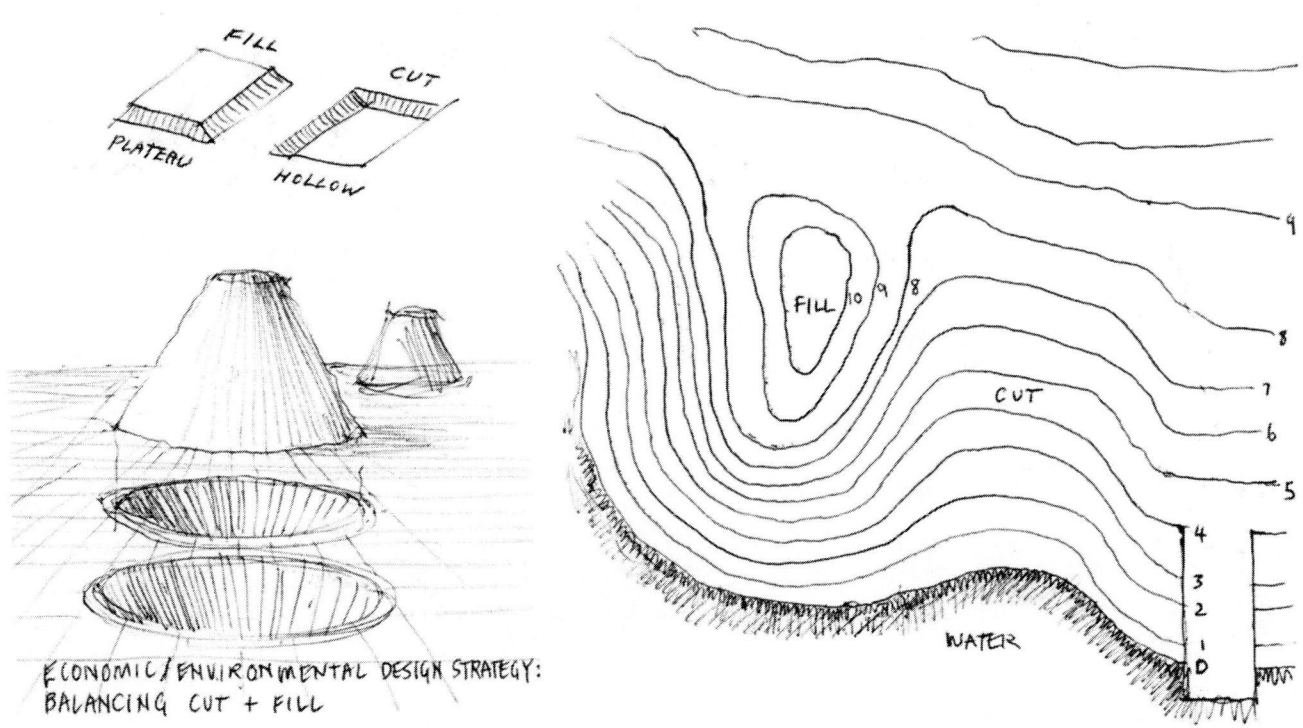

ECONOMIC/ENVIRONMENTAL DESIGN STRATEGY:
BALANCING CUT + FILL

Cut and fill

The process of taking away and adding earth to change landform is known as 'cut and fill'. Frequently the landscape architect may seek to balance the 'cut' (land removed) and 'fill' (land added) within their topographic design to reduce the need for transporting material elsewhere. Balancing cut and fill is desirable for financial and energy-saving reasons.

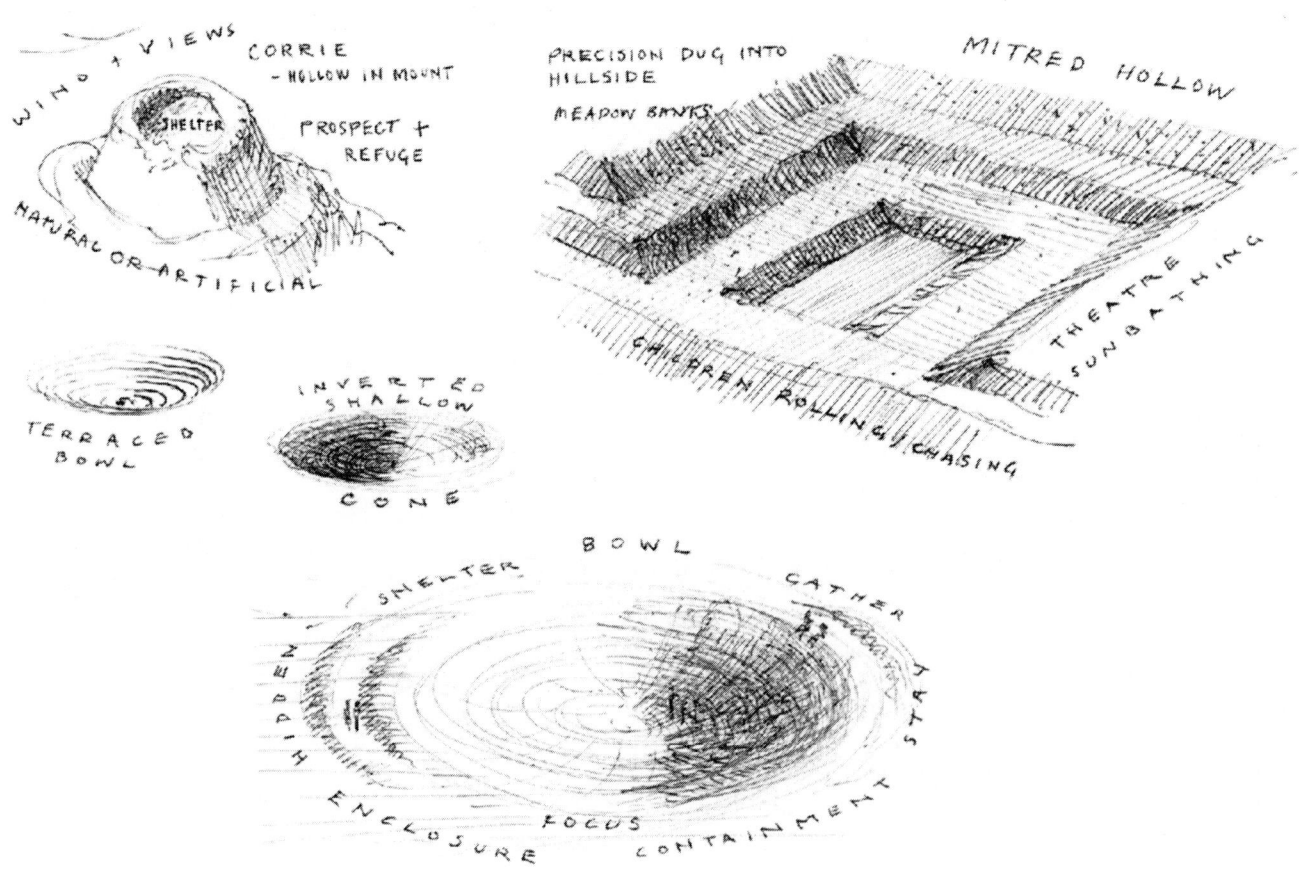

Bowls and hollows

Digging into the ground or raising banks around an area is an immediate and fundamental way of creating space within a landscape. Regular and irregular bowls and hollows in the ground plane attract people and events. The designer can modify existing depressions or artificially excavate them. Bowls form natural theatres, and endless variations on the theatre form (including the amphitheatre) provide rich themes for the design of public and collective space. As natural gathering places, bowls are focal spaces that bring people together, providing shelter and microclimatic diversity. They are play-inspiring. Hollows are smaller, more intimate spaces for secluded sitting or play, for example.

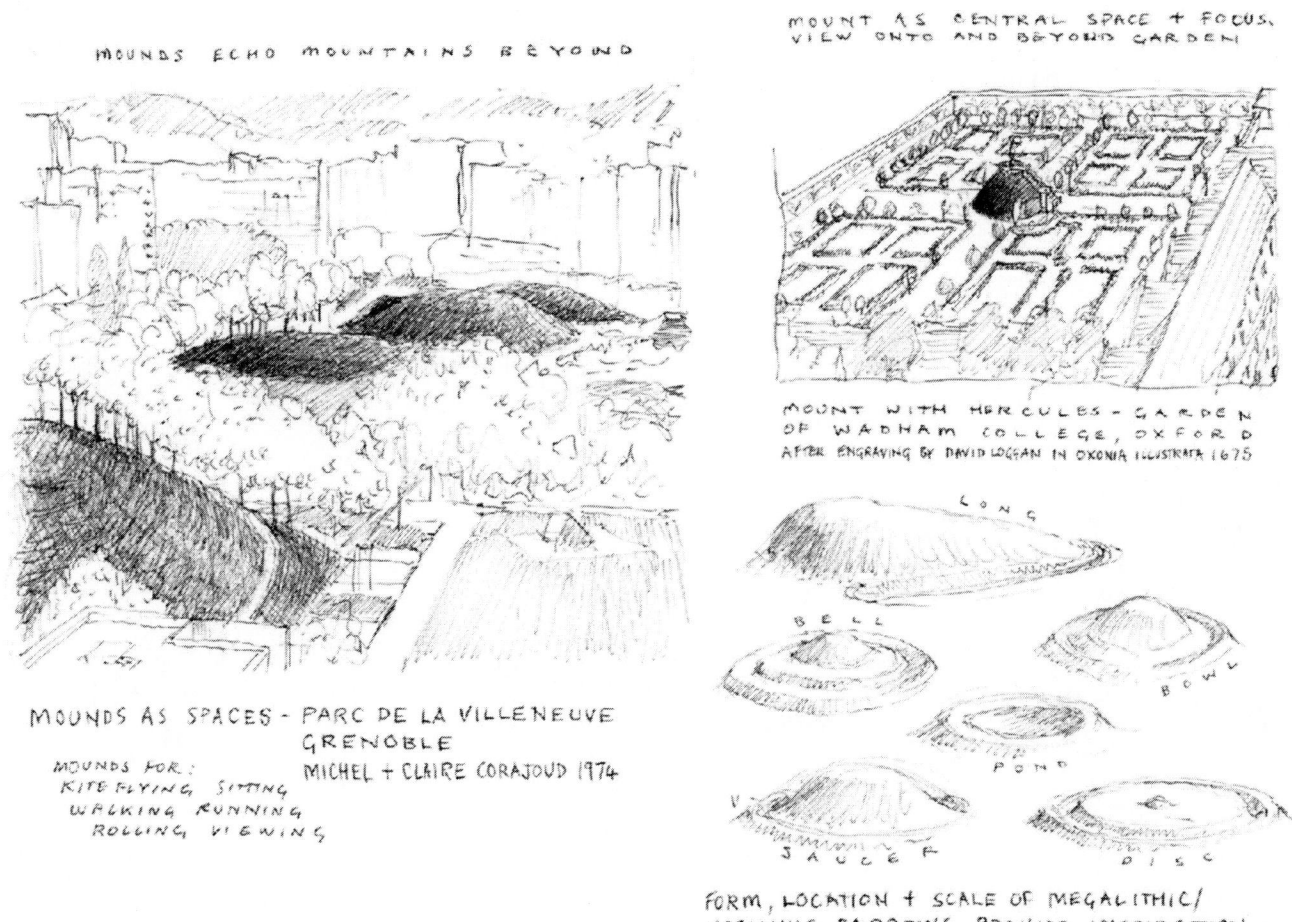

MOUNDS ECHO MOUNTAINS BEYOND

MOUNT AS CENTRAL SPACE + FOCUS,
VIEW ONTO AND BEYOND GARDEN

MOUNT WITH HERCULES - GARDEN
OF WADHAM COLLEGE, OXFORD
AFTER ENGRAVING BY DAVID LOGGAN IN OXONIA ILLUSTRATA 1675

MOUNDS AS SPACES - PARC DE LA VILLENEUVE
GRENOBLE
MOUNDS FOR :   MICHEL + CLAIRE CORAJOUD 1974
KITE FLYING SITTING
WALKING RUNNING
ROLLING VIEWING

FORM, LOCATION + SCALE OF MEGALITHIC/
NEOLITHIC BARROWS PROVIDE INSPIRATION.....

Mounds and mounts

Mound and mount spaces are created by raising ground in contrast to surrounding flatter land. Natural and artificial mounds and mounts attract people to climb, view, roll, chase and sit or fly kites. There is pleasure and security in occupying a raised position. The designer can use mounds and mounts to create distinct and focal places (see also Topographic foci), especially where views are to be had. 'Mounds' is a term used to describe relatively gentle sloping naturalistic or natural forms, while 'mounts' are steeper or more geometric and artificial forms.

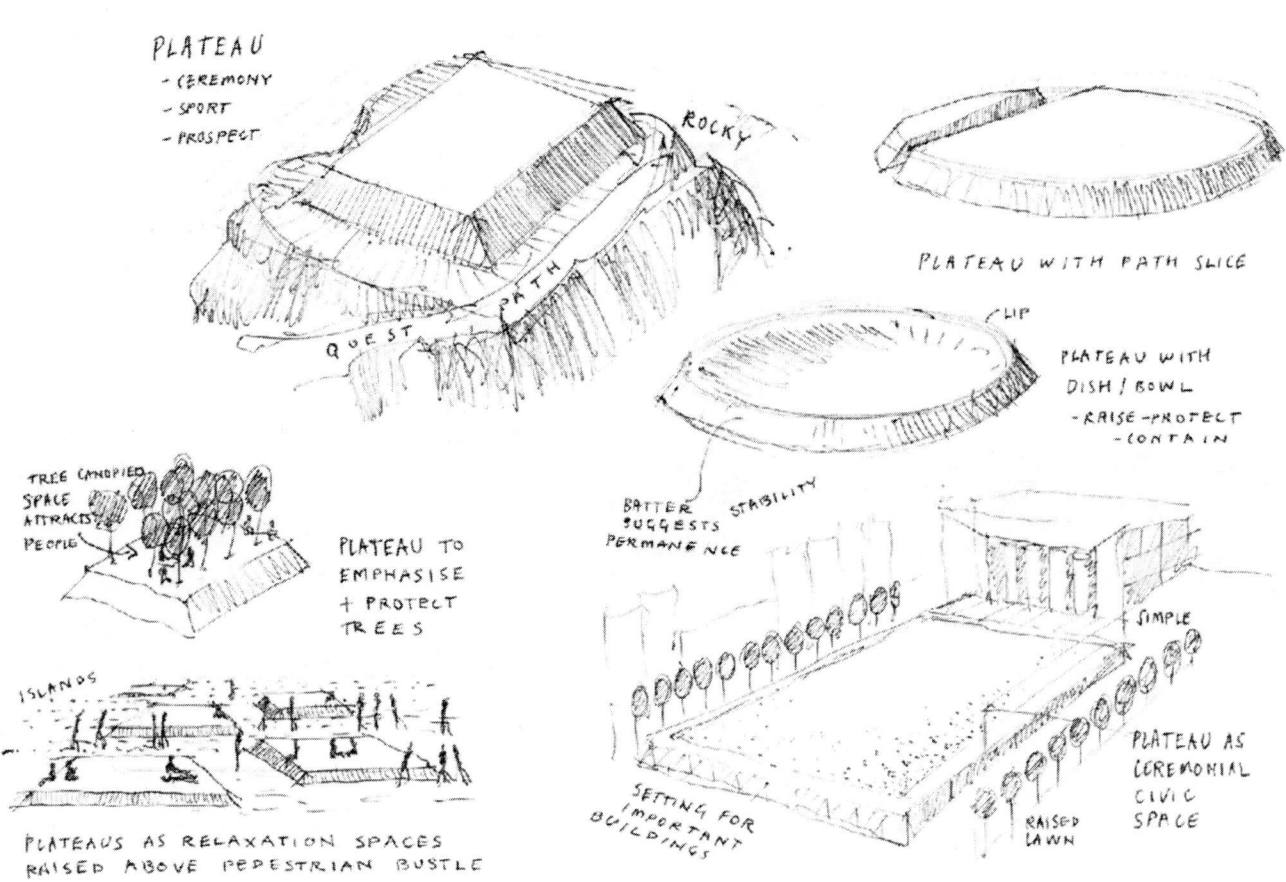

Plateaus

Like mounds and mounts the plateau is an attractive form for landscape spaces. The plateau 'suggests' both casual and ceremonial activity. It is a plinth for events because of its raised, sliced top. Plateaus can be grouped like rafts afloat amid a sea of flatness. A high plateau enables a journey of anticipation and mystery towards the unseen top. Plateaus can be places that are slightly removed from urban bustle and many small plateaus in an urban square allow groups and individuals to take possession of defensible space. Built plateaus provide small banks for skateboards or clambering children.

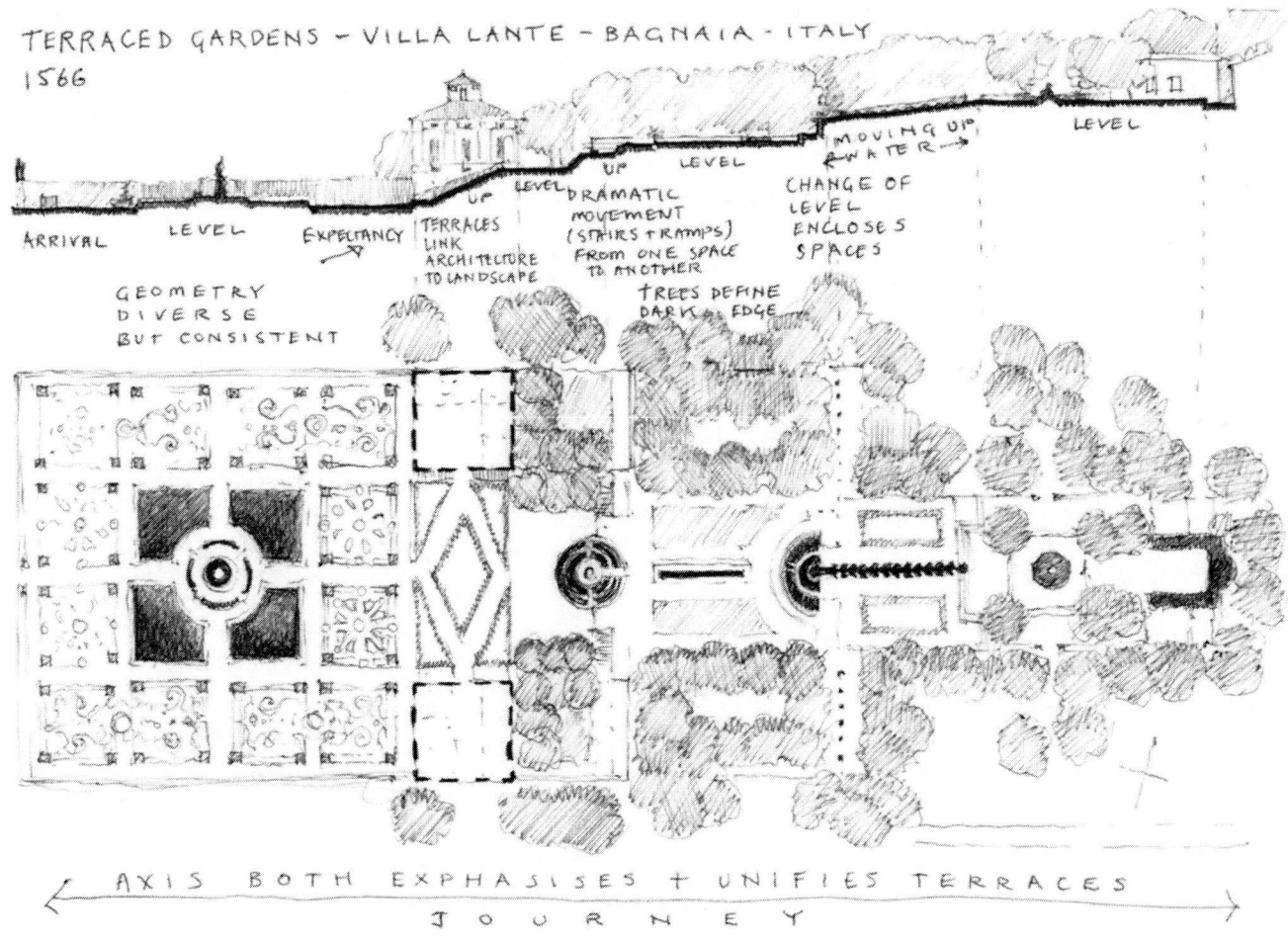

TERRACED GARDENS - VILLA LANTE - BAGNAIA - ITALY
1566

AXIS BOTH EXPHASISES + UNIFIES TERRACES

JOURNEY

Terraces

A terrace is the flat space created by digging into or building out from a hillside. Terrace spaces can 'respond' subtly and or distinctively through juxtaposition to or subordination of the contouring and scale of the existing (natural) topography. Geometric interventions can be exciting when they 'reveal' or 'balance' natural topogra-phies but are bleak when over-scaled or ineffectively juxtaposed. Terraces are commonly used to link archi-tecture with landscape, especially in gardens, and frequently become extensions of living space. Terraces can affect microclimate positively and negatively by creating both shady and sunny retaining walls.

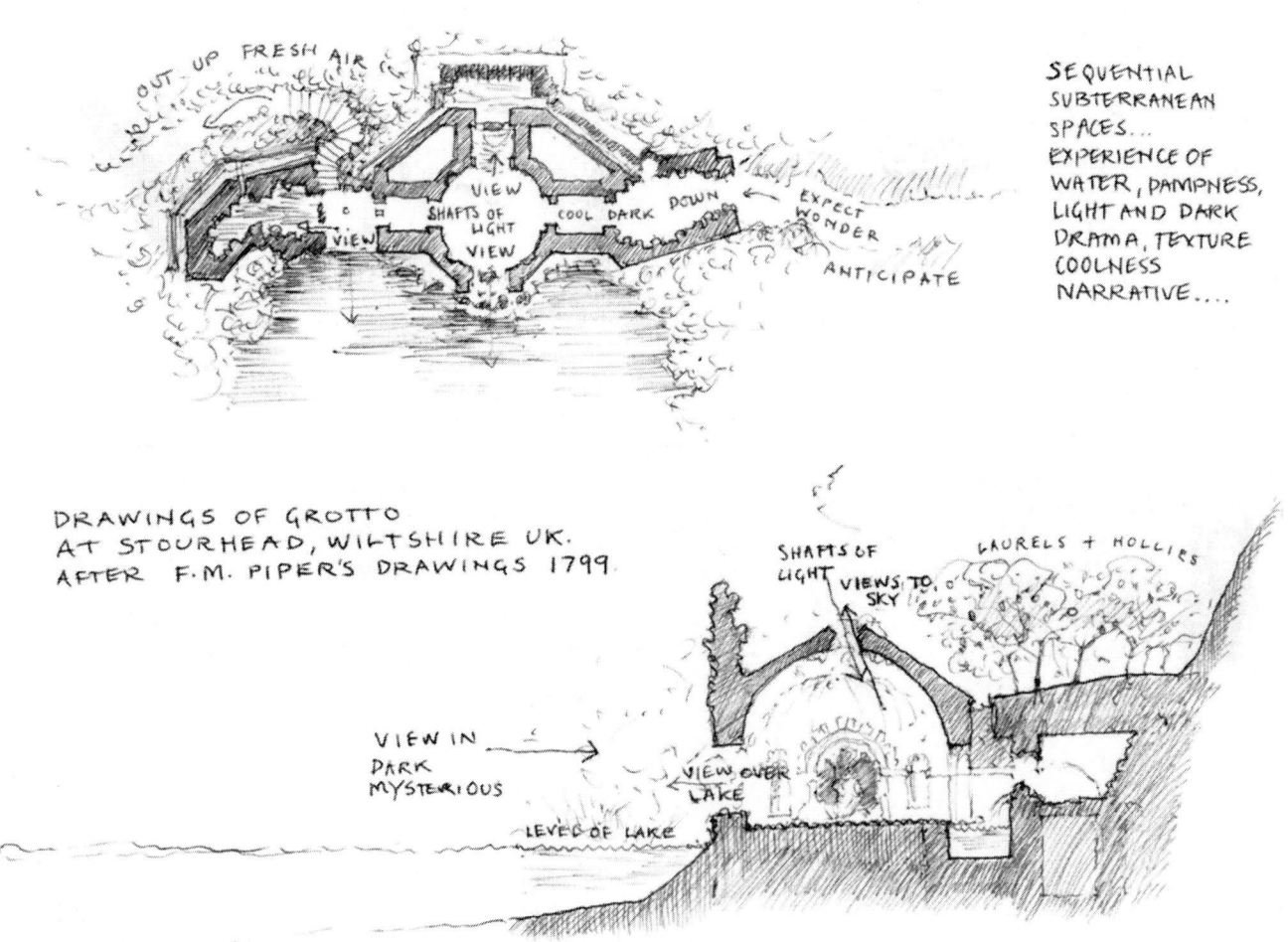

SEQUENTIAL SUBTERRANEAN SPACES... EXPERIENCE OF WATER, DAMPNESS, LIGHT AND DARK DRAMA, TEXTURE COOLNESS NARRATIVE....

OUT. UP FRESH AIR

VIEW
SHAFTS OF LIGHT
VIEW
VIEW

COOL DARK DOWN

EXPECT WONDER

ANTICIPATE

DRAWINGS OF GROTTO AT STOURHEAD, WILTSHIRE UK. AFTER F.M. PIPER'S DRAWINGS 1799

SHAFTS OF LIGHT
VIEWS TO SKY
LAURELS + HOLLIES

VIEW IN DARK MYSTERIOUS

VIEW OVER LAKE

LEVEL OF LAKE

Subterranean spaces

Secret, hidden, damp, glittering or dark, subterranean spaces in landscapes are places of both fear and attraction. Among other factors, context and gender affect response to places below ground. They can be places of urban threat or of spiritual significance. In the right context there are many design opportunities to exploit, for example, the play of light, echo sounds, closeness to water or symbolic journeys. Subterranean spaces provide the potential for architectural and landscape design to merge.

61

Vegetation spaces

PLAN GLADE STRUCTURE

Vegetation is a primary medium for defining space within landscapes. Planting design is a specialised and 'central' discipline of landscape architecture. Plants can be used and conserved as structural elements to create spaces. In these situations the ornamental properties of plants often play subsidiary roles. Plants can provide enclosure in ground, wall or sky planes and can be combined in an infinite variety of ways.

Trees and shrubs play major vertical spatial roles with herbaceous plants, grasses and bulbs often (but not always, as in the case of tall grasses) used in ground planes and for lower enclosure. Learning to mass and group plants for spatial effects is an important design skill. Treating plants as individual forms is only important when used as foci (see Vegetation foci, p. 158) or as accents. As design material, plants provide opportunities for a great deal of diversity in enclosure permeability and form. Time and vegetation management must be considered integral concepts in planting design.

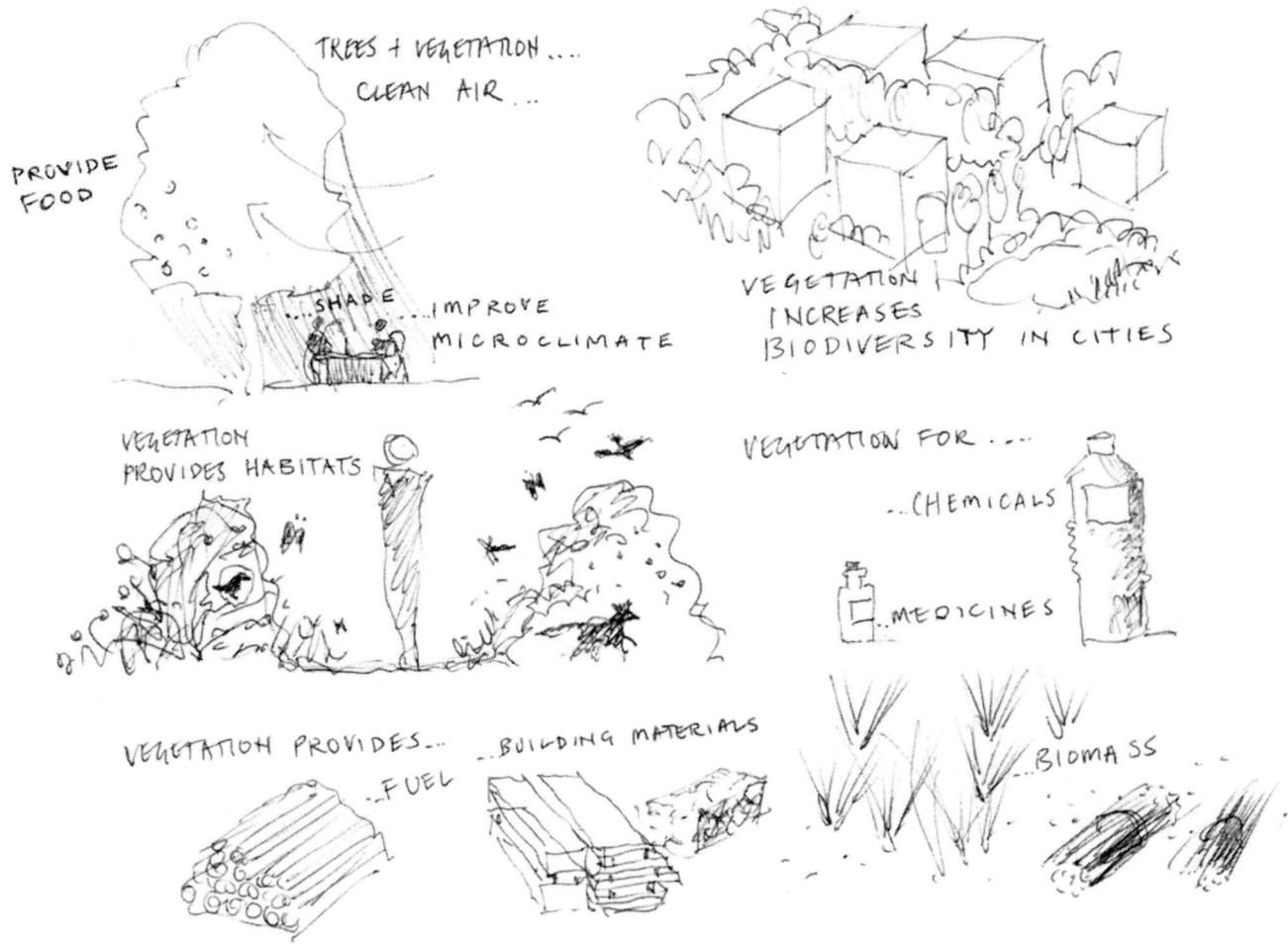

Ecological and environmental roles of vegetation

Vegetation is a primary medium of landscape architecture not only for its aesthetic and structural properties and meanings (the focus here), but also for a wide range of environmental reasons. As part of ecosystems, plants form habitats for wildlife and people and contribute to biodiversity, particularly in urban areas. They clean the air and positively influence the climate for human comfort and health. Being renewable, plants are major 'components' of sustainable living; providing food, building materials, fuel, medicines and chemicals. While this section primarily explores spatial, aesthetic and cultural aspects of plants, it is important to emphasise that their use in design always has environmental implications and potential.

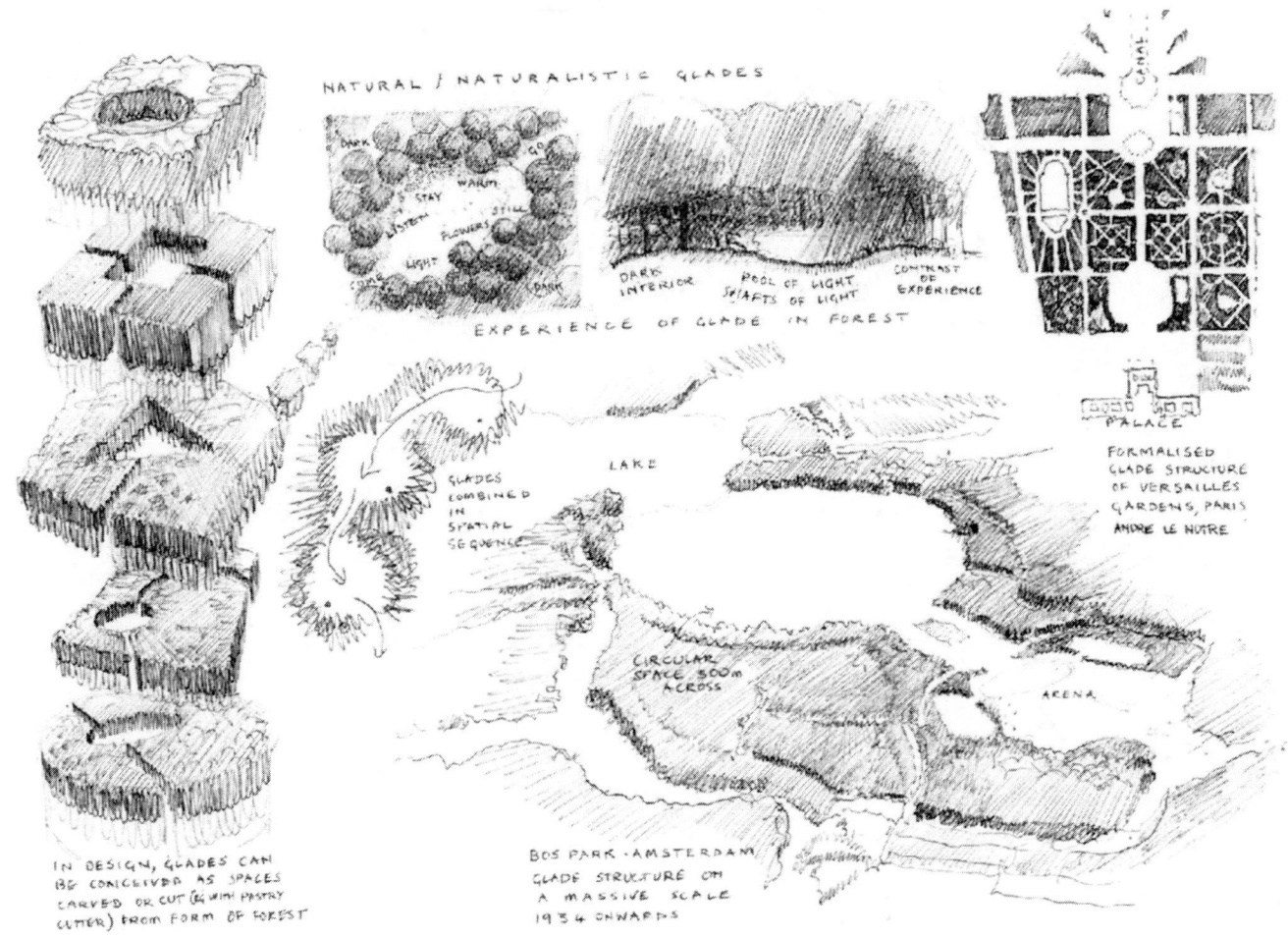

NATURAL / NATURALISTIC GLADES

DARK, STAY, WARM, LISTEN, GO, FLOWERS, STILL, LIGHT, DARK

DARK INTERIOR

POOL OF LIGHT SHAFTS OF LIGHT

CONTRAST OF EXPERIENCE

EXPERIENCE OF GLADE IN FOREST

GLADES COMBINED IN SPATIAL SEQUENCE

LAKE

CANAL

PALACE

FORMALISED GLADE STRUCTURE OF VERSAILLES GARDENS, PARIS ANDRE LE NOTRE

CIRCULAR SPACE 300m ACROSS

ARENA

IN DESIGN, GLADES CAN BE CONCEIVED AS SPACES CARVED OR CUT (eg WITH PASTRY CUTTER) FROM FORM OF FOREST

BOS PARK · AMSTERDAM GLADE STRUCTURE ON A MASSIVE SCALE 1934 ONWARDS

Glades

The glade (or forest clearing) is a dramatic and 'primeval' space type. Glades provide contrasting landscape experiences, moving from dark to light, from enclosure to openness, from shade to sun. They are natural meeting places, dwelling places, and stopping and picnic places with views of the sky and different flora thriving in the increased light. Glades have symbolic and mythic significance in many European cultures. Creating glade spaces can be conceived as 'carving space' out of a 'mass' of trees, the forest canopy a solid out of which voids are created. As a spatial form the glade has diverse guises, from naturalistic to formal, and from vast to intimate. The designer aims to integrate glade and path sequences.

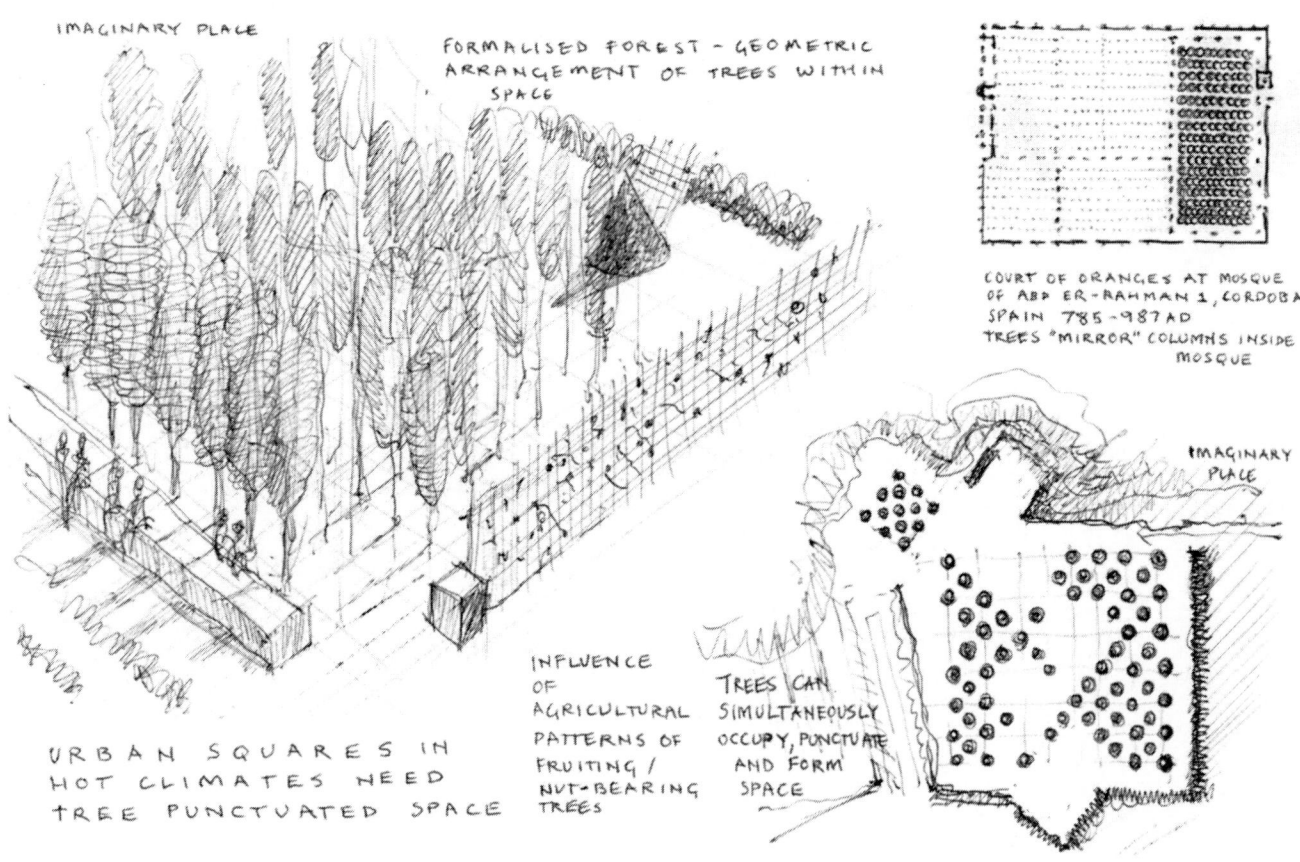

IMAGINARY PLACE

FORMALISED FOREST - GEOMETRIC ARRANGEMENT OF TREES WITHIN SPACE

COURT OF ORANGES AT MOSQUE OF ABD ER-RAHMAN 1, CORDOBA SPAIN 785-987 AD TREES "MIRROR" COLUMNS INSIDE MOSQUE

IMAGINARY PLACE

URBAN SQUARES IN HOT CLIMATES NEED TREE PUNCTUATED SPACE

INFLUENCE OF AGRICULTURAL PATTERNS OF FRUITING / NUT-BEARING TREES

TREES CAN SIMULTANEOUSLY OCCUPY, PUNCTUATE AND FORM SPACE

Forest space and the formalised forest

Forest space is complex and 'hidden' under the dense canopy of trees. Designers can underestimate the use and value of forest places because they are obscured in plan drawings. Forest space simultaneously incorporates void and mass. Space punctuated by columns of trunks is rich and structurally complex, especially when viewed while moving (see the section on Forest paths for further illustration, p. 101). Trunks are like human figures. Echoes, stillness, fear and delight, hunting, exploring, hiding, people often have ambiguous feelings in forest

space. It can be a place of menace or of longing or both. Context, gender and culture all affect the experience of forest space.

The use of 'formalised forest' in design and agriculture has a long history. The geometric organisation of trees in space in grids, quincunx and other formal arrangements can have similar spatial and experiential properties to forest space, although 'tamed' and ordered. The formalised forests of urban places can play important microclimatic roles particularly in hot climates.

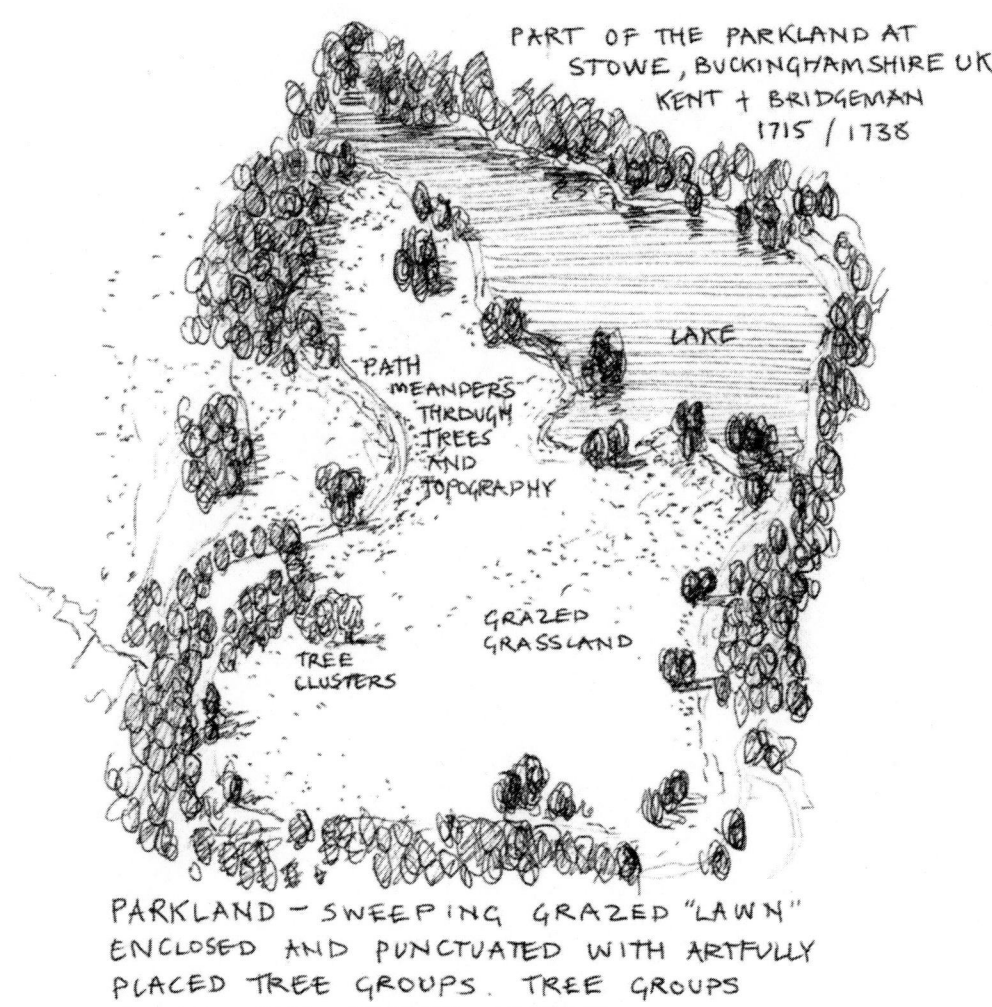

PART OF THE PARKLAND AT
STOWE, BUCKINGHAMSHIRE UK
KENT + BRIDGEMAN
1715 / 1738

LAKE

PATH
MEANDERS
THROUGH
TREES
AND
TOPOGRAPHY

GRAZED
GRASSLAND

TREE
CLUSTERS

PARKLAND — SWEEPING GRAZED "LAWN"
ENCLOSED AND PUNCTUATED WITH ARTFULLY
PLACED TREE GROUPS. TREE GROUPS
FRAME AND CREATE VISTAS

Parkland

Parkland refers to large open grassy spaces scattered with individual trees or clusters of trees, usually naturalistic in form and with rolling topography. Parkland is an enduring spatial type in landscape architecture. Its combination of openness punctuated by occasional trees appeals through simultaneous suggestions of 'naturalness' and control or order, and through its similarity to the savannah landscapes that early humans came to dwell and hunt in. As a space type it can be criticised for its blandness as an ecological, walking and visual environment. Parkland cannot be successfully created in small spaces.

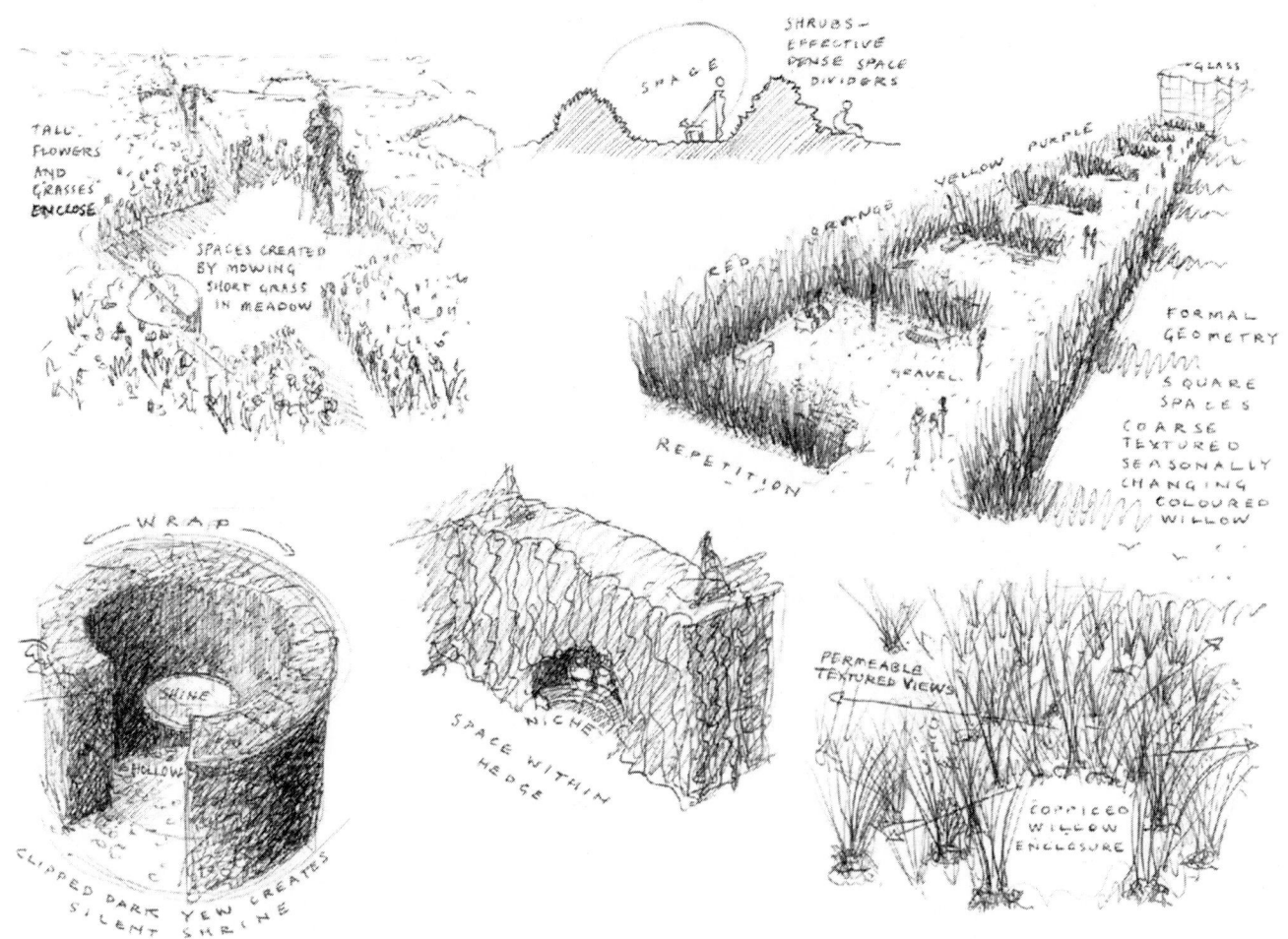

Hedged and herb enclosures

Hedges are relatively dense enclosers of space. Rough, thorny and billowing, or smooth, dark, and crisp – hedges vary in character and maintenance depending on context and intended design character. Hedges have historic and cultural roots in both garden and agriculture. They can be conceived in spatial design as green, living walls. They are long-lived. Human in scale and occupying relatively little space, hedges can be popular enclosers in urban and suburban environments, defining ownership and separating uses of land in domestic and public contexts.

Herbs and grasses can form seasonal space enclosures in temperate climates. The soft, coarse and open textures of plants can enclose space at knee height (particularly for children) and above. Scent, texture and plant movement combine to provide distinct sensory and dynamic enclosure experiences.

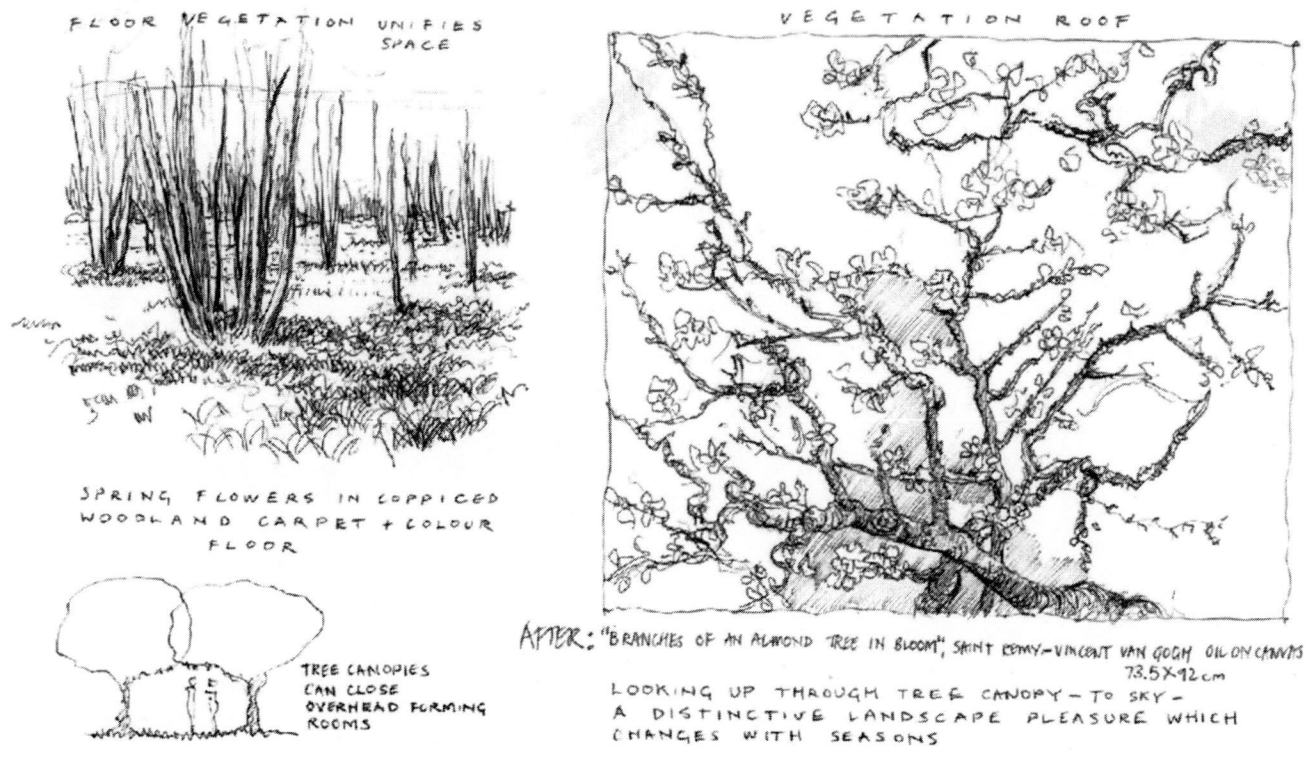

FLOOR VEGETATION UNIFIES SPACE

VEGETATION ROOF

SPRING FLOWERS IN COPPICED WOODLAND CARPET + COLOUR FLOOR

TREE CANOPIES CAN CLOSE OVERHEAD FORMING ROOMS

AFTER: "BRANCHES OF AN ALMOND TREE IN BLOOM", SAINT REMY—VINCENT VAN GOGH OIL ON CANVAS 73.5X92 cm
LOOKING UP THROUGH TREE CANOPY — TO SKY — A DISTINCTIVE LANDSCAPE PLEASURE WHICH CHANGES WITH SEASONS

Vegetated carpets

Vegetation occurs naturally and is often used in the ground plane in design. Landscape architects select species and management approaches appropriate to context, visual function and use. Floor vegetation can unify a space through the simplicity of a few dominant species (for example, lawn or moss) or through pattern and species repetition (for example, meadow or wood-land floor). Vegetation provides a soft carpet-like foil to built and rock structures and surfaces. Walking on vege-tated floors is a distinct part of the pleasure of landscape (see also Detail – Vegetation, pp. 201–3).

Leaf ceilings

By incorporating vegetation in the sky plane, designers can provide memorable landscape experiences. There is pleasure in the experience of looking up through leaf and blossom to sky above, or sheltering in shade patterned with green-brightened light. Leaf canopies create a distinct character of space which attracts people to shelter and stay especially in sunny weather.

Built spaces

ROOMS

GLASS ROOM

Structures, like vegetation and landform, play an important role in defining and enclosing spaces, particularly in urban contexts. Urban space is often partially or fully enclosed by buildings. Landscape architects work with structures in two main ways. They respond to or work with architects and urban designers to create positive building–landscape relationships and they also independently design free standing structures to enclose space. The designer considers materials and form in relation to context, function and visual intent when creating structures to define space.

Urban design, which may involve the work of landscape architects, is only briefly explored here by considering some characteristics and functions of two important urban space types: squares and courtyards. Streets are briefly considered in the section on Paths (see p. 106).

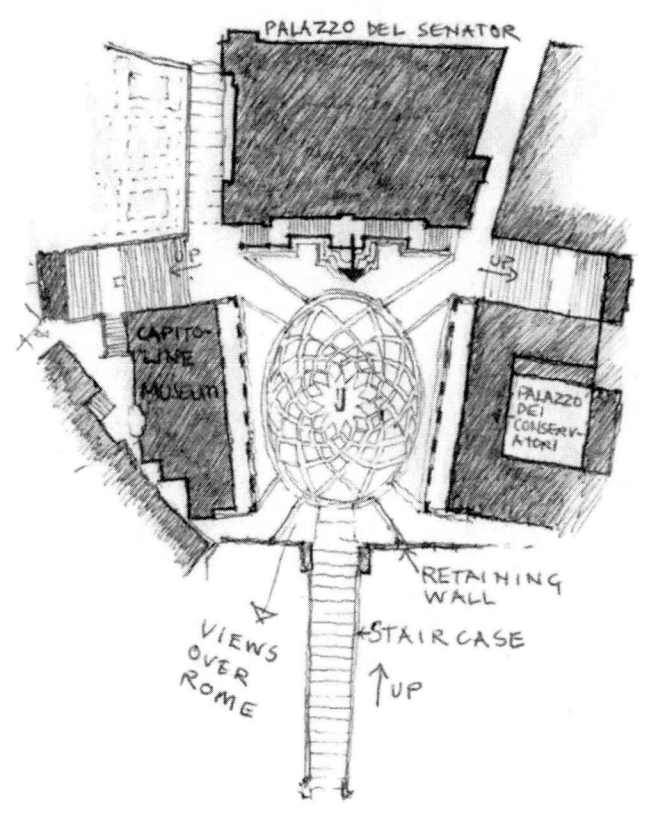

PALAZZO DEL SENATOR

CAPITO-
LINE
MUSEUM

PALAZZO
DEI
CONSERV-
ATORI

UP

UP

RETAINING
WALL

VIEWS
OVER
ROME

STAIRCASE

UP

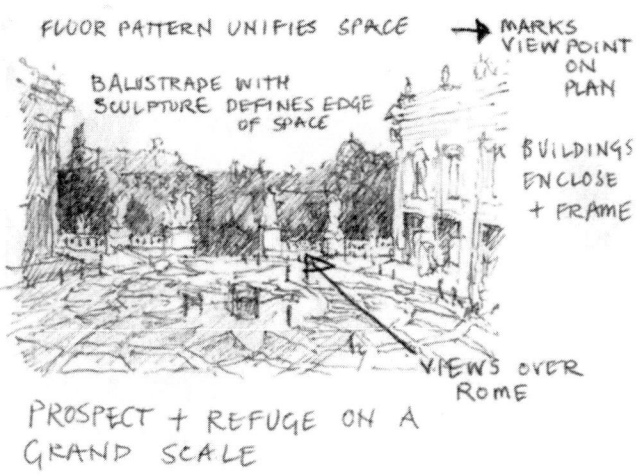

FLOOR PATTERN UNIFIES SPACE

MARKS
VIEW POINT
ON
PLAN

BALUSTRADE WITH
SCULPTURE DEFINES EDGE
OF SPACE

BUILDINGS
ENCLOSE
+ FRAME

VIEWS OVER
ROME

PROSPECT + REFUGE ON A
GRAND SCALE

PIAZZA DEL CAMPIDOGLIO, ROME

Public squares

Public squares play an important role in the cultural, social and commercial life of cities. Squares should be designed or modified for diverse and flexible public uses. The function and design of buildings that form the enclosing edge of these spaces have a great impact on the success and popularity of an urban square (see the section on Built edges, p. 137). Frequently used or symbolic public buildings, together with eating and drinking establishments, are often essential as enclosing structures for a square to be well used. The landscape design of public squares takes building form into consideration, but may also involve the creation of new forms and identity for an urban space.

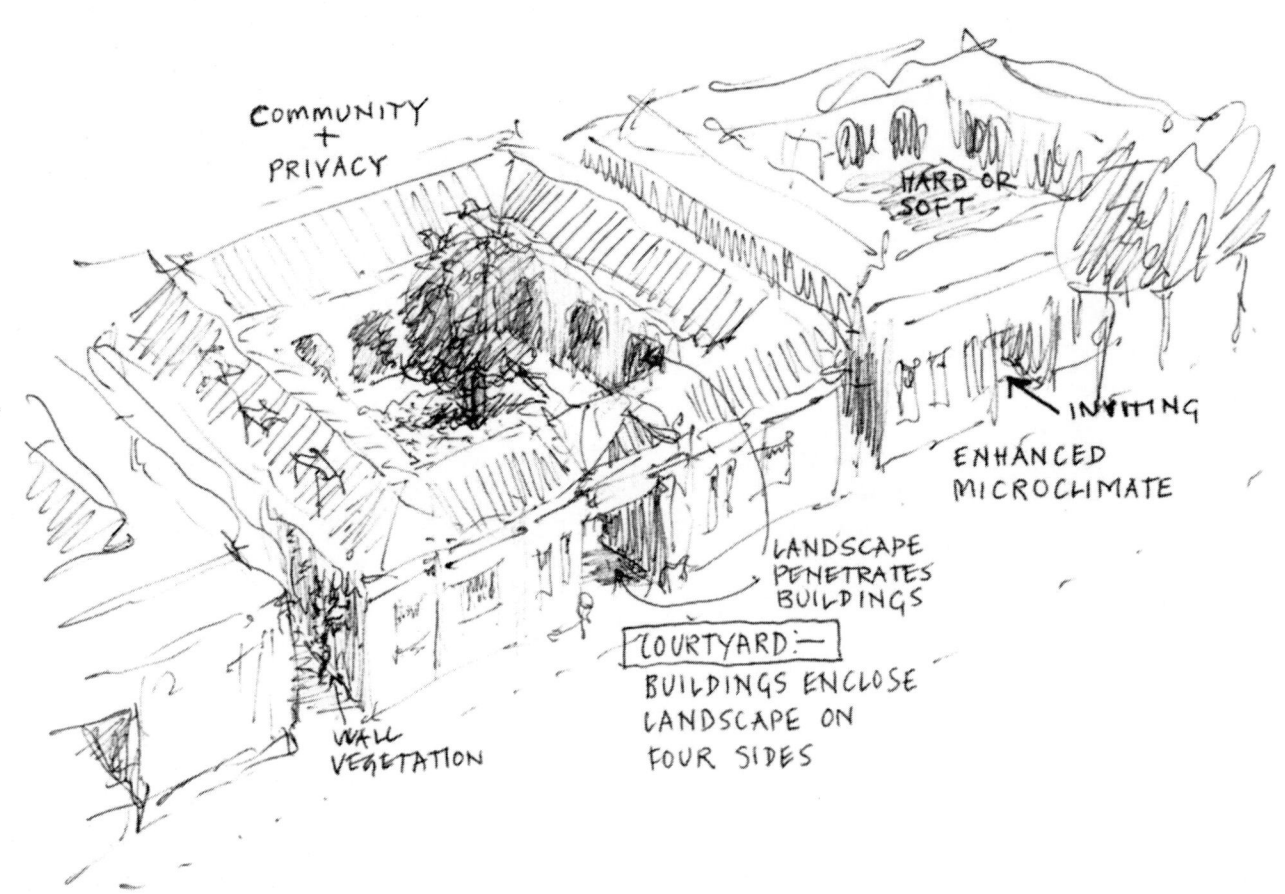

COMMUNITY + PRIVACY

HARD OR SOFT

INVITING

ENHANCED MICROCLIMATE

LANDSCAPE PENETRATES BUILDINGS

COURTYARD:— BUILDINGS ENCLOSE LANDSCAPE ON FOUR SIDES

WALL VEGETATION

Courtyards

Courtyards provide a private and domestic spatial counterpart to public squares and streets in urban environments. As an urban form, the landscape of courtyards provides space, light and greenery for social and private activities. Courtyards potentially enable close interaction between indoor and outdoor life because the architectural and landscape spaces are interwoven.

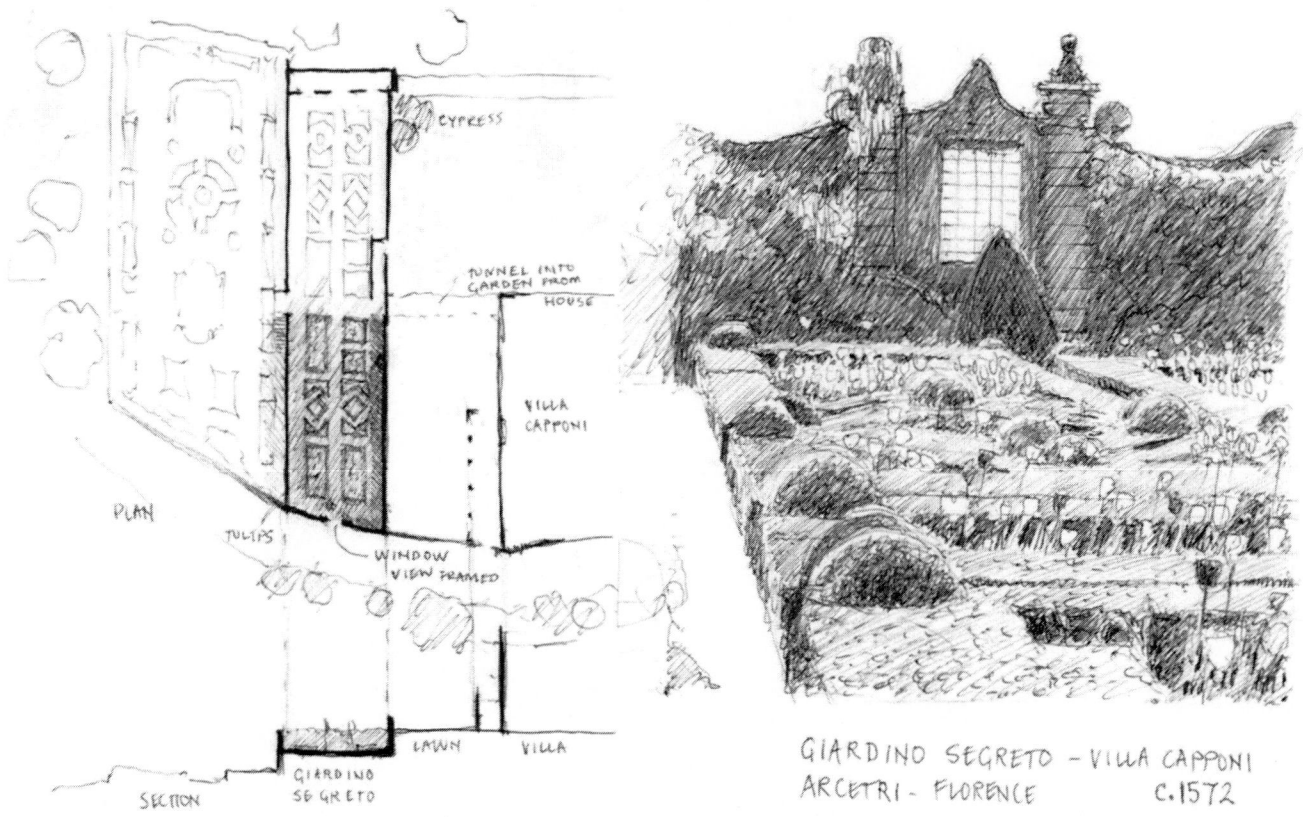

GIARDINO SEGRETO - VILLA CAPPONI
ARCETRI - FLORENCE   C.1572

Walls and walled gardens

As impermeable space dividers, walls play important roles in providing privacy and seclusion. As landscape structures they can be used in design to link architecture and landscape or to 'connect' a site to its underlying geology, thereby creating regionally distinct space. Walls provide sculptural and textural design opportunities. They strongly affect microclimate by absorbing sun and radiating warmth or providing shade and dampness. Walls can be homes for vegetation. They have diverse social and cultural uses in cities, in particular as surfaces for communication. Walls can be conceived of as backdrops onto which images may be projected, words written or dramas and games played out. Walls can also obscure, intimidate, obstruct and threaten, especially if too high or used unnecessarily in design.

The walled garden is an enduring landscape archetype with many manifestations in history. The popularity of this form lies in its potential for food production and horticulture, and in its associated aesthetic and recreational uses, including ornament with vegetation, seclusion and privacy and warmth or shade.

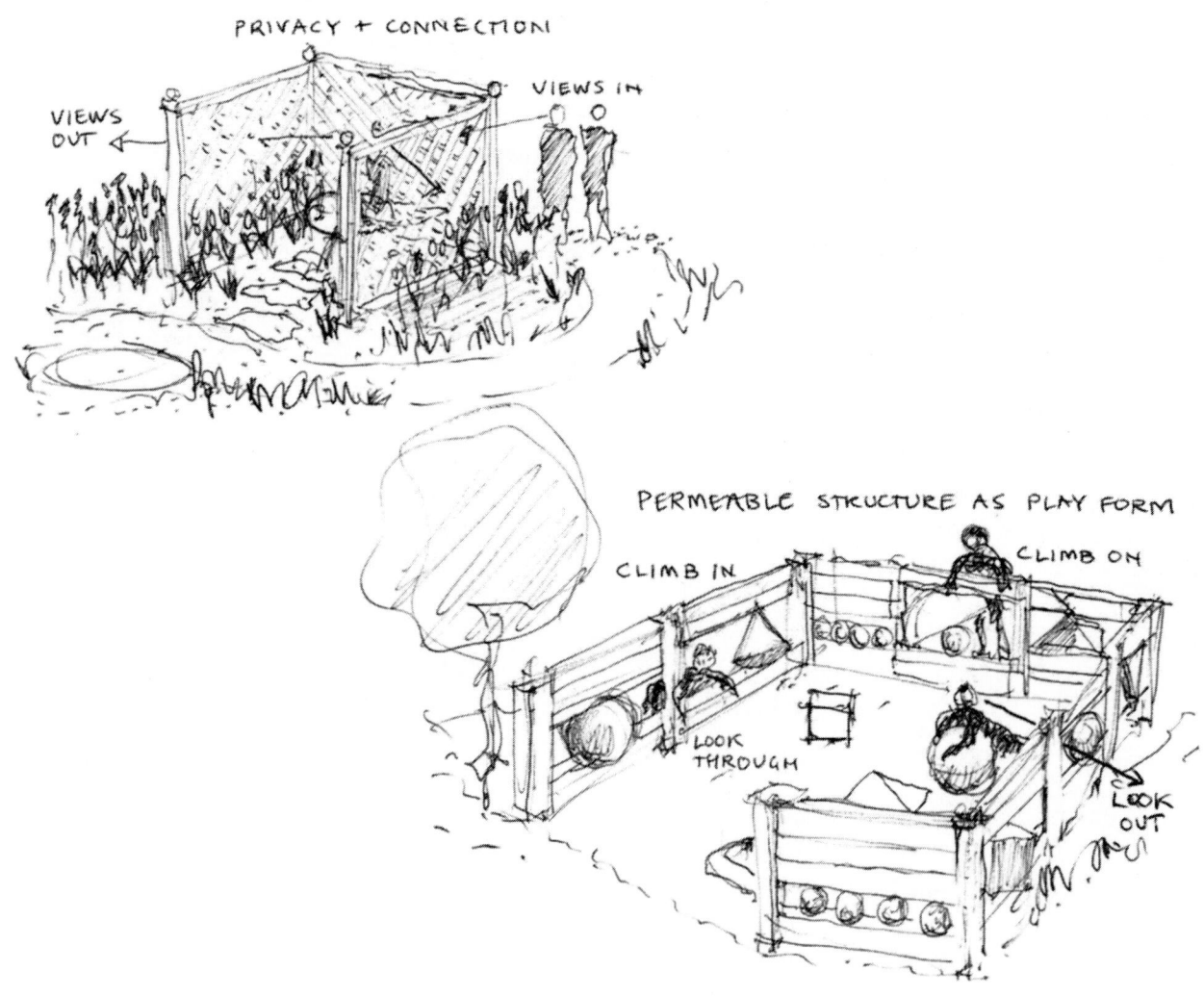

Permeable enclosing structures

Permeable built boundaries such as fences, trellis and railings enable the visually linking of one space to another. Their use in design is often desirable where physical division of space is desired but complete visual separation is not. Permeable structures play important roles as domestic–public dividers such as street–garden or yard edges. Permeable structures are often associated with plants as supports for climbers or as forms whose texture or colour is juxtaposed to vegetation. The materials used in permeable structures strongly influence their form, character and pattern.

ROOF STRUCTURES — TEMPORARY AND PERMANENT-
FORM IMPORTANT OUTDOOR HABITATS —
MODIFYING MICROCLIMATE, ENCLOSING, DRAMATISING

DRAWING AFTER : "THE COURT OF KHAN KUYUK" 1438 ANONYMOUS
TIMURID STYLE OF SHIRAZ .. BRITISH MUSEUM

Canopies

The design of canopies or roof-like structures for enclosing the sky plane within landscape may be considered part of landscape architecture or of architecture depending on the size, complexity and context of the structure. Landscape architects should be aware of the potential for their use in landscapes for protection from the weather, linking to buildings or to create secluded outdoor space.

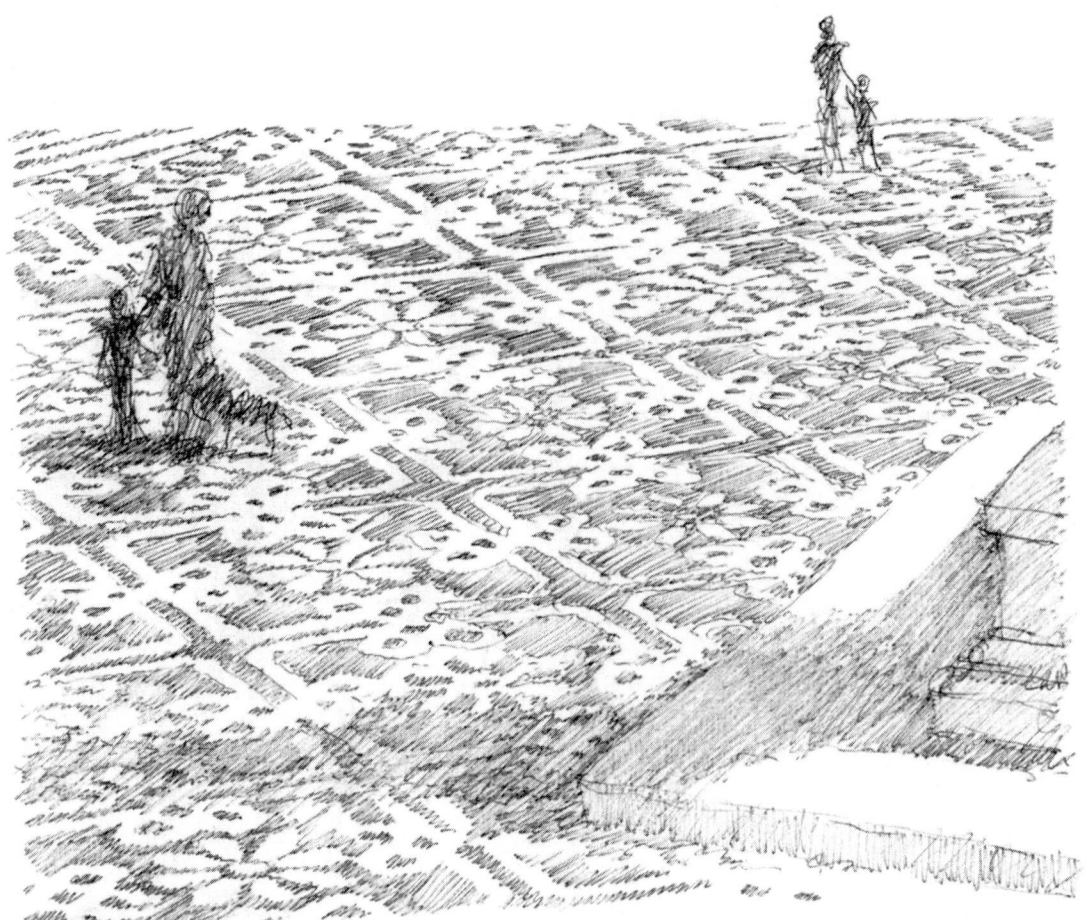

FLOORS - PATTERN OF PAVING CAN PROVIDE PRIMARY CHARACTER OF SPACE
CARPET-LIKE - CONTRAST WITH FOCAL VERTICAL ELEMENTS - AND MOVING PEOPLE
BLACK + WHITE LIMESTONE SETS IN TRADITIONAL BOW PATTERN
PORTUGAL

Floors

In urban contexts the ground plane often needs a built surface. Floors and the quality of pavements have a strong influence on the daily experience of city dwellers. The importance of surfaces in contributing to good landscapes is often underestimated. Materials used for floors and their composition in design are extremely diverse and the design of floors is a specialised area of landscape architecture that goes beyond the scope of this introduction. A summary of design considerations includes pattern, movement, uses, texture, drainage systems, safety, durability, maintenance, context, character, permeability and flexibility.

Water spaces

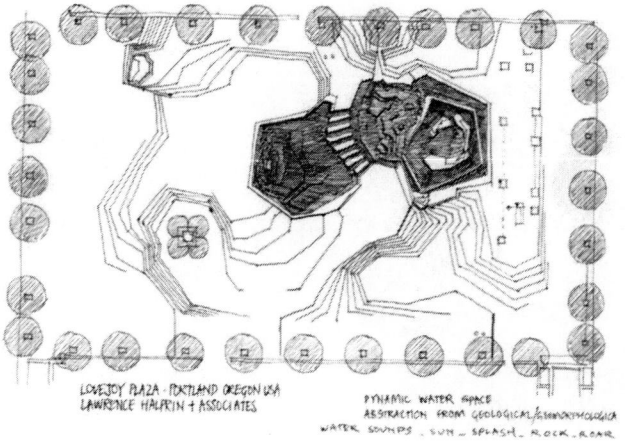

LOVEJOY PLAZA · PORTLAND OREGON USA
LAWRENCE HALPRIN + ASSOCIATES

DYNAMIC WATER SPACE
ABSTRACTION FROM GEOLOGICAL/geomorphologica
WATER SOUNDS . SUM — SPLASH — ROCK — ROAR

Water is a primary element of landscape architecture. 'Water spaces' refers to places in which water is a dominant element or simply to a waterbody along with its enclosing topography. The complex relationship between topography and water is not fully explored in this section. Large water spaces are very commonly 'natural' or modified natural environments. Water spaces attract people because of their diverse recreational potential, and they are often important habitats for wildlife. As a source of life, water has fundamental and enduring cultural meanings. The purpose of this section is to illustrate some of the spatial and experiential potential of water in recreational landscapes.

Linear waterbodies are explored in the section on Paths (see p. 111).

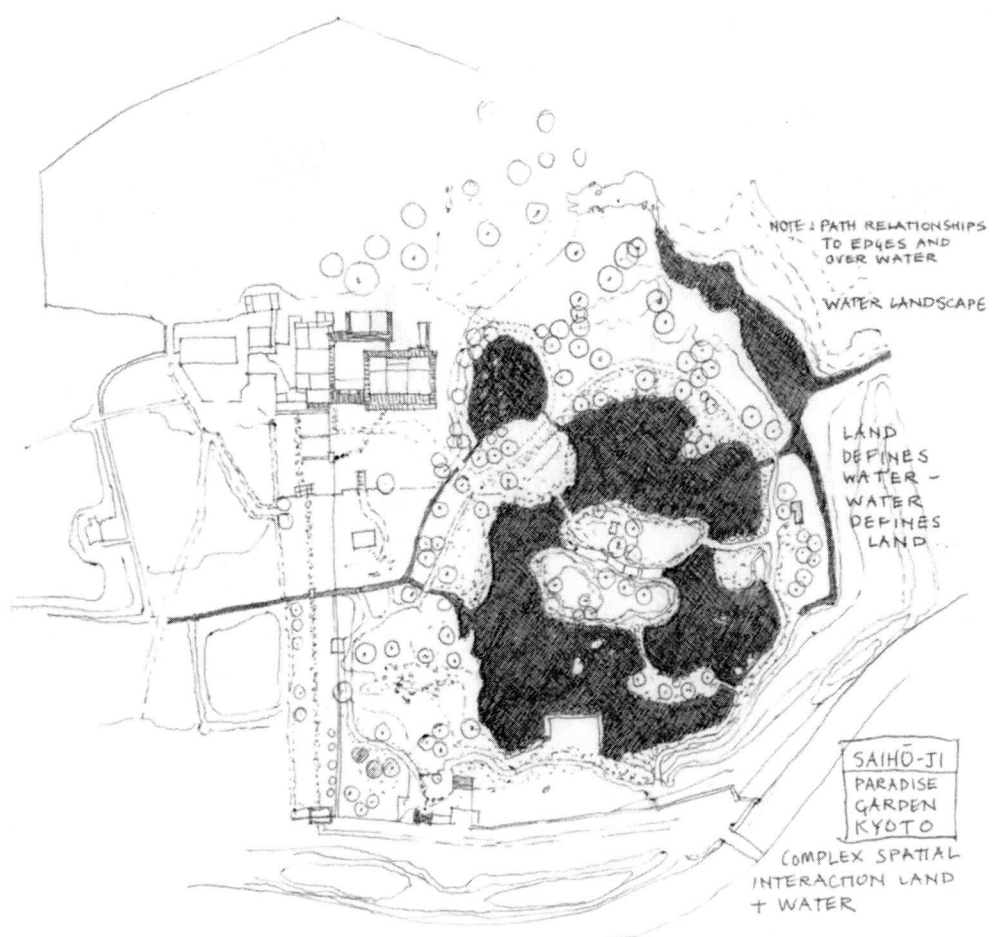

NOTE: PATH RELATIONSHIPS TO EDGES AND OVER WATER

WATER LANDSCAPE

LAND DEFINES WATER – WATER DEFINES LAND

SAIHŌ-JI PARADISE GARDEN KYOTO

COMPLEX SPATIAL INTERACTION LAND + WATER

Lakes and waterscapes

Large inland waterbodies such as lakes are valued for their breadth, their openness and characteristics that provide contrast to land. They have important environmental roles in water conservation and providing wildlife habitats. Water environments are visually and sensorily dynamic because they reflect the sky and weather. Waterbodies change their appearance dramatically in sun, rain or cloud, wind or calm. For all these reasons they are attractive places for recreation. Design provides

for diverse recreation on and around a waterbody, and for creating or protecting wildlife habitats. Visual and experiential considerations include, among others: waterbody form and topographic–water relationships, vistas, scale, diversity and complexity of edge and path relationship to water (see Water paths, p. 112), stopping places and thresholds (see Water thresholds, p. 186), refuge and prospect, and exposure and shelter, as well as functional requirements associated with water sports.

LUIS BARRAGÁN'S
FUENTE DEL BEBEDERO
LAS ARBOLEDAS, MEXICO
1958-61

WATER USED AS MIRROR
OF LIGHT AND SHADE –
JUXTAPOSED
WHITE WALL
HORIZONTALITY + VERTICALITY BALANCED

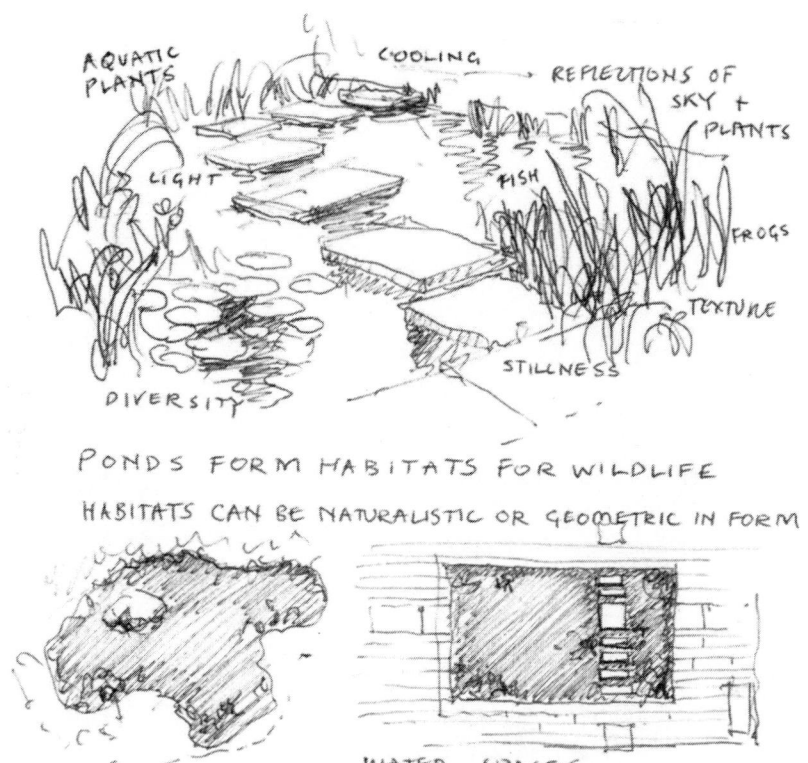

AQUATIC PLANTS
COOLING
REFLECTIONS OF SKY + PLANTS
LIGHT
FISH
FROGS
TEXTURE
STILLNESS
DIVERSITY

PONDS FORM HABITATS FOR WILDLIFE

HABITATS CAN BE NATURALISTIC OR GEOMETRIC IN FORM

WATER SPACES

Pools and ponds

In contrast to lakes, ponds and pools are defined as relatively small (human) scale waterbodies that provide both recreational potential and wildlife habitats. 'Pool' is used to describe a waterbody that has bathing and/or merely visual and cooling functions. Alternatively 'pond' describes a waterbody that provides a habitat for plants and associated wildlife and is predominantly green in character. As water spaces, both pools and ponds have the potential to provide distinct and contrasting (to land) landscape experiences. A summary of some important design considerations to maximise experiential qualities of pools and ponds includes:

- enabling people to have contact with water as often as possible for bathing or touching
- manipulating light and darkness
- manipulating stillness and movement; silence and splash
- juxtaposition of texture, colour and forms of landform, vegetation and structures with water
- exploiting reflection
- providing for wildlife and plants.

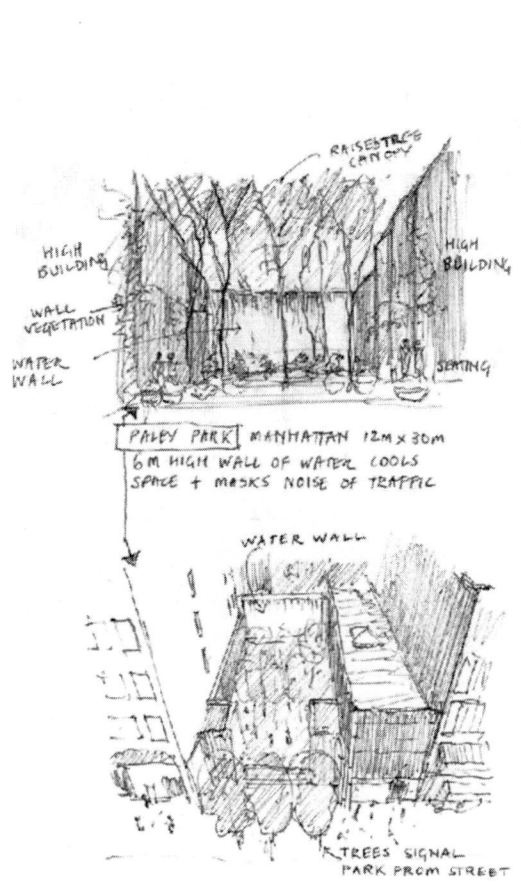

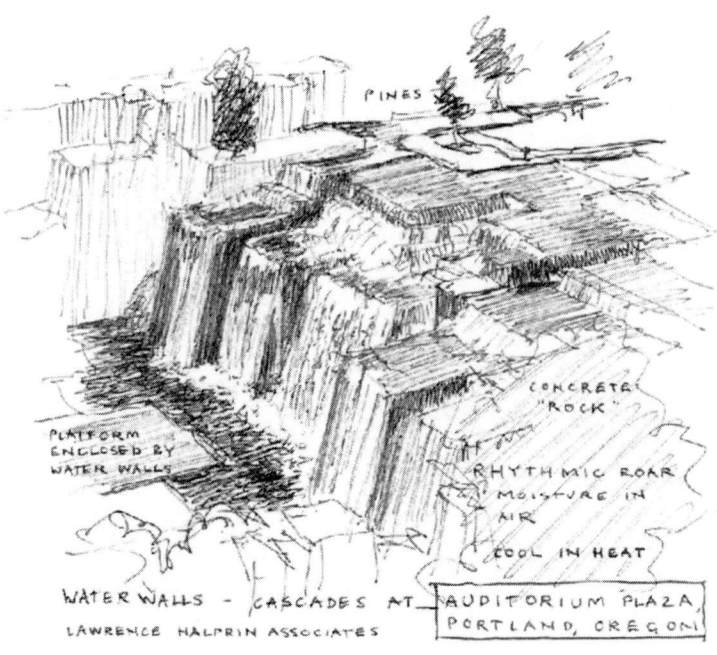

Water walls and moving water

In urban contexts, water can be used in wall planes to enclose space. Water walls and other types of moving water cool, visually animate and create sound in spaces. They have a very strong physical presence and create exhilarating or peaceful experiences in a similar way to waterfalls in natural environments (see Water foci, p. 168). There are many different design considerations affecting experience of water walls. In particular, the dramatic or calming nature of such an experience is affected by the speed and quantity of water, together with the texture of the structure over which water passes. In places with moving water the air becomes full of fine mist which changes the atmosphere through sound, light, touch and taste.

79

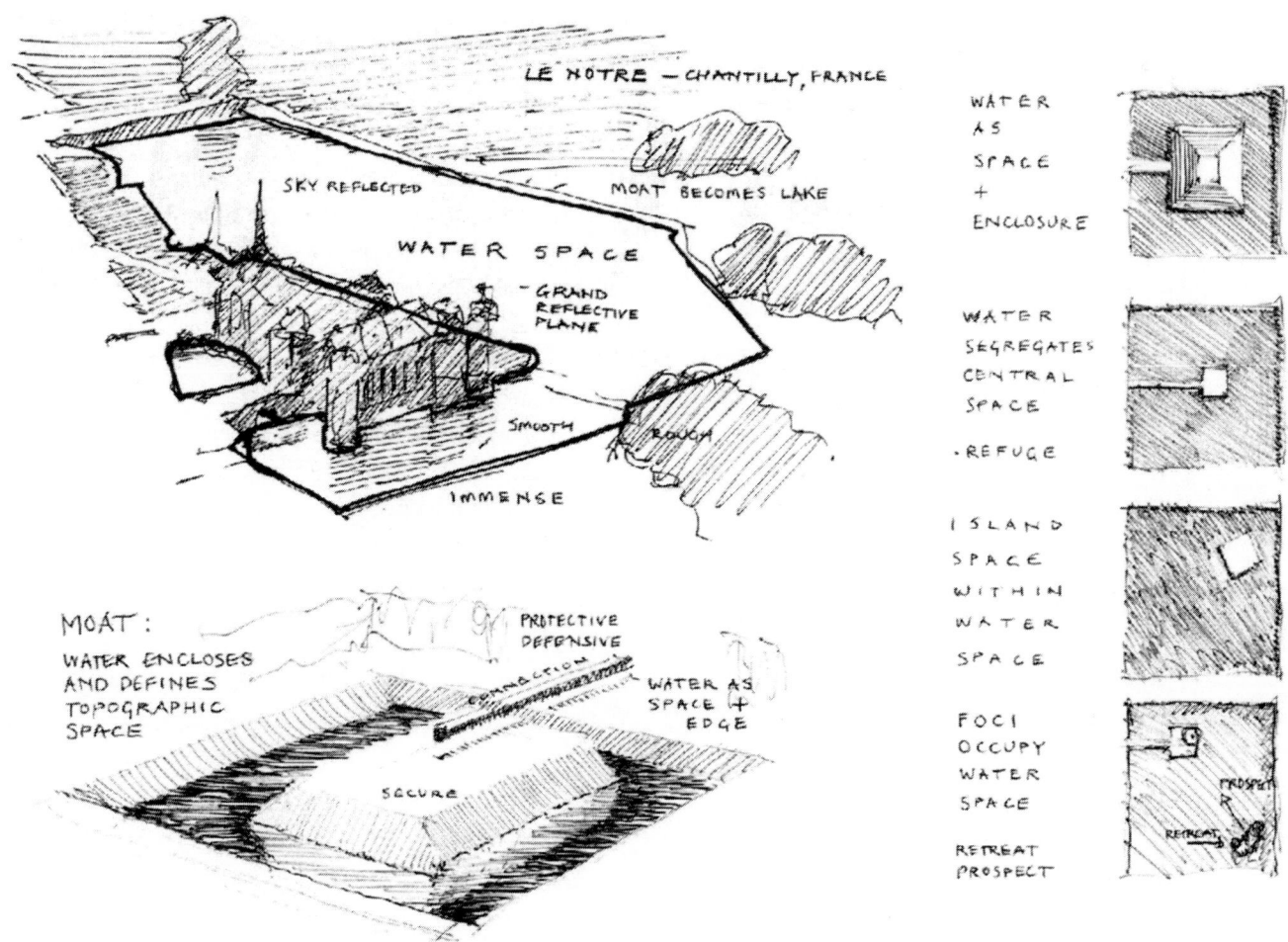

LE NOTRE – CHANTILLY, FRANCE

SKY REFLECTED

MOAT BECOMES LAKE

WATER SPACE

– GRAND REFLECTIVE PLANE

SMOOTH   ROUGH

IMMENSE

MOAT:
WATER ENCLOSES AND DEFINES TOPOGRAPHIC SPACE

PROTECTIVE DEFENSIVE

CONNECTION

WATER AS SPACE + EDGE

SECURE

WATER AS SPACE + ENCLOSURE

WATER SEGREGATES CENTRAL SPACE
• REFUGE

ISLAND SPACE WITHIN WATER SPACE

FOCI OCCUPY WATER SPACE

RETREAT PROSPECT

PROSPECT

RETREAT

Moats – water as enclosing element

Water can be used to enclose space in the horizontal plane by separating land mass or building from surrounding landscape. Differing from their previous defensive function, moats can today play a wide range of aesthetic and recreational roles. When people are isolated by a moat with prospects over the reflective surface, or are entering a place by boat or bridge, feelings of security and separateness are promoted.

3 Paths

This section explores the roles, potential and design of paths in the landscape. Together with spaces, paths are considered to be principal structural components of designed landscapes because they play a crucial role in mediating or facilitating the experience and use of landscapes.

This section provides a conceptual framework for considering path design informed by social, aesthetic and environmental aspects. The potential use of topography, vegetation, structures and water in creating path forms is illustrated. The focus is primarily on pedestrian environments and their experience.

GARDEN, GRAND ISLE, VERMONT, USA
LANDSCAPE ARCHITECT - SUSAN CHILD

Definitions

Paths can be defined as:

- linear landscape spaces for travel
- linking forms that create networks of circulation
  in the landscape
- linear surfaced areas.

82

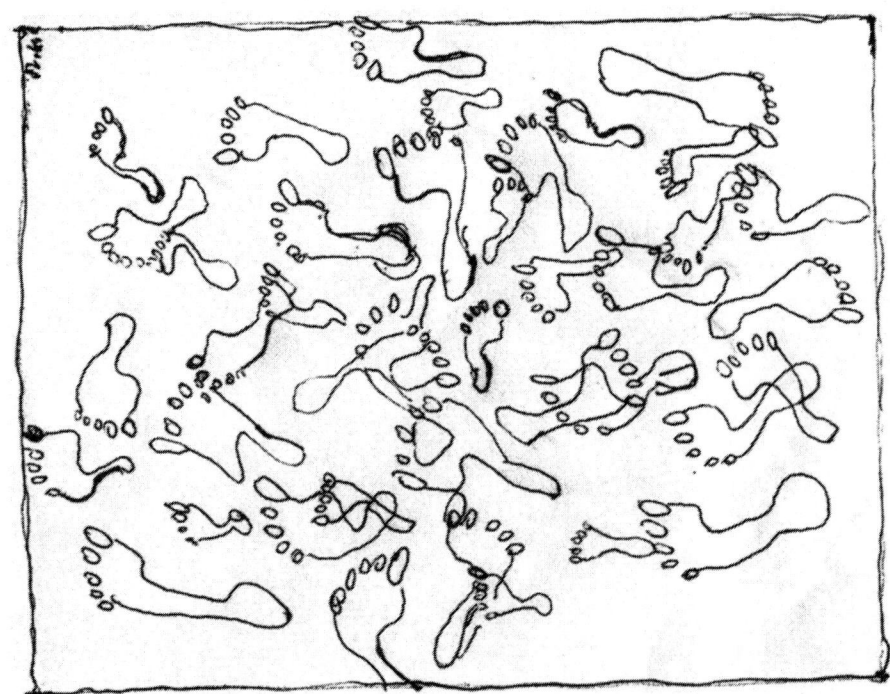

DRAWING AFTER
JEAN DUBUFFET "TRACES DE PAS SUR LE SABLE" 1948

People's use and experience of paths

Paths are adopted and made to enable people and wild-life to travel easily between and within places. Paths are not only places of movement but, for example in cities, streets become social and recreational places. Paths are also places of recreation when they are travelled for pleasure. In design, the landscape architect considers both movement for pleasure and necessity alongside the static social activities that may occur and can be facilitated on paths. Good path design is thus a primary method of enabling and encouraging access and enjoyment of the landscape. As paths play this key role, they are considered – together with spaces – part of the fundamental structure of landscapes.

Movement – kinetic experience of landscape

The kinetic experience of moving requires different design considerations and strategies to those necessary for a more static experience of landscape. Moving through the landscape makes us acutely aware of space–time relationships. The designer must be aware that what is sensed during movement in landscapes is constantly changing, with different views, sounds, scents, warmth, coolness, brightness and shade layered into the experience of a journey.

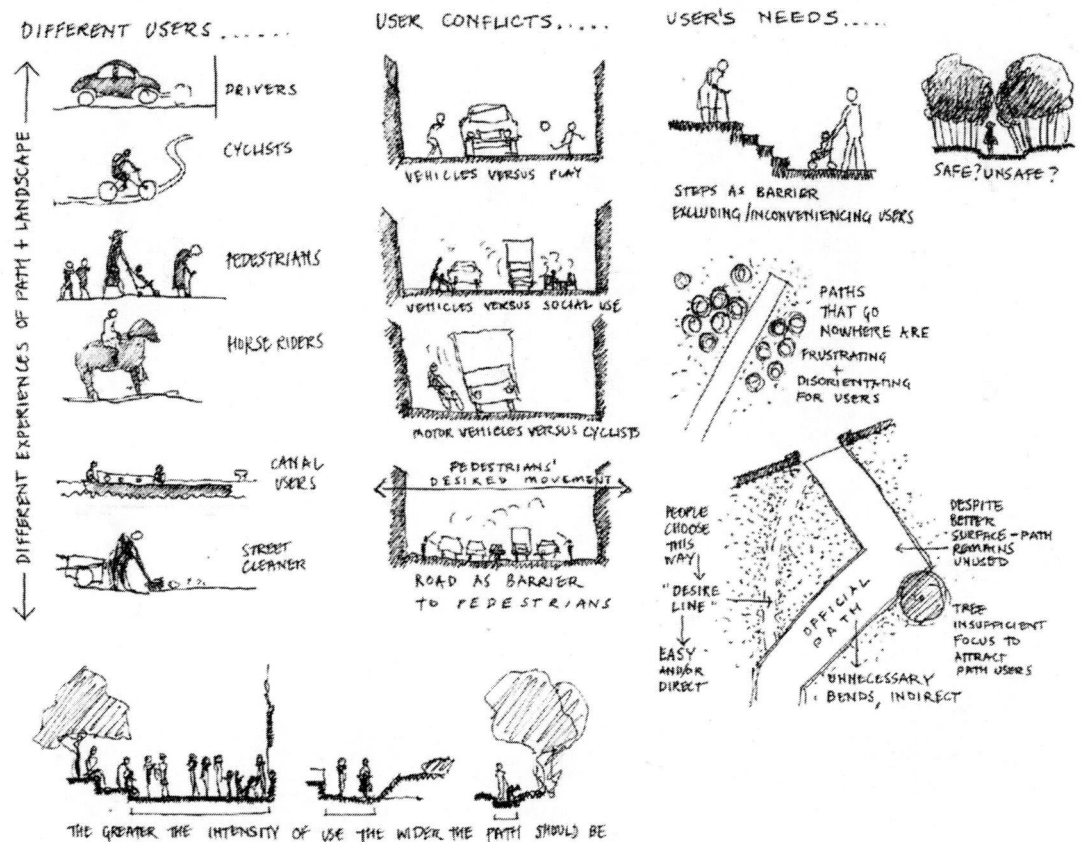

Different users, uses and modes of transport

Different users, uses and modes of transport have diverse design requirements. Landscape architecture involves the consideration of different modes of travel and also of different users and means of accommodating these and reducing conflict between them. In many urban landscapes the designer must resolve conflicts between motor vehicles and pedestrians.

Intensity and frequency of use of a path influence a designer's choice of width, form and surface. Perceived and actual safety and security are also important factors in path design.

Official and unofficial paths

A vital consideration in design is to facilitate people's movement with appropriate surfacing. Grass, other planted surfaces and earth are not resistant to heavy foot traffic. 'Desire lines' are tracks worn across unsurfaced ground that indicate frequent pedestrian use. If a surfaced route has been made but does provide (or appear to provide) the easiest way, desire lines occur. Desire lines can also indicate where paths are needed. The landscape architect must, in these situations, be sensitive to the effects of topography on people's choice of route. People often prefer to walk on steeply-sloping ground rather than use steps with high risers, and will also make short cuts if a path on sloping ground appears to be too indirect.

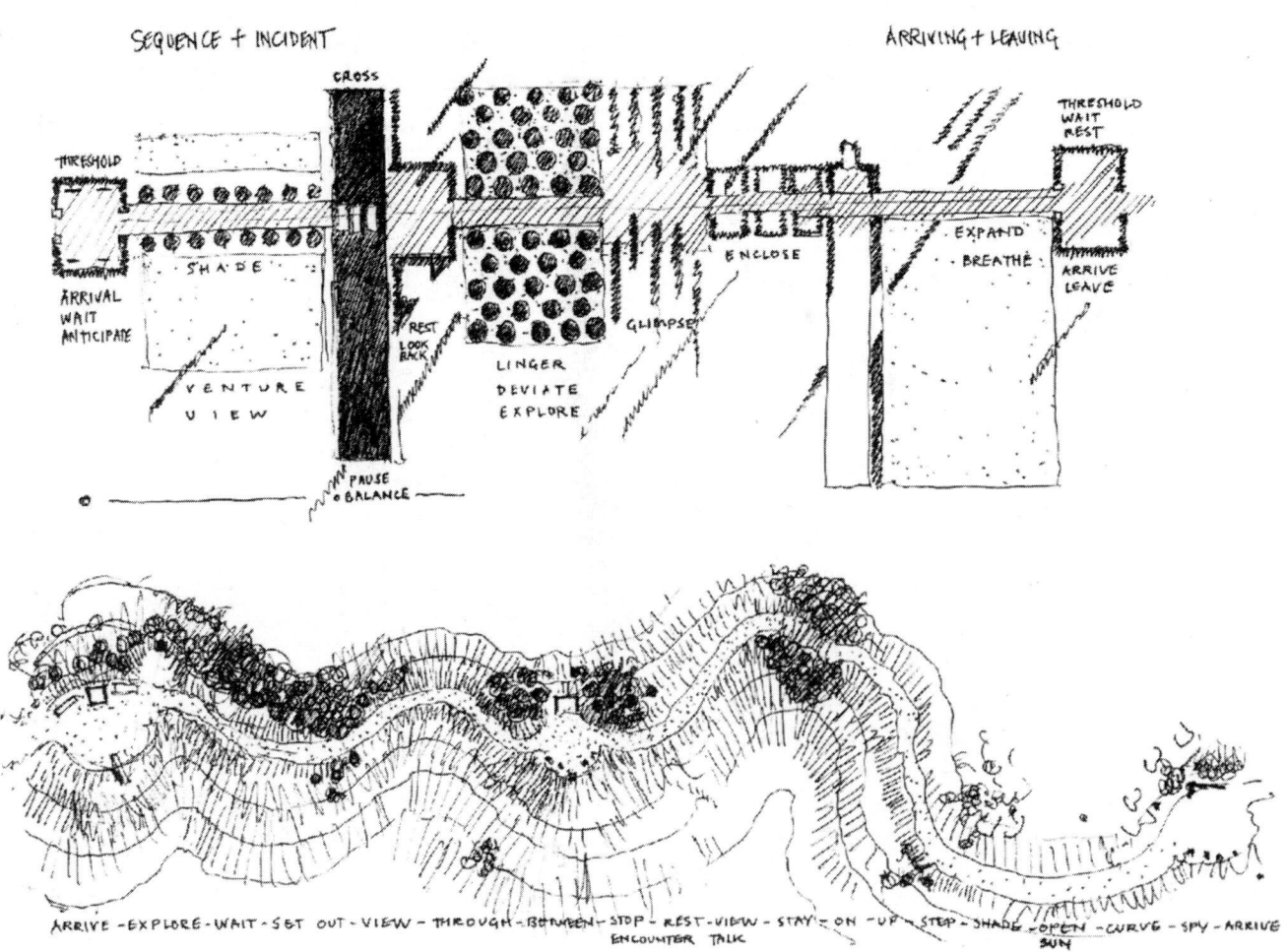

Sequence and incident

Long periods of travel though similar terrain can be tedious. In design, the variety, incident and sequence of a journey must be considered. Path form, space and edge relationships can be organised to avoid monotony or for dramatic or symbolic effects.

Arriving and leaving

Places of arrival and departure are also experientially important and thus of prime concern to designers. Arriving in and departing from places can be emotional and symbolic experiences for social and cultural reasons. The landscape architect can enhance the aesthetic and social experience of arrival and departure by creating appropriate forms and sequences at the beginning and end of paths.

ECOLOGICAL CORRIDOR —
RIVER IN CITY — RECREATION AND
WILDLIFE — VEGETATION
ALTERNATIVE PEDESTRIAN PATH

Ecological corridors

Ecological 'corridors' are important path concepts for urban landscape planning. Linear linking spaces of vegetation and water between built environments allow flora and fauna species to move, reproduce and colonise freely. Ecological corridors can form networks across cities, link to countryside and, if large enough, also provide recreational paths and resources.

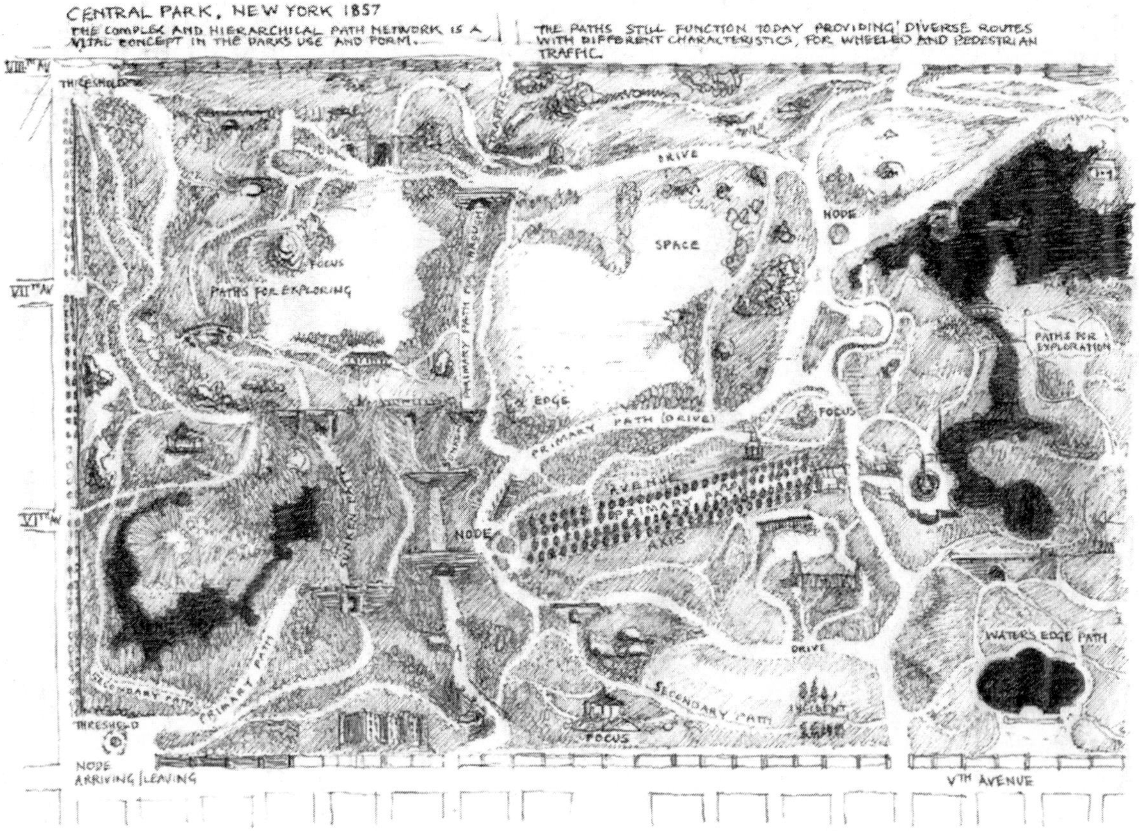

CENTRAL PARK, NEW YORK 1857
THE COMPLEX AND HIERARCHICAL PATH NETWORK IS A VITAL CONCEPT IN THE PARKS USE AND FORM.

THE PATHS STILL FUNCTION TODAY PROVIDING DIVERSE ROUTES WITH DIFFERENT CHARACTERISTICS, FOR WHEELED AND PEDESTRIAN TRAFFIC.

Path systems and hierarchies

Path design not only involves the creation of individual paths but path systems or networks. Consideration must often be given to hierarchical arrangements in which intensively-used paths are designed and linked in different ways to those used occasionally. Different paths will have different functional purposes; some for direct access, others for slower meandering exploration of the landscape. The design of path systems involves the organisation of relationships of these different types of paths.

Networks, nodes and foci

When paths are formed into networks, junctions become important stopping, meeting and waiting locations. These nodes (Lynch 1960) therefore need design consideration to accommodate the activities that naturally occur where paths meet. Nodes often need to be designed as small spaces in their own right

Path network designs also respond to and integrate with foci (which are often located at nodes). As visual and symbolic attractors in the landscape, foci (see the section on Foci, p. 147) have a very important relationship with paths as endpoints to journeys or as incidents in a sequence.

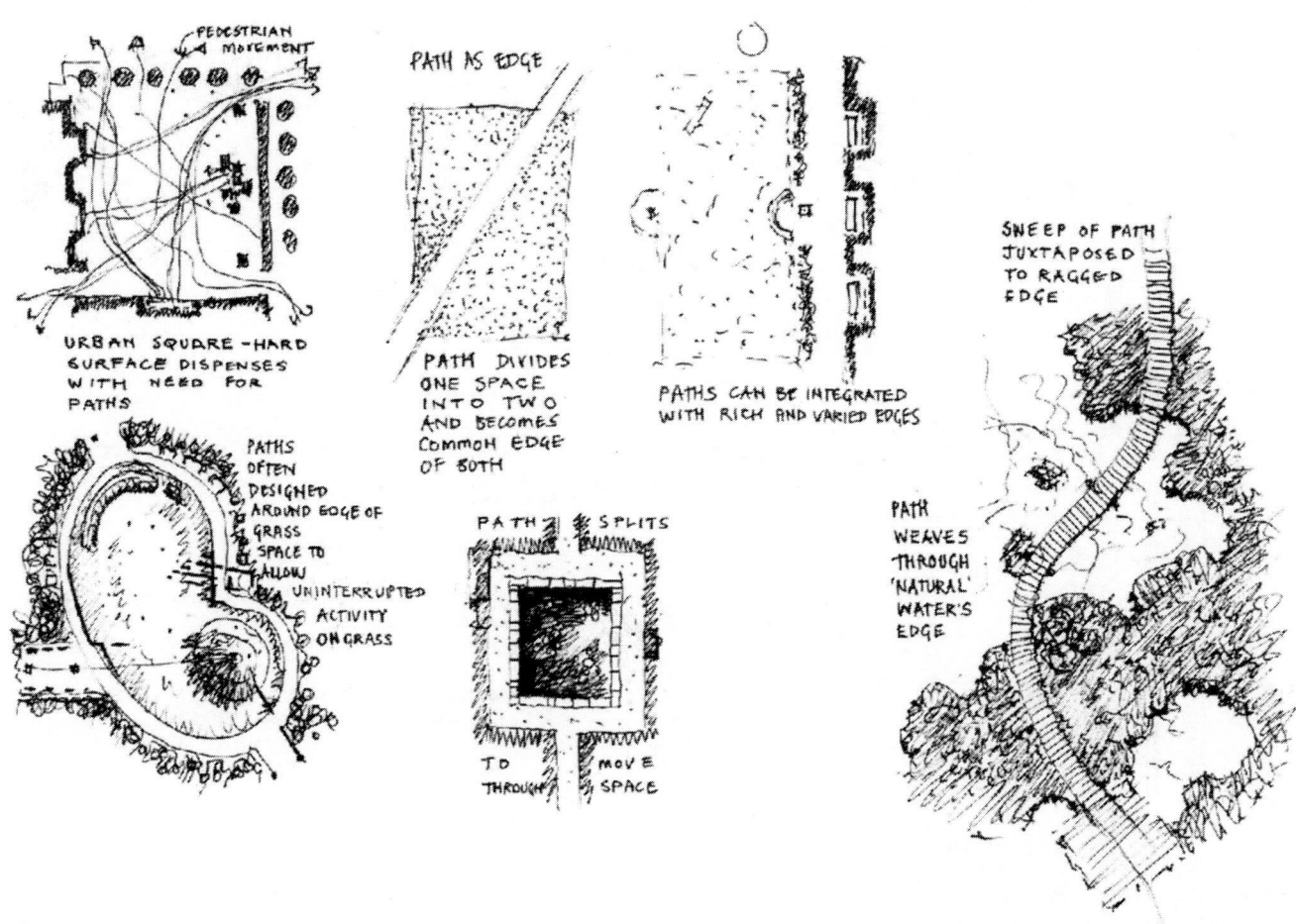

URBAN SQUARE – HARD SURFACE DISPENSES WITH NEED FOR PATHS

PATH AS EDGE

PATH DIVIDES ONE SPACE INTO TWO AND BECOMES COMMON EDGE OF BOTH

PATHS CAN BE INTEGRATED WITH RICH AND VARIED EDGES

PATHS OFTEN DESIGNED AROUND EDGE OF GRASS SPACE TO ALLOW UNINTERRUPTED ACTIVITY ON GRASS

PEDESTRIAN MOVEMENT

PATH SPLITS

TO MOVE THROUGH SPACE

SWEEP OF PATH JUXTAPOSED TO RAGGED EDGE

PATH WEAVES THROUGH 'NATURAL' WATER'S EDGE

Paths, spaces and edges

A complex and vital aspect of landscape architecture is the spatial integration of paths and spaces. In surfaced spaces such as urban squares it is unnecessary to consider paths as separate landscape forms. However, in many vegetated and grassy landscapes, decisions must be made on how to locate paths in relation to spaces. Paths may often 'hug' the edge of places to preserve the openness of spaces for activities. Paths are commonly experienced as edges and boundaries which define space. For example, a centrally located path 'splits' a space in two. The landscape architect does not consider the design of paths, spaces and edges separately but as integrated wholes (see the sections on Edges, p. 123 and Landscape fabric, pp. 26–9).

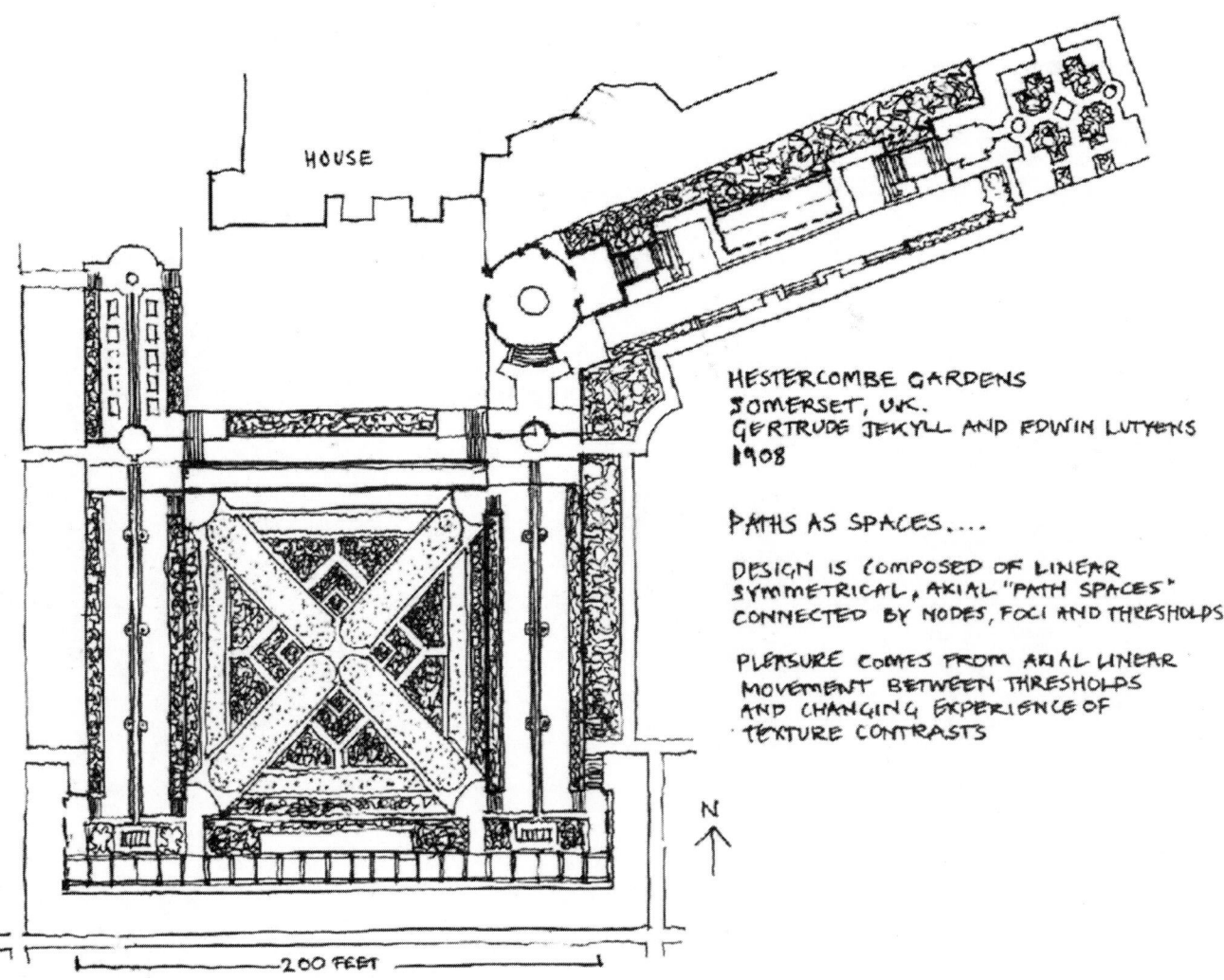

HOUSE

HESTERCOMBE GARDENS
SOMERSET, U.K.
GERTRUDE JEKYLL AND EDWIN LUTYENS
1908

PATHS AS SPACES....

DESIGN IS COMPOSED OF LINEAR
SYMMETRICAL, AXIAL "PATH SPACES"
CONNECTED BY NODES, FOCI AND THRESHOLDS

PLEASURE COMES FROM AXIAL LINEAR
MOVEMENT BETWEEN THRESHOLDS
AND CHANGING EXPERIENCE OF
TEXTURE CONTRASTS

N

200 FEET

Paths as spaces

Wide paths – particularly urban streets and promenades – are potentially more than just places of movement and can therefore be designed as spaces that facilitate static activities. Busy urban streets are places for sitting, buying selling and performance. Long linear spaces can be designed to function simultaneously as paths and spaces.

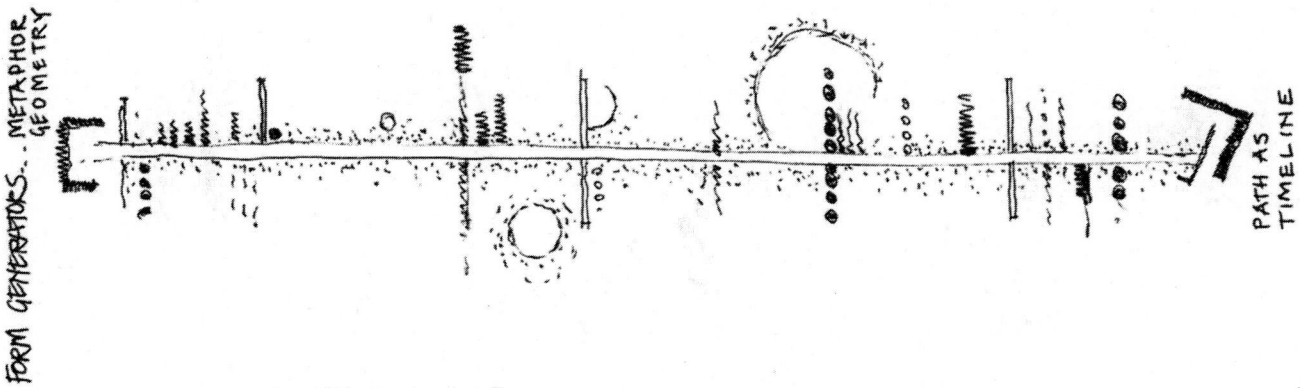

Form

The following pages illustrate influences on and considerations for the design of path form.

Form generators

Design generators for path forms have many similarities with those identified for spaces (see Spaces/Form, p. 37). Existing site forms and uses, geometry, metaphor, symbolism, archetype, vernacular and historic paradigms can all be used to inspire and generate path form. Path forms can also be generated through narrative (telling a story through design forms) which may draw heavily on metaphor and symbolism.

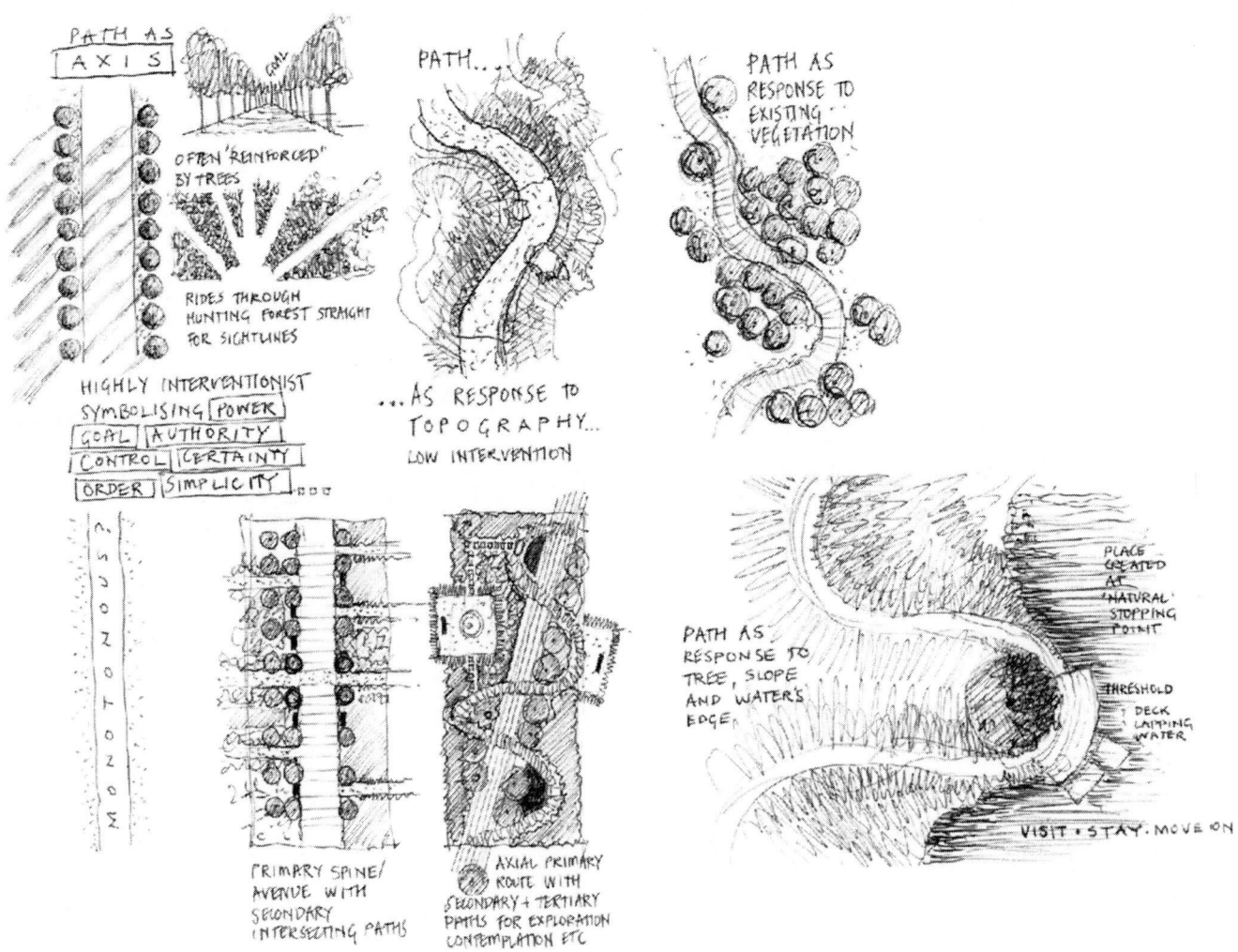

Axis and meander

Directness and 'indirectness' in path form have both functional and aesthetic connotations. Axial and meandering path forms thus have different use, character and associations and provide distinct experiences. Path forms strongly influence the character and form of spaces and may often be the dominant form generators for a site.

Axis has associations with order, power and control, while meandering paths have associations with 'naturalness'. There are many path form variations that combine qualities of the meander and the axis. Designers may also deliberately juxtapose and combine axial and meandering forms for design purposes.

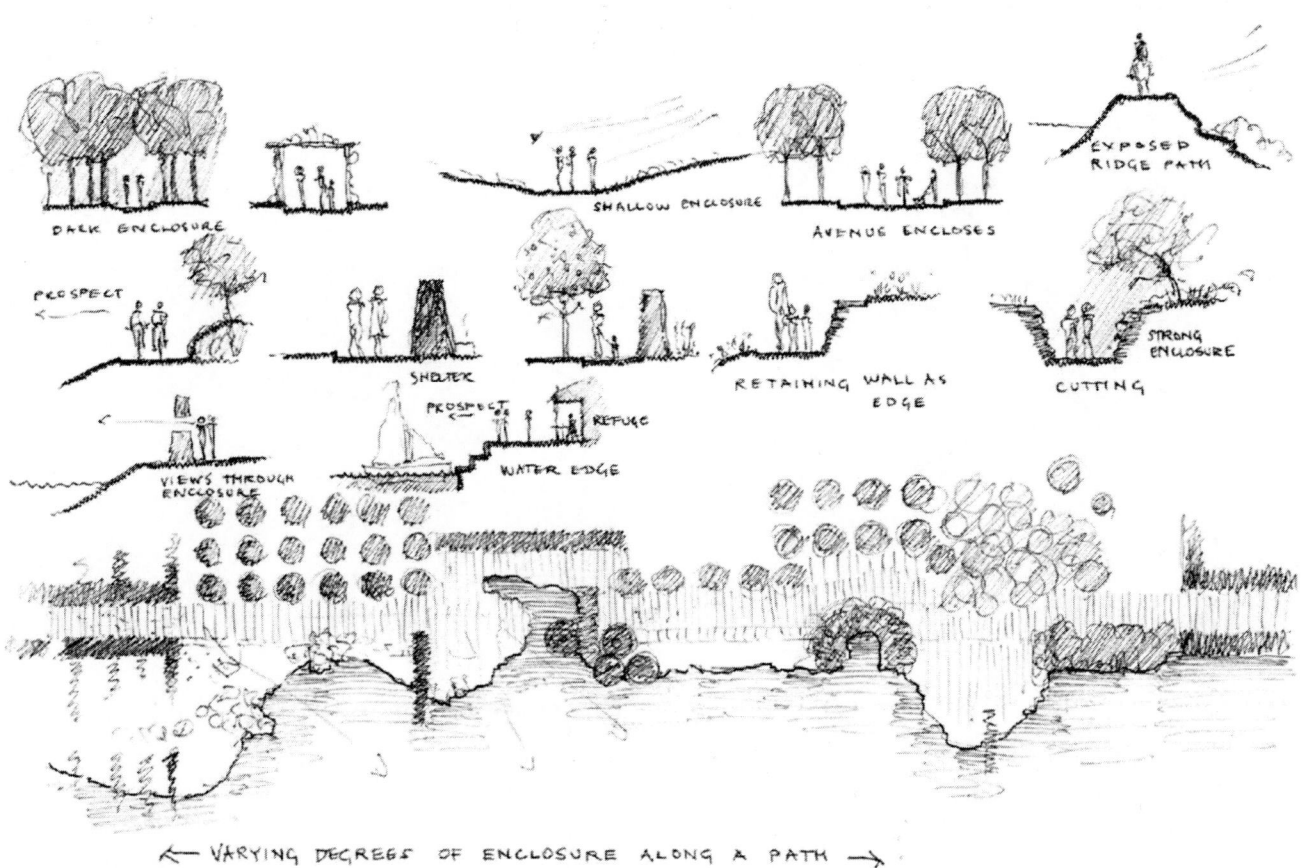

DARK ENCLOSURE

SHALLOW ENCLOSURE

AVENUE ENCLOSES

EXPOSED RIDGE PATH

PROSPECT

SHELTER

RETAINING WALL AS EDGE

STRONG ENCLOSURE

CUTTING

VIEWS THROUGH ENCLOSURE

PROSPECT

REFUGE

WATER EDGE

← VARYING DEGREES OF ENCLOSURE ALONG A PATH →

Degrees of enclosure

Varying the degrees of enclosure in the 'wall' and 'sky' planes of a path is an important design consideration. The experience of walking a path can be enlivened and made comfortable for example by controlling views, opening and closing glimpses, protecting from the elements and providing refuge along one edge.

Topographic paths

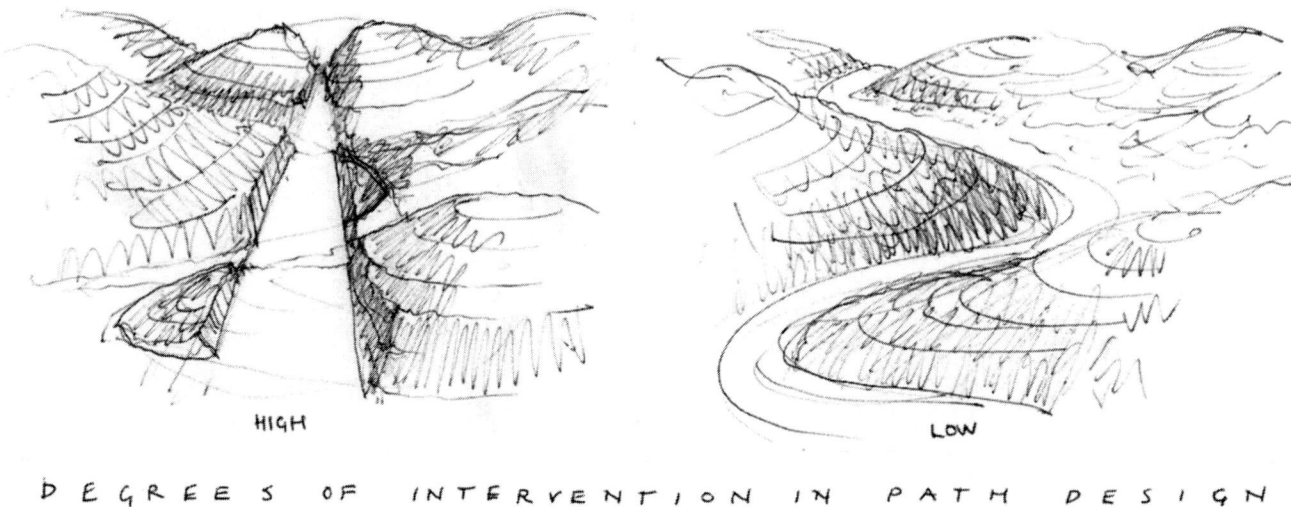

HIGH   LOW

D E G R E E S   O F   I N T E R V E N T I O N   I N   P A T H   D E S I G N

A significant dimension of landscape architecture is the opportunity for inventive and subtle topographic path design.

Degrees of intervention

As with topographic space design, landscape architects must decide on how much to intervene and change existing topography in path design. Paths may make small interventions in natural topography and accommodate the lie of the land or require dramatic remodelling of the existing landform. Design decisions are informed by functional and aesthetic considerations already discussed (see pp. 83–92).

Over the following pages, examples of topographic path forms are explored that offer distinct landscape experiences.

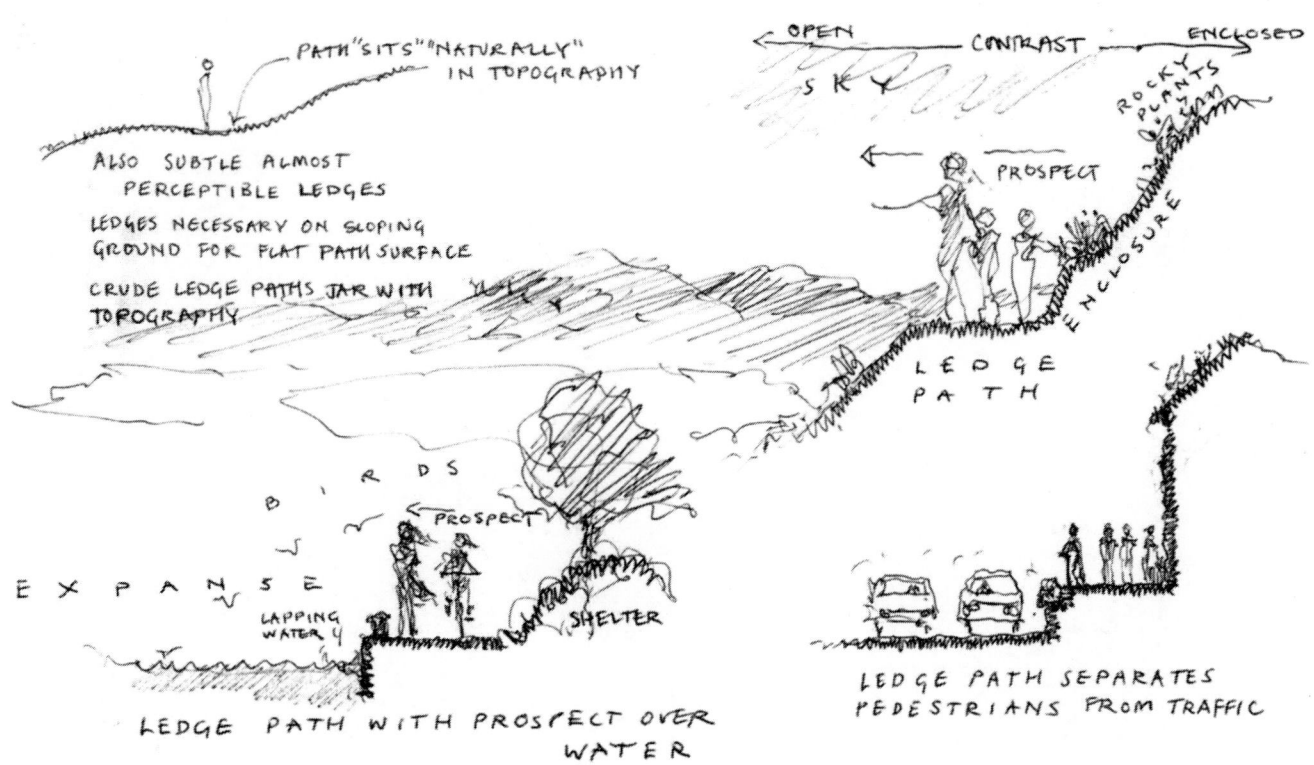

PATH "SITS" "NATURALLY" IN TOPOGRAPHY

ALSO SUBTLE ALMOST PERCEPTIBLE LEDGES

LEDGES NECESSARY ON SLOPING GROUND FOR FLAT PATH SURFACE

CRUDE LEDGE PATHS JAR WITH TOPOGRAPHY

OPEN ← CONTRAST → ENCLOSED

SKY

ROCKY PLANTS

PROSPECT

ENCLOSURE

LEDGE PATH

BIRDS

PROSPECT

EXPANSE

LAPPING WATER

SHELTER

LEDGE PATH WITH PROSPECT OVER WATER

LEDGE PATH SEPARATES PEDESTRIANS FROM TRAFFIC

Ledge paths

Ledge paths provide attractive landscape experiences as they afford users prospect (views over surrounding landscape) on one side while providing enclosure on the other. A ledge path may be as simple as a single step up from the space it surrounds, or as dramatic as a cliff-hugging route. Ledge paths are often desirable or necessary next to seas, rivers, lakes and canals, enabling walks with prospect of water or fishing (See also the section on Water paths, p. 112). Pavements with kerbs are ledge paths that protect users from vehicles. Ledge paths can enclose spaces.

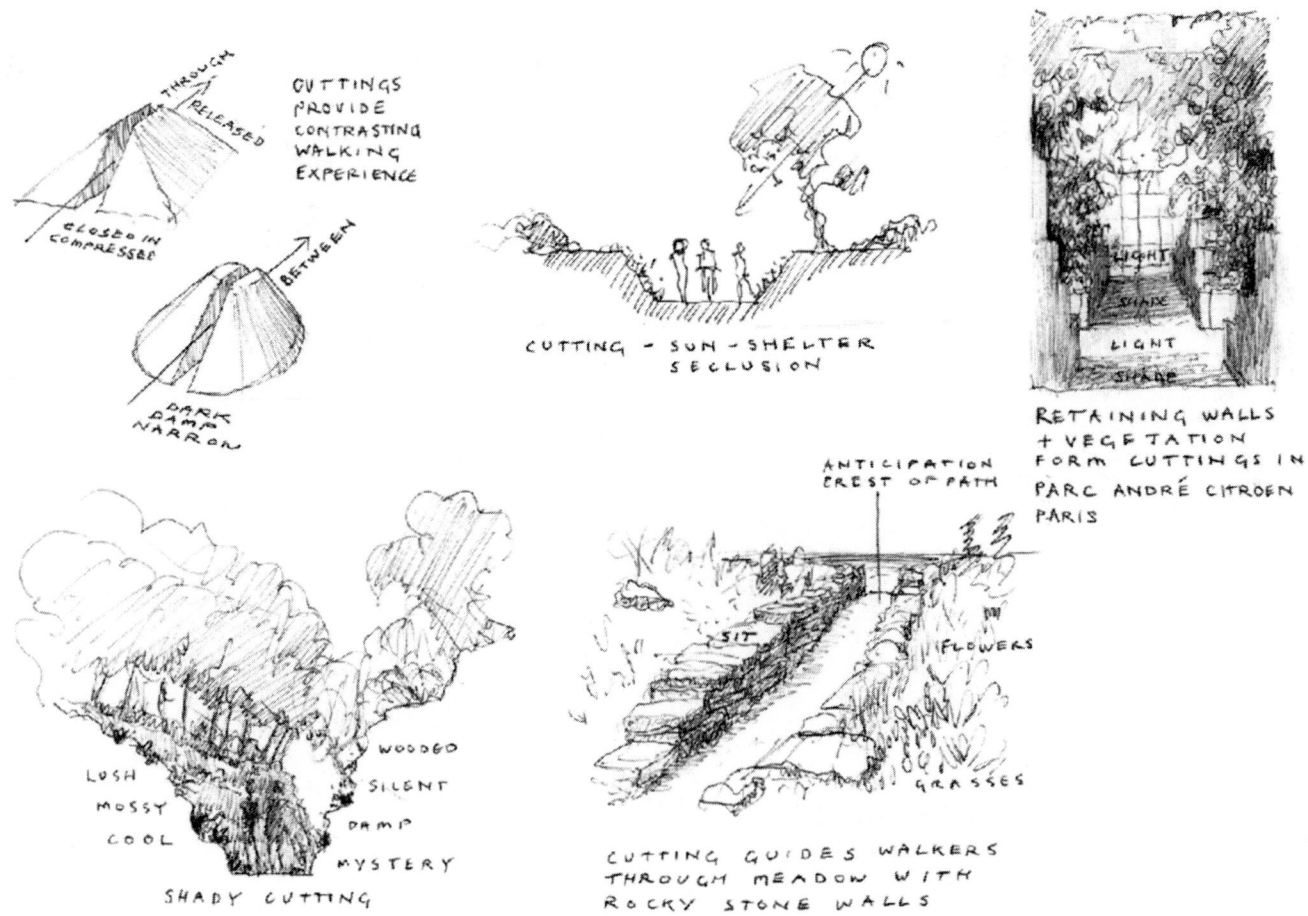

CUTTINGS PROVIDE CONTRASTING WALKING EXPERIENCE

CUTTING - SUN - SHELTER SECLUSION

RETAINING WALLS + VEGETATION FORM CUTTINGS IN PARC ANDRÉ CITROEN PARIS

SHADY CUTTING

CUTTING GUIDES WALKERS THROUGH MEADOW WITH ROCKY STONE WALLS

Cuttings

Cuttings are paths enclosed by landform or retaining walls on both sides. They provide distinct landscape experiences for symbolic, spatial and microclimatic reasons. The microclimate is often still and silent; damp and cool if deep and vegetated; warm and sunny if shallow. Cuttings offer opportunities for dramatic contrast of spatial experience, moving from open expansive spaces to 'closed in' territory and vice versa. As hidden places, cuttings encourage exploration but can also be places of fear.

95

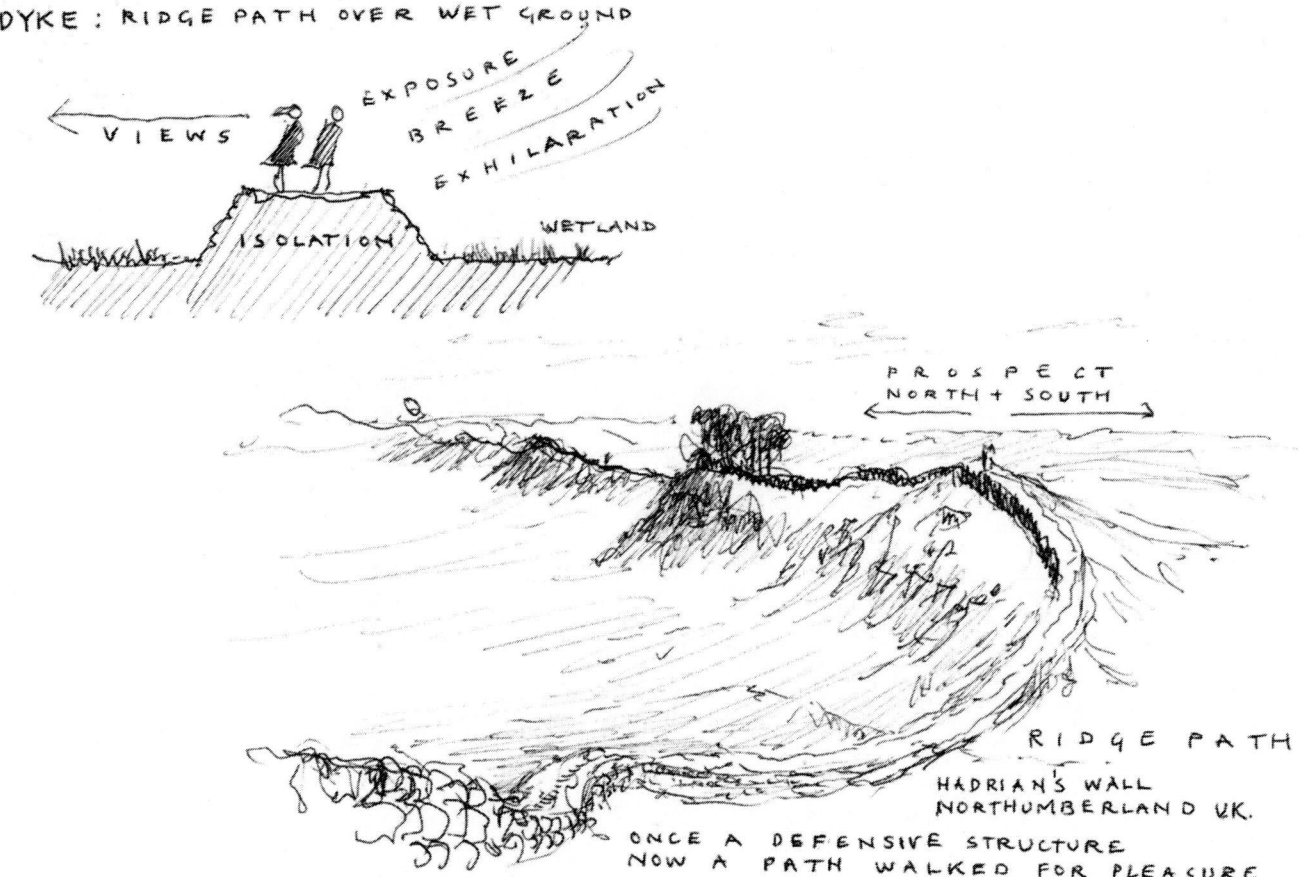

DYKE : RIDGE PATH OVER WET GROUND

VIEWS

EXPOSURE

BREEZE

EXHILARATION

ISOLATION

WETLAND

PROSPECT NORTH + SOUTH

RIDGE PATH

HADRIAN'S WALL
NORTHUMBERLAND UK.

ONCE A DEFENSIVE STRUCTURE
NOW A PATH WALKED FOR PLEASURE

Ridge paths

Ridge paths form routes raised on both sides above the surrounding topography. In their use, pleasure is derived from the prospect they allow in all directions and the feeling of exposure to wind, sky and sometimes water. Ridge paths can enclose and define space. Ridge path networks are developed on and are distinctive to wetland landscapes.

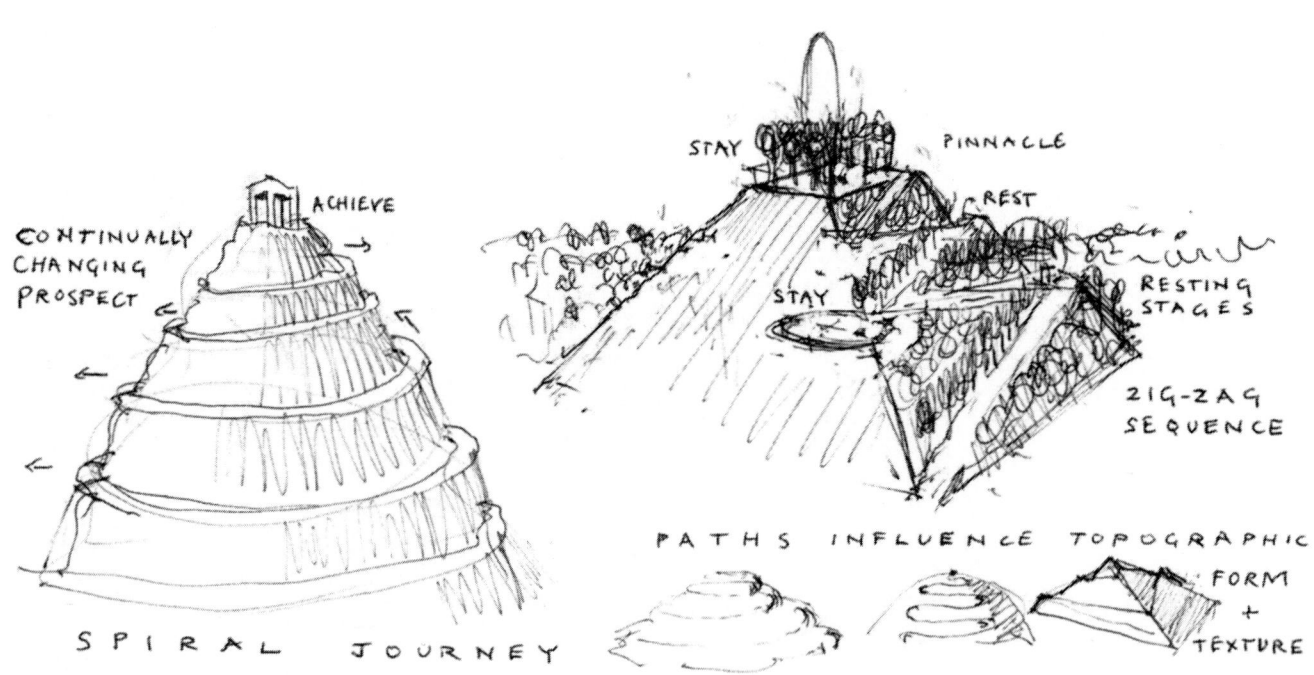

Spiral and zig-zag paths

To access the top of high or steep landforms, topographic paths often need to spiral around the landform or zig-zag up its side. The constraints of topography offer design opportunities for distinctive journey sequences. Spiral paths can have a smooth dynamic flowing char-

acter, but can also be disorienting and provide no 'natural' stopping places. Zig-zag paths can integrate stopping platforms for rest and prospect. The potential frustration of repeatedly moving back and forward can be avoided by developing narrative sequences for the path.

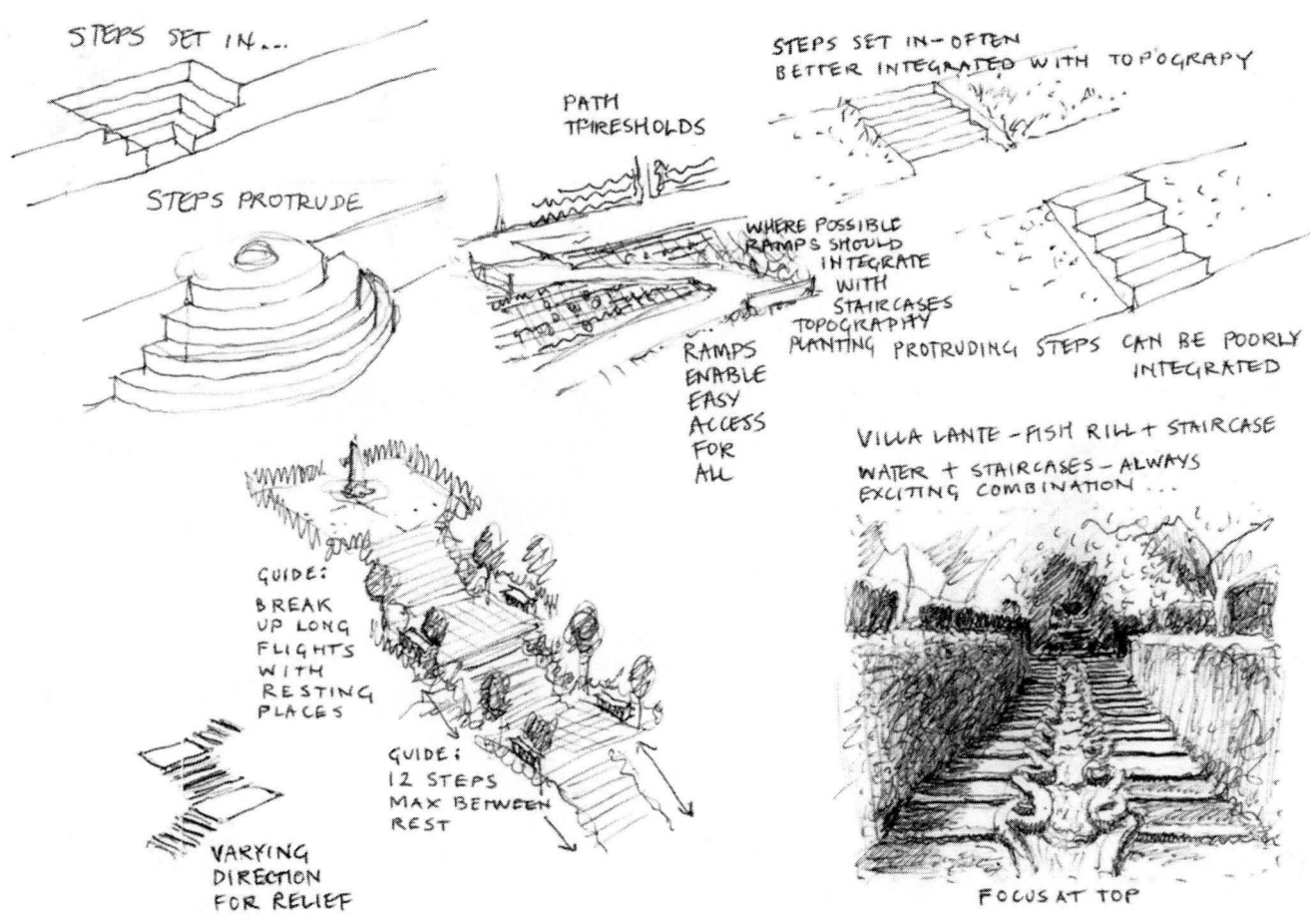

STEPS SET IN...

STEPS PROTRUDE

PATH
THRESHOLDS

STEPS SET IN - OFTEN
BETTER INTEGRATED WITH TOPOGRAPY

WHERE POSSIBLE
RAMPS SHOULD
INTEGRATE
WITH
STAIRCASES
TOPOGRAPHY

RAMPS
ENABLE
EASY
ACCESS
FOR
ALL

PLANTING PROTRUDING STEPS CAN BE POORLY
INTEGRATED

GUIDE:
BREAK
UP LONG
FLIGHTS
WITH
RESTING
PLACES

GUIDE:
12 STEPS
MAX BETWEEN
REST

VARYING
DIRECTION
FOR RELIEF

VILLA LANTE - FISH RILL + STAIRCASE

WATER + STAIRCASES - ALWAYS
EXCITING COMBINATION ...

FOCUS AT TOP

Stepped paths, staircases and ramps

On steep ground paths become staircases or ramps. Ramps should be fully integrated in designs to enable full access to all. Steep staircases can be barriers to access but equally can be exciting landscape experiences, depending on context. Landings within staircases are always desirable (even in short ones, and vital in long staircases) where space allows. Landings and staircases are often threshold spaces (see the section on Topographic thresholds, p. 178), which enable transition as well as sitting, resting and viewing.

Vegetation paths

AFTER "THE AVENUE" HOBBEMA

Vegetation can be used for surface, and for vertical and overhead enclosure of paths. In this section, examples of paths enclosed in these three planes are explored. The presence of vegetation is reason enough alone for walking; to smell plants and touch leaves, to move from dappled shade to sunlight or be amid the rustle of dry grasses. Vegetated paths provide highly sensory experiences. In addition, vegetation can play important structural and spatial roles forming paths by emphasising direction, thus separating or integrating paths with adjacent spaces. Roads in particular can be integrated into rural and urban contexts, and environmental effects can be mitigated with vegetation. Vegetation can also play way-marking, sequential, rhythmic and focal roles in paths. Vegetation also plays an important ecological and environmental as well as recreational role in greenways or ecological corridors (see Paths/Ecological corridors, p. 86).

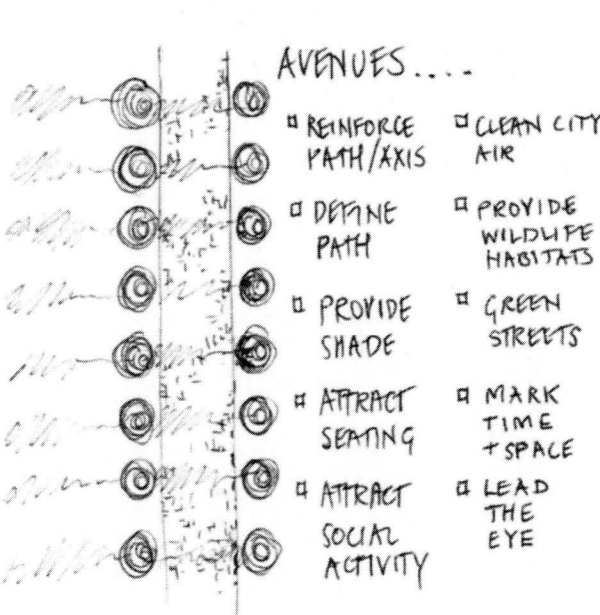

AVENUES....

▢ REINFORCE PATH/AXIS

▢ DEFINE PATH

▢ PROVIDE SHADE

▢ ATTRACT SEATING

▢ ATTRACT SOCIAL ACTIVITY

▢ CLEAN CITY AIR

▢ PROVIDE WILDLIFE HABITATS

▢ GREEN STREETS

▢ MARK TIME + SPACE

▢ LEAD THE EYE

WINTER CANOPY

LONG SHADOWS

GRANDEUR — TALL FOREST TREES FORM HIGH NARROW PATH SPACE

Avenues

The avenue is an enduring landscape form. Its popularity may be due to the many functions that avenues can perform. They shade, orient people by emphasising axis, provide transitional edges between road and buildings and can mediate between large and human scales. They provide habitats and play environmental roles in narrow urban spaces. Older avenues give a sense of place and time. Historically and in rural places, avenues also have economic and agricultural functions.

Forest paths

Forest paths provide distinctive walking experiences. Dark and gloomy in cloudy weather or animated and dappled in sunlight, forest paths are dynamic. Ground becomes soft, mossy and damp. These paths are strangely silent. As they are walked, tree trunks orbit, slide and migrate from view, grouping behind each other like figures in a crowd. Timelessness is somehow conveyed in the extent of repeated trunks (see also Spaces/Formalised forest, p. 65). Forest paths form systems and networks associated with nodal glades (see Spaces/Glades, p. 64).

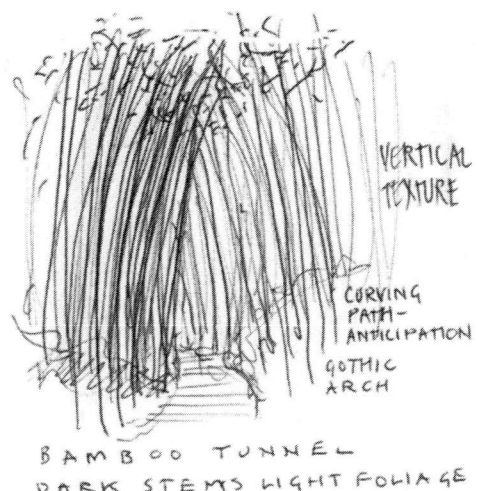

VERTICAL TEXTURE

CURVING PATH – ANTICIPATION

GOTHIC ARCH

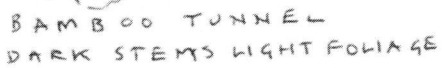

BAMBOO TUNNEL
DARK STEMS LIGHT FOLIAGE

LIGHT PENETRATES FROM SIDES

EXPECTANCY

SMOOTH SCULPTED YEWS
ACCENTUATE VISTA

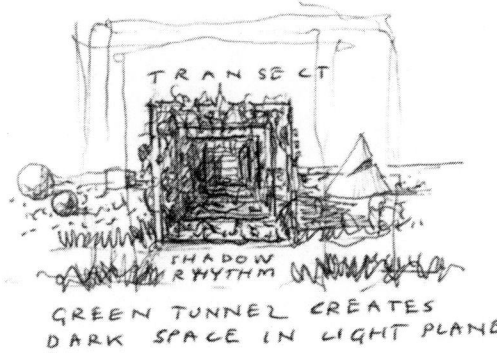

TRANSECT

SHADOW RHYTHM

GREEN TUNNEL CREATES
DARK SPACE IN LIGHT PLANE

Green tunnels

Paths through vegetated 'tunnels' provide very green and distinct experiences because of the total enclosure and seclusion created by leaves and branches. Like cutting paths they provide contrasting walking experiences by enabling people to move between light and dark, warmth and cool, openness and enclosure.

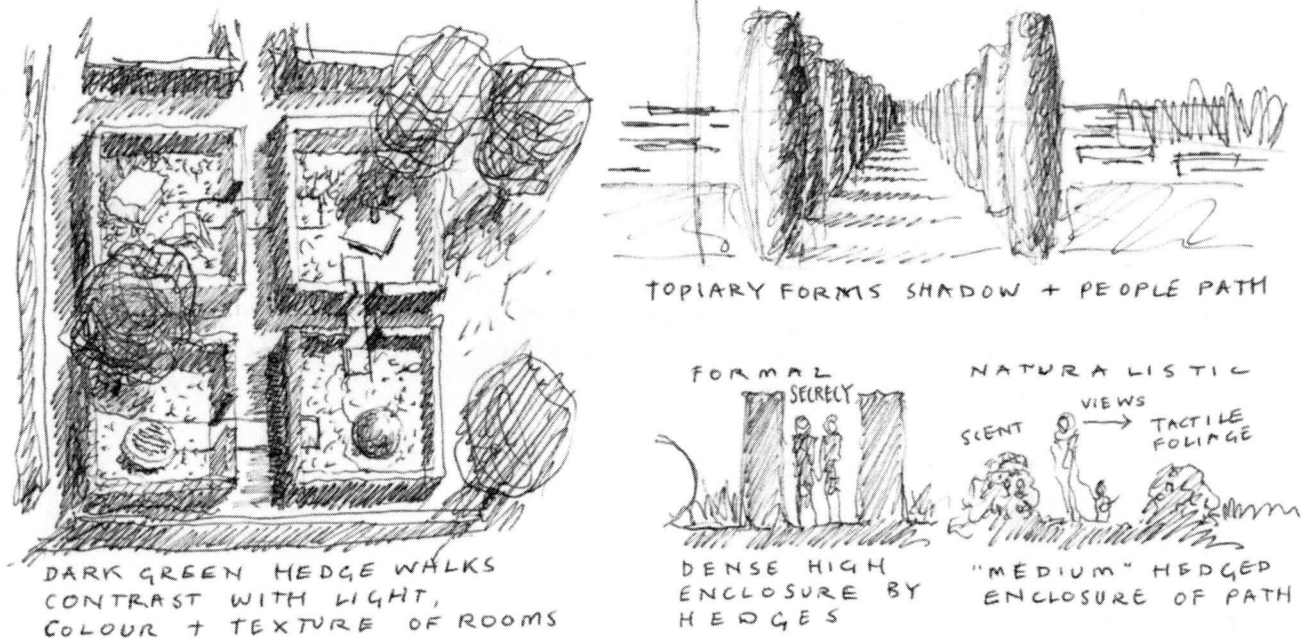

DARK GREEN HEDGE WALKS CONTRAST WITH LIGHT, COLOUR + TEXTURE OF ROOMS

TOPIARY FORMS SHADOW + PEOPLE PATH

FORMAL
SECRECY

NATURA LISTIC

SCENT
VIEWS → TACTILE FOLIAGE

DENSE HIGH ENCLOSURE BY HEDGES

"MEDIUM" HEDGED ENCLOSURE OF PATH

Hedged walks

Hedges can enclose paths on one or both sides, providing secrecy, shelter and scent. Like avenues, hedges reinforce the direction of paths but if a path curves, it can also obscure a destination. Depending on context, hidden destinations in hedged walks can be threatening or engaging through mystery and seclusion.

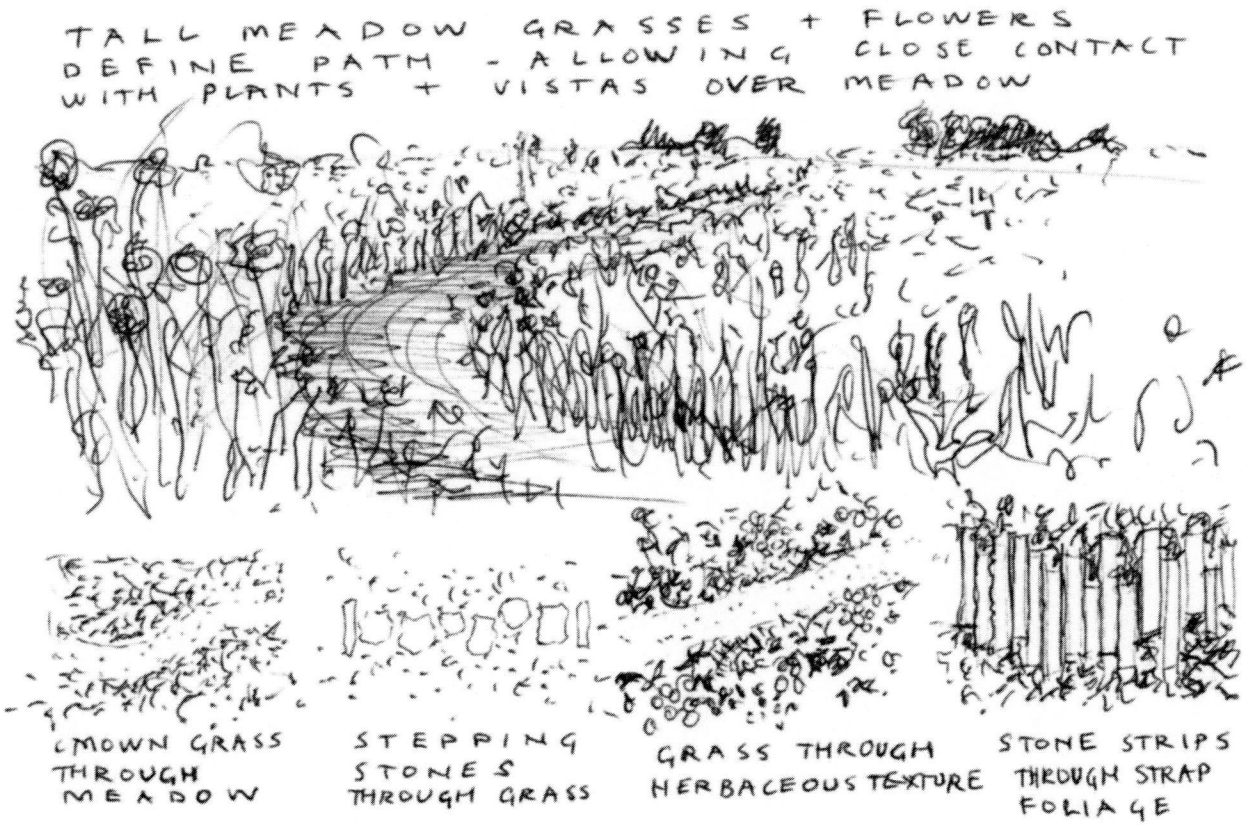

TALL MEADOW GRASSES + FLOWERS
DEFINE PATH - ALLOWING CLOSE CONTACT
WITH PLANTS + VISTAS OVER MEADOW

MOWN GRASS THROUGH MEADOW

STEPPING STONES THROUGH GRASS

GRASS THROUGH HERBACEOUS TEXTURE

STONE STRIPS THROUGH STRAP FOLIAGE

Grass, vegetated floors and meadow paths

Vegetation is a vulnerable surface in places of heavy public use. In less intensely used recreational places it is always desirable if management resources are available and climate allows. Paths can be created simply through grassland by using different mowing regimes.

Built paths

Path surfaces are of course structures. In this section, surfaces as well as enclosing structures are briefly illustrated.

NARROW PEDESTRIAN STREET
PATH ENCLOSED BY CHANGING TEXTURE
AND FORM OF BUILDINGS

TREES PROVIDE
SECONDARY ENCLOSURE

PEDESTRIAN
DOMINATED
STREET

SHOPS   VEHICULAR   PEDESTRIAN   VEHICULAR   SHOPS
BARS   TRAFFIC   PROMENADE   TRAFFIC   BARS
CAFES   WITH MARKET   CAFES
                         TRADE STANDS

LAS RAMBLAS - BARCELONA
SECTION SHOWS BUILDING ENCLOSURE OF
STREET AND WIDTH / HEIGHT RELATIONSHIPS

STREET AS HIGHLY USED URBAN "GREENSPACE"

Streets

The landscape design of streets is primarily concerned with detailing the space between buildings, but it may also involve working at earlier stages with urban designers or architects and engineers to develop concepts and strategies for networks and building space relationships. Pedestrianised streets and pedestrian zones on vehicular roads offer great potential as recreational 'greenspaces'. The diversity of approaches to landscape and urban design of streets goes beyond the scope of this book.

NARROW BACKS CAN BE ATTRACTIVE
PEDESTRIAN PATHS - GLIMPSES OF
YARPS AND GARDENS IN RESIDENTIAL
AREAS. CAN BE LITTER STREWN,
VANDALISED IF NEGLECTED/UNUSED/UNPERSONALISED

REFUSE COLLECTION....
SERVICE ACCESS....
CAR MAINTENANCE....
PLAY.. ETC....
ALL IMPORTANT DESIGN
CONSIDERATIONS

'Backs'

'Back streets' and pedestrian-only paths are important paths in urban environments as they provide quieter alternative routes and settings for domestic and recreational activities. They are included here as an important path type in cities, with distinct design potential and character.

SECTION OF PEDESTRIAN "STREAM" PATH BY WATER
NAGAKUTE TOWN, JAPAN
GEOMETRIC ORDER AND ORGANIC/RANDOM PATTERNING EFFECTIVELY COMBINED - GRANITE + KISO STONE

Path floors

The design of path floors is a major part of landscape
architecture. The diversity of approaches to designing the
built surface of paths is beyond the scope of this book.
An illustration is included here because surface plays a
very important but often neglected part of urban experience (see also Spaces/Built spaces/Floors, p. 75).

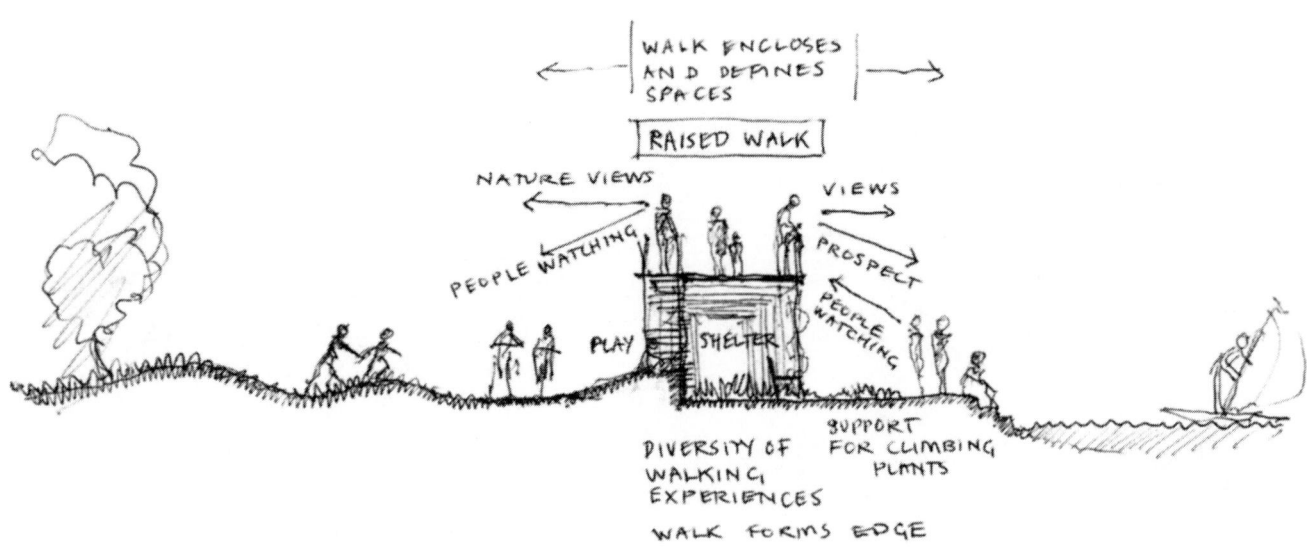

The labels within the diagram read:

WALK ENCLOSES AND DEFINES SPACES

RAISED WALK

NATURE VIEWS

VIEWS

PEOPLE WATCHING

PROSPECT

PEOPLE WATCHING

PLAY

SHELTER

DIVERSITY OF WALKING EXPERIENCES

SUPPORT FOR CLIMBING PLANTS

WALK FORMS EDGE

Raised walks

Raised walk structures can provide exciting landscape experiences in giving prospect over surrounding spaces and can enhance the recreational potential of places with 'bland' topography. However, they can also become barriers to many users, especially if they are the only means to travel through or to a place. Lightweight structures avoid dark 'dead' space below.

COVERED WALKS CAN BE :... ...

···GLOOMY   PLEASANTLY COOL
STAGNANT   OR   + SHADED
COLD   SHELTERED
THREATENING   SECURE
DINGY   PATTERNED
CLAUSTRAPHOBIC
DIRTY

TOO HOT   OR   LIGHT
AIRLESS   AIRY
UNCOMFORTABLE   COMFORTABLE
                     WARM
                     SHELTERED......

·······DEPENDING ON CONTEXT, FUNCTION
CLIMATE, STRUCTURE + MATERIALS.

Covered walks

Canopied walks extend the use of places by improving microclimate through the provision of shelter or shade from rain, wind or sun. As edges, covered walks can be important social and recreational places (see for example Edges/Built/Colonnades, p. 137). Lightness through transparency and visually open structures are desirable in temperate climates, while density of structure to provide shade is an important consideration in hot environments. Covered walks are meaningless additions to landscape unless they connect places of destination.

Water paths

Landscape architecture involves the design of linear waterbodies and the design of pathways adjacent to natural or constructed waterbodies. The following pages briefly illustrate the design considerations and potential of these water paths.

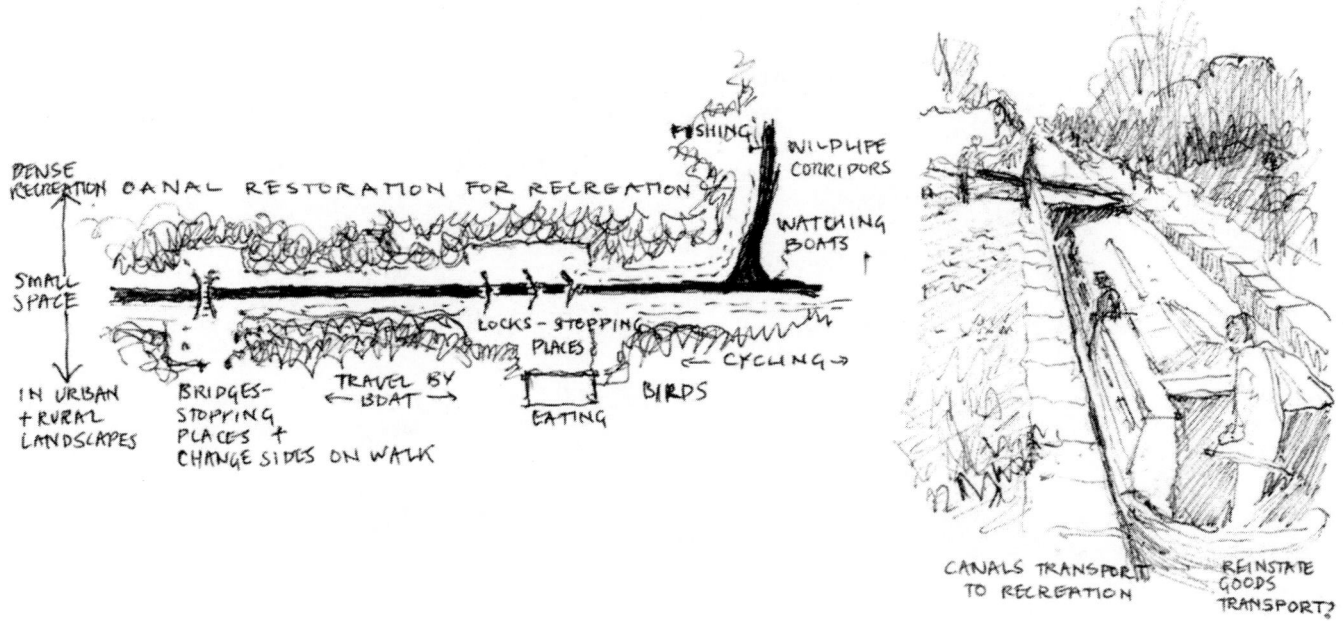

The design of paths adjacent to water

Water intrinsically attracts people, and recreational walking is commonly associated with rivers, canals, coast or inland waterbodies. Waterside paths are vibrant edge places. They require strong integration with thresholds, edges and sequenced stopping spaces along the path. Monotony can be avoided by creating a diversity of path relationships to the water's edge and incident along the path. Paths and people can conflict with wildlife. Paths can be organised to protect vulnerable landscapes by directing people around sensitive places or over water and back again.

DRAWING AFTER DETAIL FROM "AERIAL VIEW OF LONDON DOCKS" BY WILLIAM LIONEL WYLLIE 1851-1932

Rivers and canals in urban environments

Rivers, canals and river corridors act as paths in cities for transport and travel for pleasure and potentially as ecological corridors. They are fundamentally important parts of the urban environment. Considering fully their environmental benefits and problems and recreational potential and implications for design is not possible here.

113

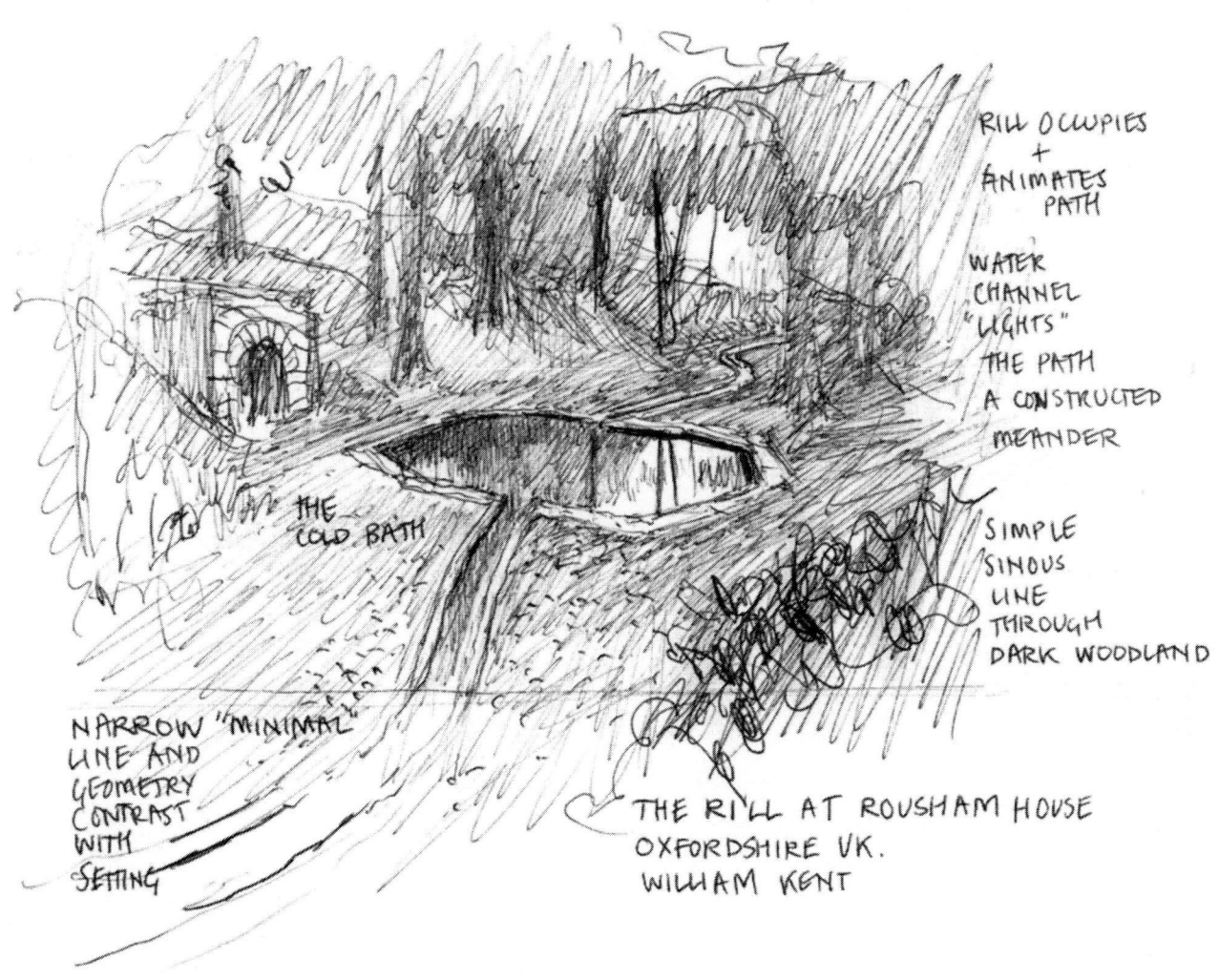

RILL OCCUPIES
+
ANIMATES
PATH

WATER
CHANNEL
"LIGHTS"
THE PATH
A CONSTRUCTED
MEANDER

SIMPLE
SINOUS
LINE
THROUGH
DARK WOODLAND

THE
COLD BATH

NARROW "MINIMAL"
LINE AND
GEOMETRY
CONTRAST
WITH
SETTING

THE RILL AT ROUSHAM HOUSE
OXFORDSHIRE UK.
WILLIAM KENT

Designed linear waterbodies

Small-scale linear waterbodies such as rills and channels are not paths in themselves, but attract movement and interaction along their length. In design they are often therefore integrated with pathways. Water enhances the pleasure of walking by animating a route. The experience of sequence, variation, repetition and incident are all important qualities in linear waterbodies.

4 Edges

In this section, edges are explored as distinct physical components of landscape and also as spatial concepts in design. Edges are interlocking forms or places of transition that enclose and separate different spaces. Thinking about edges as physical and conceptual entities within landscapes provides the opportunity to be integrative, complex, rich and subtle in the design of spatial transitions. Edges 'knit' the fabric of the landscape together and connect architecture to landscape and vice versa.

Edges are also considered important spatial concepts because of their potential to support or detract from social activity in public places.

The use of topography, vegetation, structures and water to create edges is illustrated.

DRAWING AFTER:
GIOVANNI GUERRA

"MOUNT PARNASSUS"
THEATRE
VILLA MEDICI
PRATOLINO 1604

EDGE OF
SEATING
+ TREES
BECOMES
SIGNIFICANT
PLACE OF
USE

Definitions

An edge can be defined as:

- the linear interface between two spaces or regions of a landscape that have different functions and/or physical characters
- a thickened permeable 'wall' plane
- a transitional or 'in-between' linear zone
- a seam of 'interlock' in landscape
- an ecotone
- a boundary
- a horizon.

People's use and experience of edges

Edges are of immense importance conceptually and physically in landscape design because they can support diverse human uses and have important experiential and cultural meanings. They are also important because, as spatial components, they are often neglected or ignored by designers. This neglect may be due in part to binary thinking that categorises mass and space as opposites and negates the possibility of designing 'hybrid' spaces that are neither mass nor space but are both simultaneously.

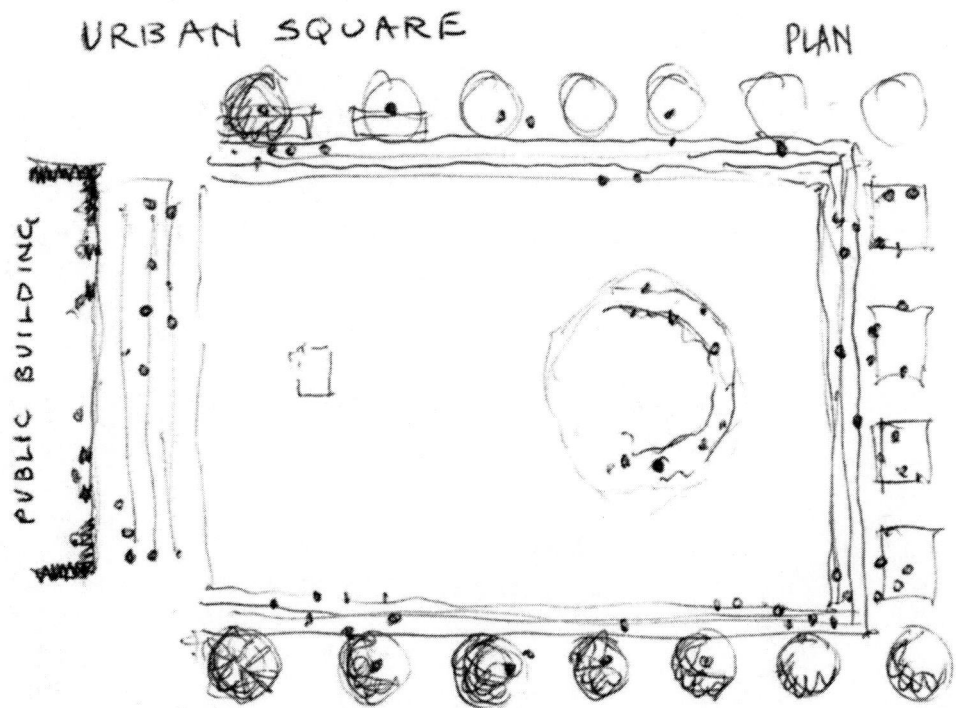

URBAN SQUARE PLAN

PUBLIC BUILDING

DOTS REPRESENT LIKELY STOPPING AND
SITTING / WAITING PLACES FOR PEOPLE

Edges as social places

Edges are potentially vibrant social environments. In public spaces (depending on the cultural context), people frequently choose to sit, wait or occupy edges of spaces rather than positioning themselves more centrally. Various theories and research work help to explain this

behaviour including Appleton's (1996) 'prospect–refuge' theory. Designers can also observe this for themselves. Landscape architecture involves facilitating potential social activities (especially sitting) with appropriate physical forms, elements and relationships for edges.

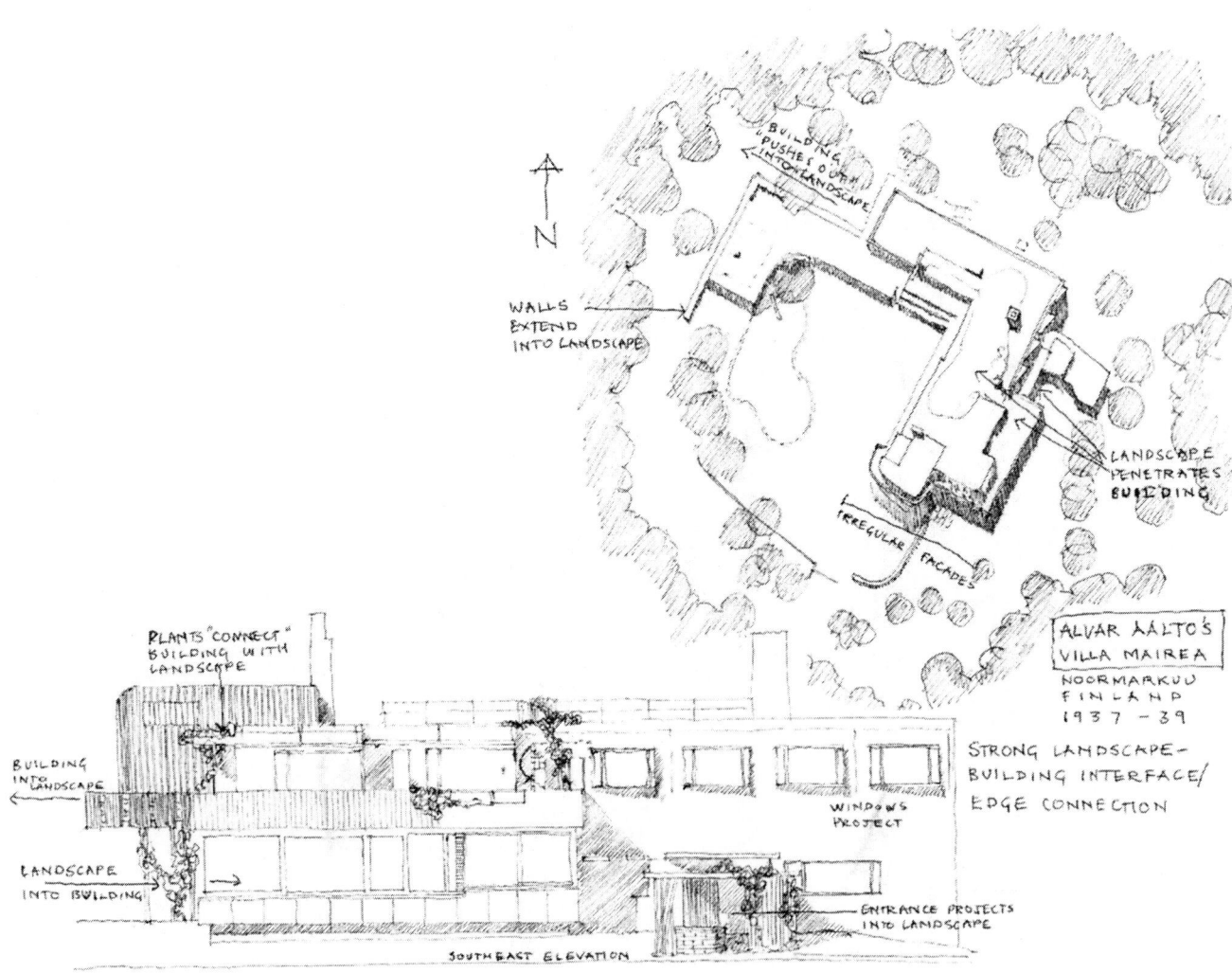

Architecture–landscape interface

The 'hybrid linear space' around buildings that is both landscape and architecture is an edge. The design of this physical interface can be thought of as the dual task of architect and landscape architect. Too often architect and landscape architect fail to work together creatively to realise the design potential for this transitional space. For aesthetic and social reasons, strong physical connections between indoors and outdoors – where landscape penetrates buildings and interiors or facades project out into landscape – are often desirable.

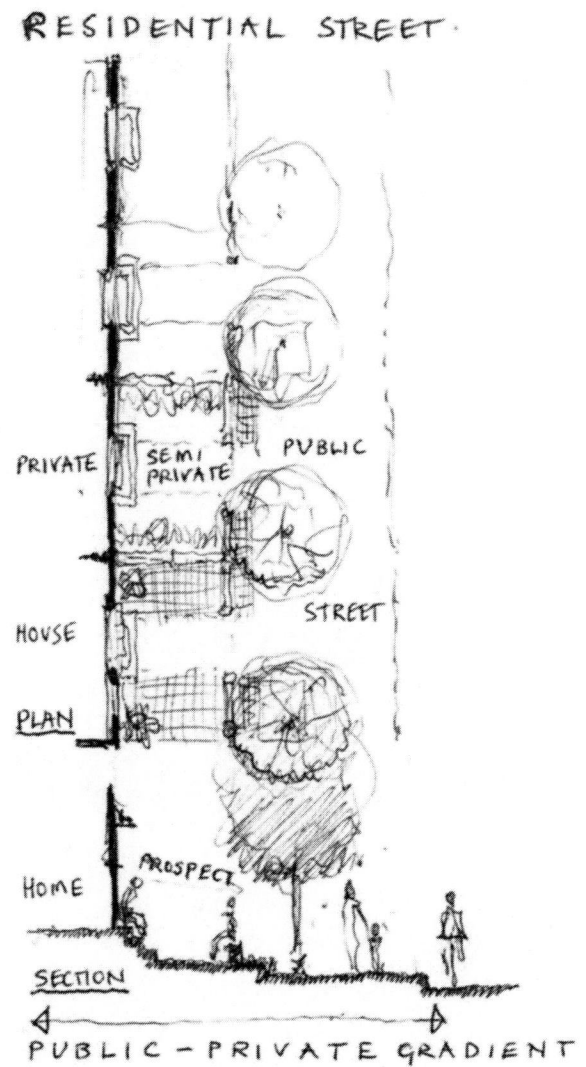

RESIDENTIAL STREET

PRIVATE   SEMI PRIVATE   PUBLIC

HOUSE   STREET

PLAN

HOME   PROSPECT

SECTION

PUBLIC — PRIVATE GRADIENT

Public, private and semi-private interfaces

Spaces are often defined by boundaries of ownership. Indeed, ownership could be described as the single most influential factor in determining the physical form of landscape spaces. The landscape architect is therefore often faced with the task of indicating the edges of public and private space with form. Transitional edges between public and private landscapes are important for social as well as aesthetic reasons, particularly in residential environments, and designers need to respond to this by providing for the distinct functions of these places.

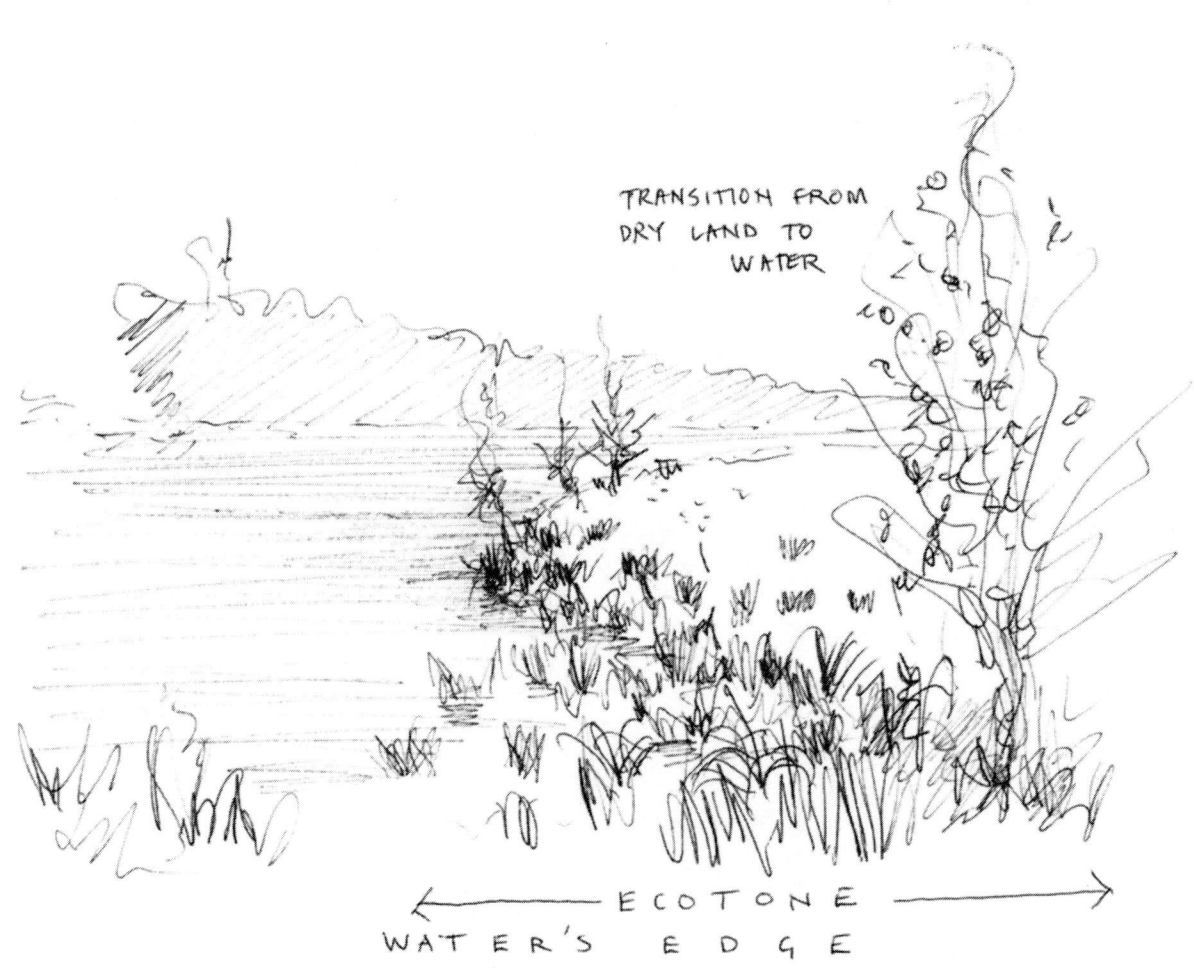

TRANSITION FROM
DRY LAND TO
WATER

← ——— E C O T O N E ——— →
W A T E R ' S   E D G E

Ecotones

In natural environments, vegetation, soils, climate and topography combine to form distinct landscape types, patterns and habitats. These change over time and space and therefore do not have abrupt physical edges but instead are bound by transitional zones where one landscape gradually becomes another. These transitions can occur over kilometres or metres and are known as 'ecotones'. It is important for designers to understand these ecotones for aesthetic and environmental reasons. They provide visual as well as ecological richness, dynamism and complexity for example in woodland edges or the gradient of a beach.

DRAWING AFTER PHOTOGRAPH BY JOHN DILLWYN LLEWELYN "KENNETH HOWARD IN BRANDY COVE" 1854

Edge meanings

The word edge has both negative and positive connotations when used in different cultural contexts. For example 'on the edge of' can describe the marginal status of people and groups in a society, or it can refer to the positive anticipation of a discovery or solution to a problem. Cultural meanings of words influence the meanings and experience of landscape forms and vice versa, and edges can therefore have quite specific and varied cultural interpretations by different people.

Horizons

Horizons are visual and symbolic edges where earth or sea meets sky. As physical places that cannot be occupied, horizons may connote future aspirations but also loss and separation. Visually complex horizons mesh and link earth and sky. This visual stitching of earth and sky in design is often more desirable than abrupt separation because it can increase our enjoyment of the sky as part of a landscape.

DRAWING AFTER "HARBOUR SCENE" BY ALFRED WALLIS (1855-1942) OIL ON CARD
PAINTING ILLUSTRATES RELATIONSHIPS OF EDGES, SPACES, PATHS +
FOCI... FORMING COMPLEX WHOLES OR LANDSCAPE FABRIC...

Edges and spaces, paths, thresholds and foci

As thickened 'wall' planes, edges enclose and separate spaces as well as contain 'sub-spaces' within their form. Paths are similarly often either enclosed by an edge or form part of the edge of a space. Thresholds have transitional and integrative functions that are similar to edges but are 'centred' spatial entities rather than linear forms. Foci may be located as visual sequential incidents along edges.

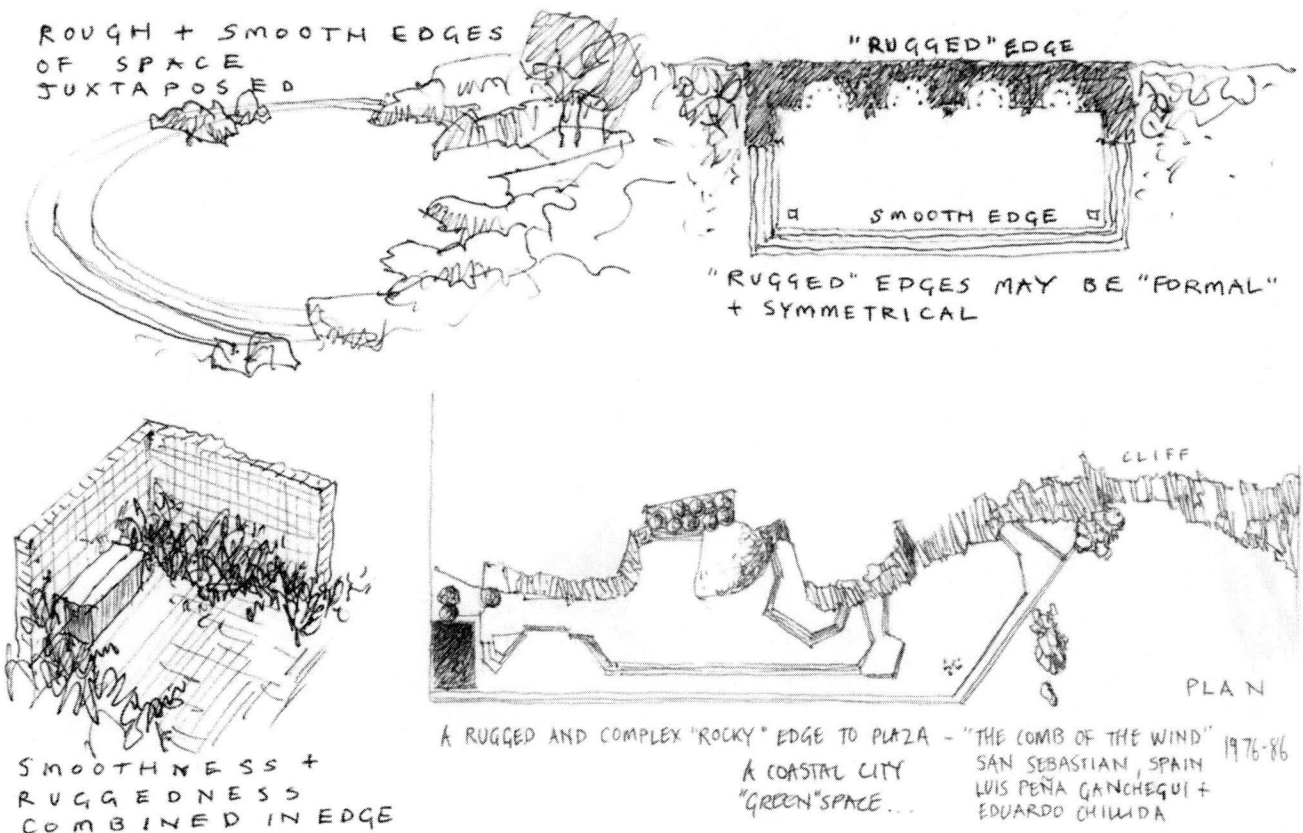

ROUGH + SMOOTH EDGES OF SPACE JUXTAPOSED

"RUGGED" EDGE

SMOOTH EDGE

"RUGGED" EDGES MAY BE "FORMAL" + SYMMETRICAL

SMOOTHNESS + RUGGEDNESS COMBINED IN EDGE

A RUGGED AND COMPLEX "ROCKY" EDGE TO PLAZA – A COASTAL CITY "GREEN" SPACE...

"THE COMB OF THE WIND" 1976-86 SAN SEBASTIAN, SPAIN LUIS PEÑA GANCHEGUI + EDUARDO CHILLIDA

CLIFF

PLAN

Forms

The following pages illustrate varying approaches to and considerations for the form generation of edges.

Rugged and smooth edges and their juxtaposition

Edges can be 'rugged' or 'smooth' in form in horizontal and vertical planes. Rugged edges are diverse and enclose sub-spaces as part of their form. Smooth edges are simple, minimal and without sub-spaces. It is often desirable to juxtapose or combine both smooth and rugged edges in the different enclosing planes of a space. Smoothness has value in visual simplicity and continuity. Ruggedness is textural and supports the social activity of small groups and individuals by incorporating sub-spaces – 'niches'.

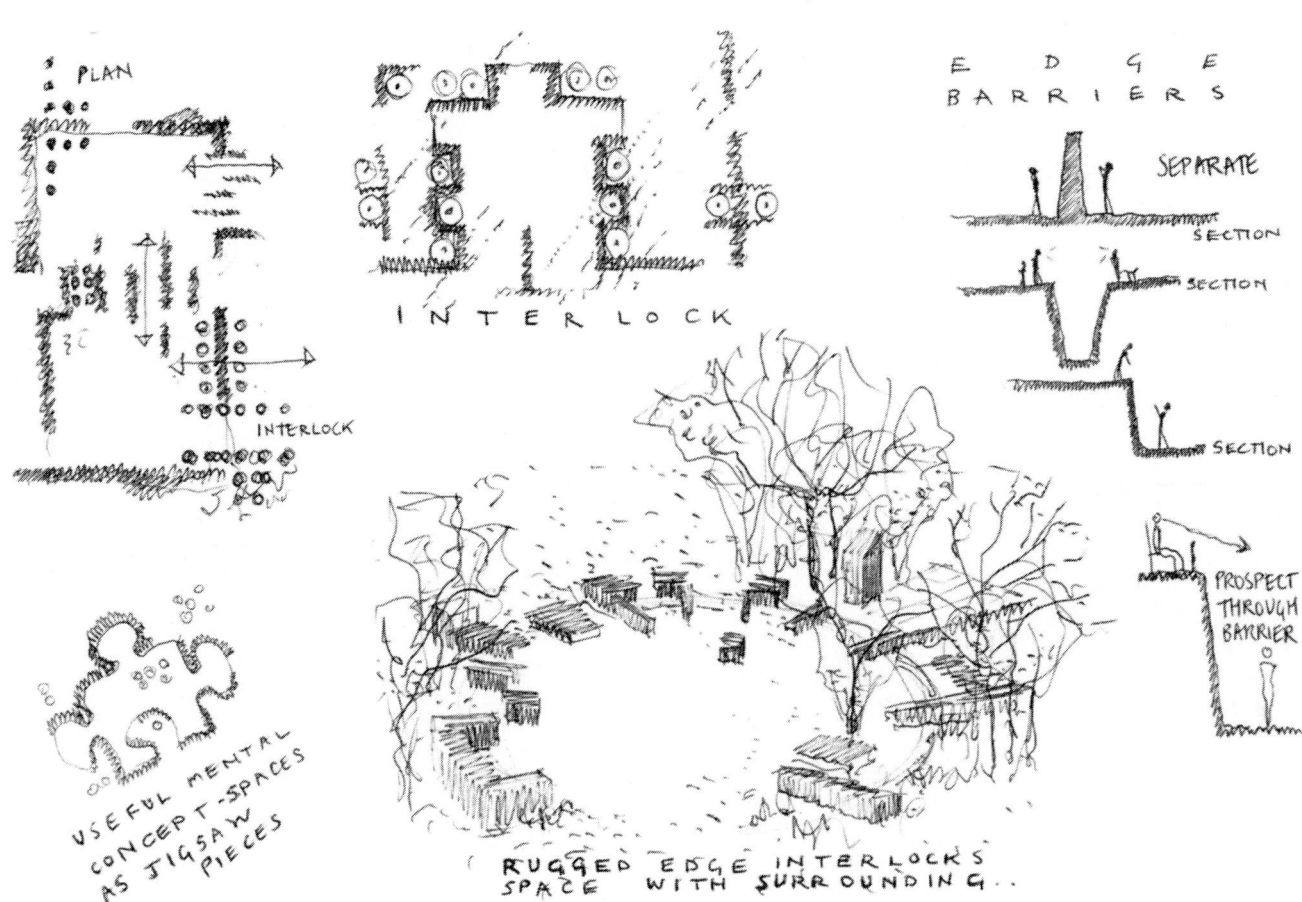

Interlock

'Rugged' edges provide strong 'interlock' between one place and another by pushing out or pulling in physical forms and characteristics of one space into another. Interlocking edges knit together the fabric of the landscape with overt physical texture. Smooth edges provide minimal visual and physical interlock and can be physical and perceptual barriers.

Barriers – intentional and unintentional

Dramatic or abrupt physical separation between one space and another creates psychological and physical barriers in the landscape. Designing edges as barriers is an important design skill, but it is equally important to ensure that edges do not unintentionally act as barriers. Building facades can act as barriers by reducing interaction between outdoors and indoors (see Edges/Built, p. 137).

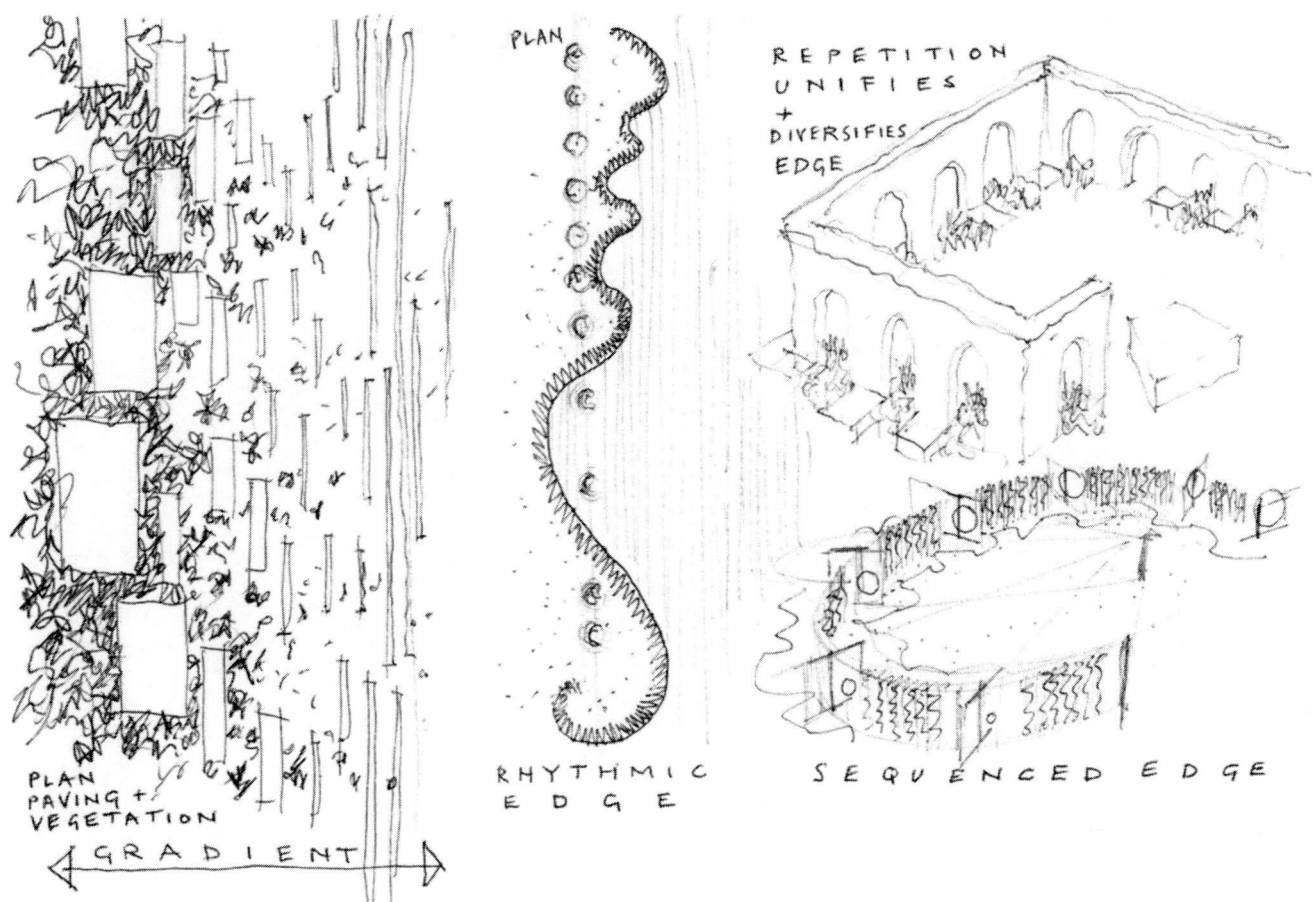

PLAN

REPETITION
UNIFIES
+
DIVERSIFIES
EDGE

PLAN
PAVING +
VEGETATION

⟨ G R A D I E N T ⟩

R H Y T H M I C
E D G E

S E Q U E N C E D   E D G E

Gradients

As well as being a topographic term, 'gradient' refers also to the gradual transition in form, texture, materials and vegetation over horizontal distance. Ecotones (see p. 121) are natural gradients. As edges, 'gradients' enable one space to merge with another in a seamless and subtle fashion.

Rhythm, sequence, repetition

Edges provide opportunities for diversity and unity in their overall form through use of repeated textures, forms and colours to create rhythms and sequences along their length.

126

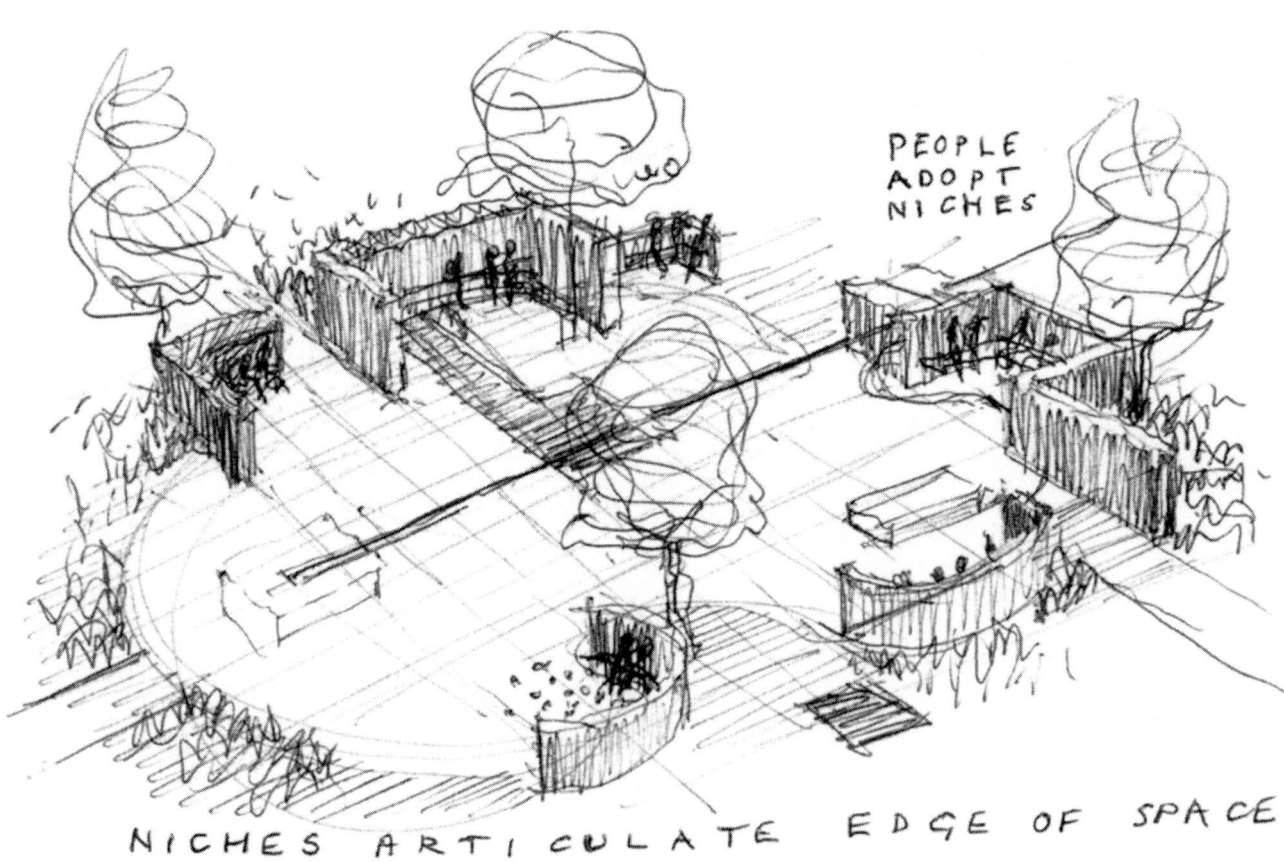

PEOPLE
ADOPT
NICHES

NICHES ARTICULATE EDGE OF SPACE

Edge sub-spaces – niches

An important characteristic of interlocking and 'rugged edges' is the 'sub-space' created in their form. These sub-spaces are small and intimate in character and can be adopted by small groups in public places for diverse social activities. Niche (from the French for 'to nest') is a good descriptive term for this type of edge space.

127

Topographic edges

The following pages illustrate the design of different types of topographic edges.

Spurred edges

'Spurred' refers to the topographic arrangement of an edge where higher ground projects in repeated fingered form (spurs) into a lower space. Spurs create niches at the lower level while the 'fingers' become vantage points and structures for play and sitting. Spurred edges can be naturalistic or geometric in form, or be combinations of both.

Stacked edges

'Stacked' describes a topographic edge in which a change of level incorporates clusters of strongly vertical forms similar to (in form not scale) geological stacks. Stacks provide stepped forms which enable movement between levels and can be arranged in random or rhythmic groups suggesting 'naturalness'. They have the potential for incorporating plants and water. A stacked edge provides diverse forms for sitting, climbing and children's exploration.

129

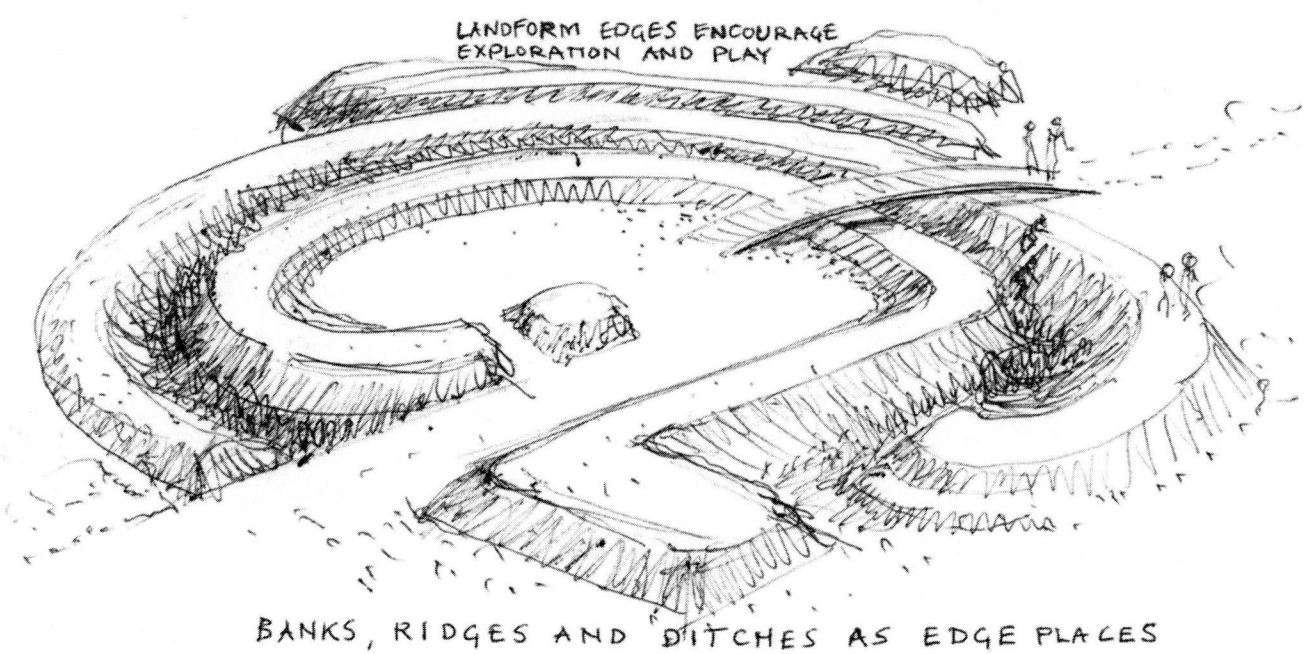

BANKS, RIDGES AND DITCHES AS EDGE PLACES

Banks

Sloping ground that separates or encloses space can provide an edge space to accommodate use. Mown grass and built banks provide play environments for a wide range of age groups. Banks often become habitats for wild plants through lack of, or different, management approaches. If they are too steep, they can be uncomfortable places to sit for long periods of time.

Ridges

Two banks 'back to back' become a ridge that, while separating spaces, also becomes a place of use in its own right especially for walking, sitting, watching/viewing, hiding, sunbathing and rolling.

Ditches

Ditches separate spaces through lower ground. Often damp, watery and concealed places, they are attractive to children for play, hiding and for wildlife, but are less attractive to adults as places to stay. Ditches often signal their presence in the landscape through the strapped texture of rushes and reeds.

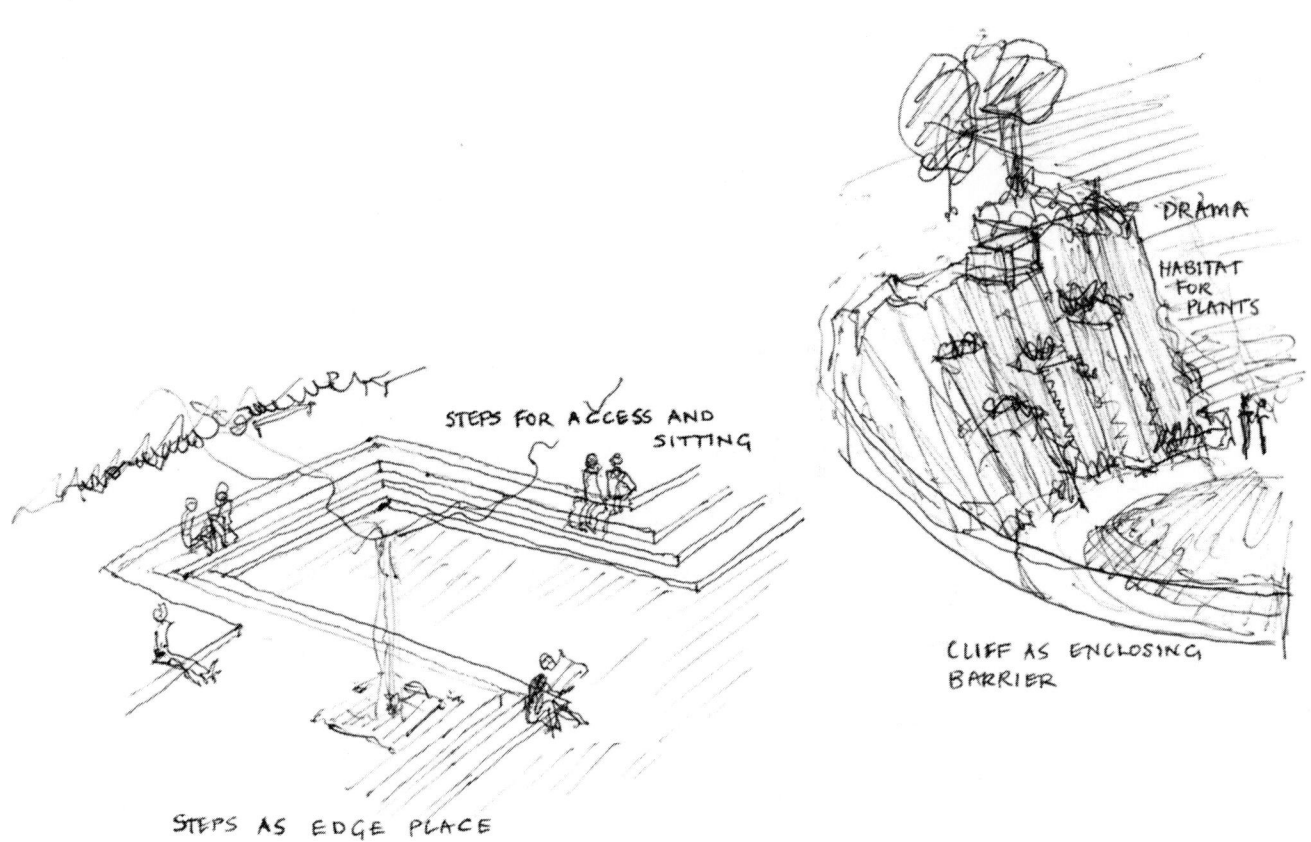

STEPS FOR ACCESS AND SITTING

DRAMA

HABITAT FOR PLANTS

CLIFF AS ENCLOSING BARRIER

STEPS AS EDGE PLACE

Steps as edges

Broad flights of steps can wrap around spaces to enclose them. These stepped edges often create positive social environments that are adopted by people for sitting, eating and drinking, as well as enabling access to the space they enclose.

Cliffs and chasms

Occasionally in urban places cliff and chasm forms are sometimes necessary and can be used to create distinctive and dramatic edge places. 'Cliffs' and high retaining walls can provide settings for theatre, video or digital light projections, ball games and recreational climbing. Cliffs and chasms are of course barriers to easy movement and can therefore be alienating and disorientating for people.

131

Vegetation edges

The following pages explore the use of vegetation to create edges.

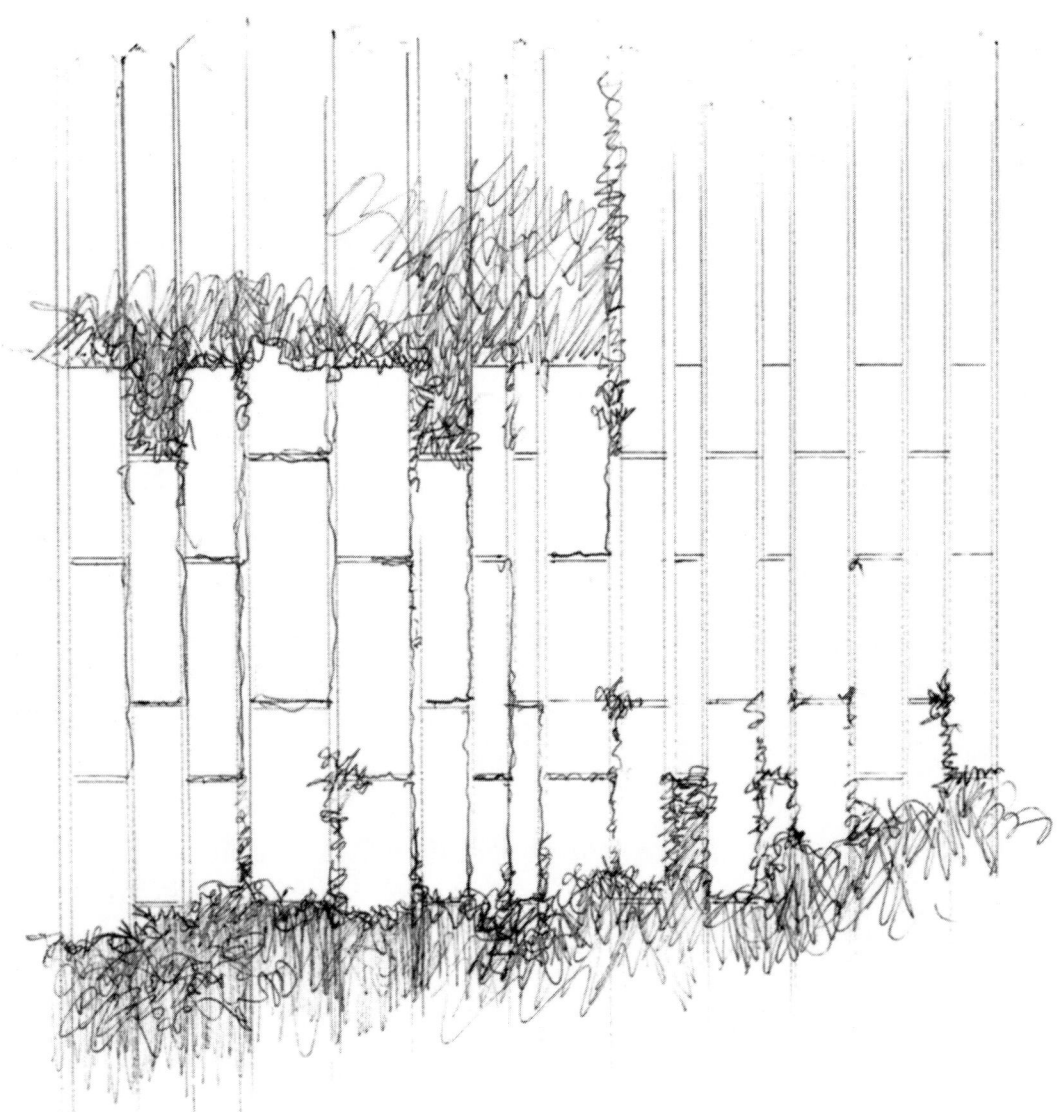

'Soft' and 'colonising' edges

Vegetation 'softens' edges. The texture and form of foliage and plants play important visual roles in inter-locking and transitional edges. The mass of individual and grouped plant forms is loose and coarse as it incorpo-rates 'space' within forms. The 'colonising' aesthetic of planted edges is of great appeal especially as counter-point to built and minimal structures. Ecotones are 'colonising edges'.

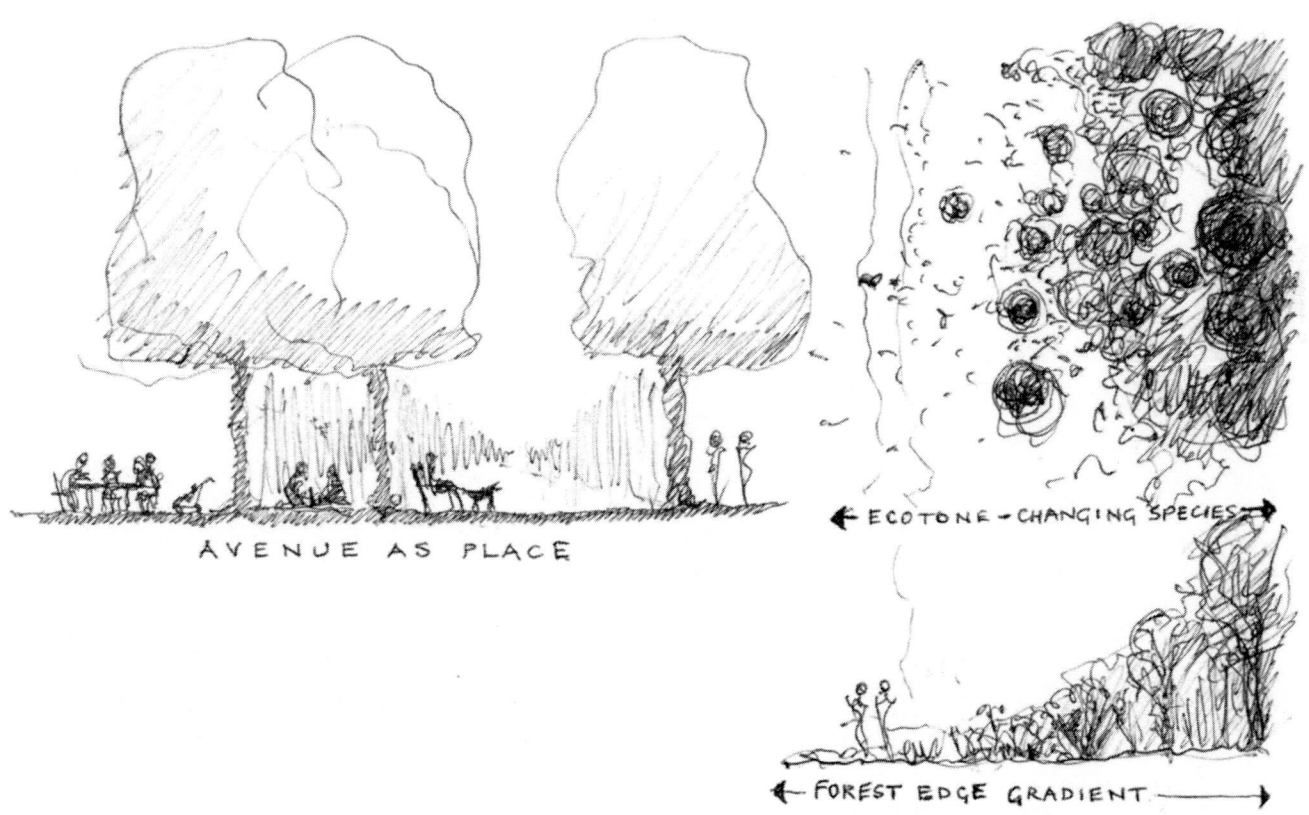

AVENUE AS PLACE

← ECOTONE - CHANGING SPECIES →

← FOREST EDGE GRADIENT →

Forest edge

The forest edge is a place of gradient from high tree canopy to low grassland. This ecotone incorporates changing species related to shade tolerance and competition. The forest edge provides distinct habitats for flora and fauna. It is a place of visual richness and complexity for landscape experience. Fruit and birds thrive. It is a sheltered place to look out from and a place to look into dark forest space.

Avenue as place to be

Avenues which line paths or the edge of spaces can become places to stay, eat, sit, park, sell, and to watch traffic or pedestrians pass by. The tree canopy demarcates and encloses a floor space below, especially in hot climates. In temperate climates, avenues can be gloomy, damp and dripping edges.

HEDGED AND SHRUBBY
EDGES ENABLE CLOSE CONTACT
WITH SCENTS, TEXTURES AND
PATTERN OF PLANTS

CENTRE FREE
FOR BALLGAMES
ETC

PATH

CLOSE MOWN
GRASS SPACES WITH
"MEADOW" EDGES

"MEADOW" ENRICHES
EDGES

Hedges and shrubby edges

Hedges and shrubs provide human-scale edge structures. Formal hedges with indented and alcove forms encourage sitting and sheltering uses. Shrubs can be massed to provide niches within indented edges allowing people to sit among the scent, colour and texture of plants.

Meadowed edges

On edges where people do not need to walk meadows can flourish. With their associated texture, flowering colour and seasonal change meadow edges can provide dynamic visual counterpoint to simple smooth lawn or paved spaces. Meadow edges provide transitional gradients between lawn and forest or shrub edge.

135

Built edges

The following pages explore different types of built edges and their design potential.

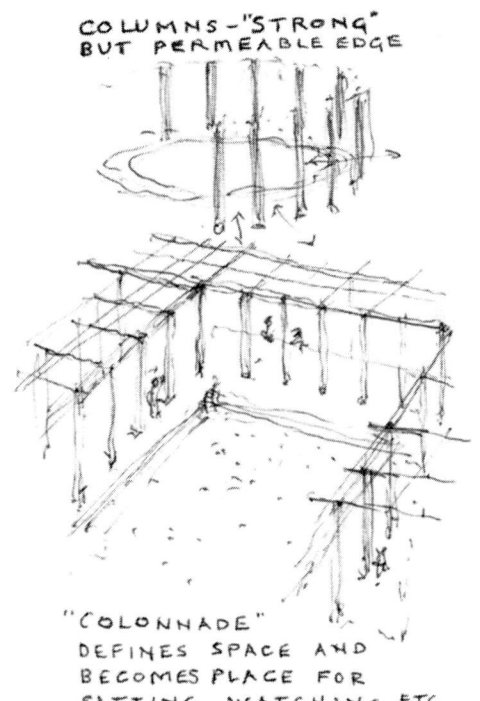

COLUMNS - "STRONG" BUT PERMEABLE EDGE

"COLONNADE" DEFINES SPACE AND BECOMES PLACE FOR SITTING, WATCHING ETC

STRONG INTERFACE BETWEEN LANDSCAPE AND BUILDING INTERIOR IN JAPANESE DESIGN DUE TO CULTURAL/AESTHETIC, CLIMATIC AND SOCIAL FACTORS

Building–landscape interface

There is infinite variation in the way that buildings and landscape may form interfaces. Design considerations for this interface might include creation of positive (useable) outdoor as well as indoor space; bringing visual themes and forms from outside in and vice versa or a deliberate juxtaposition and contrast of built and natural forms (see also Edges/Architecture–landscape interface, p. 119).

Colonnades and columns

Colonnades form strong yet permeable enclosing edges either as extensions of buildings or as freestanding structures. Colonnades often have classical associations or form, but they don't have to. They can provide a covered edge to important public spaces for people to sit, eat, talk and trade. Columns that enclose spaces have similar functions. The grand scale and vertical form of columns and colonnades provide a permanent and often theatrical character to spaces.

137

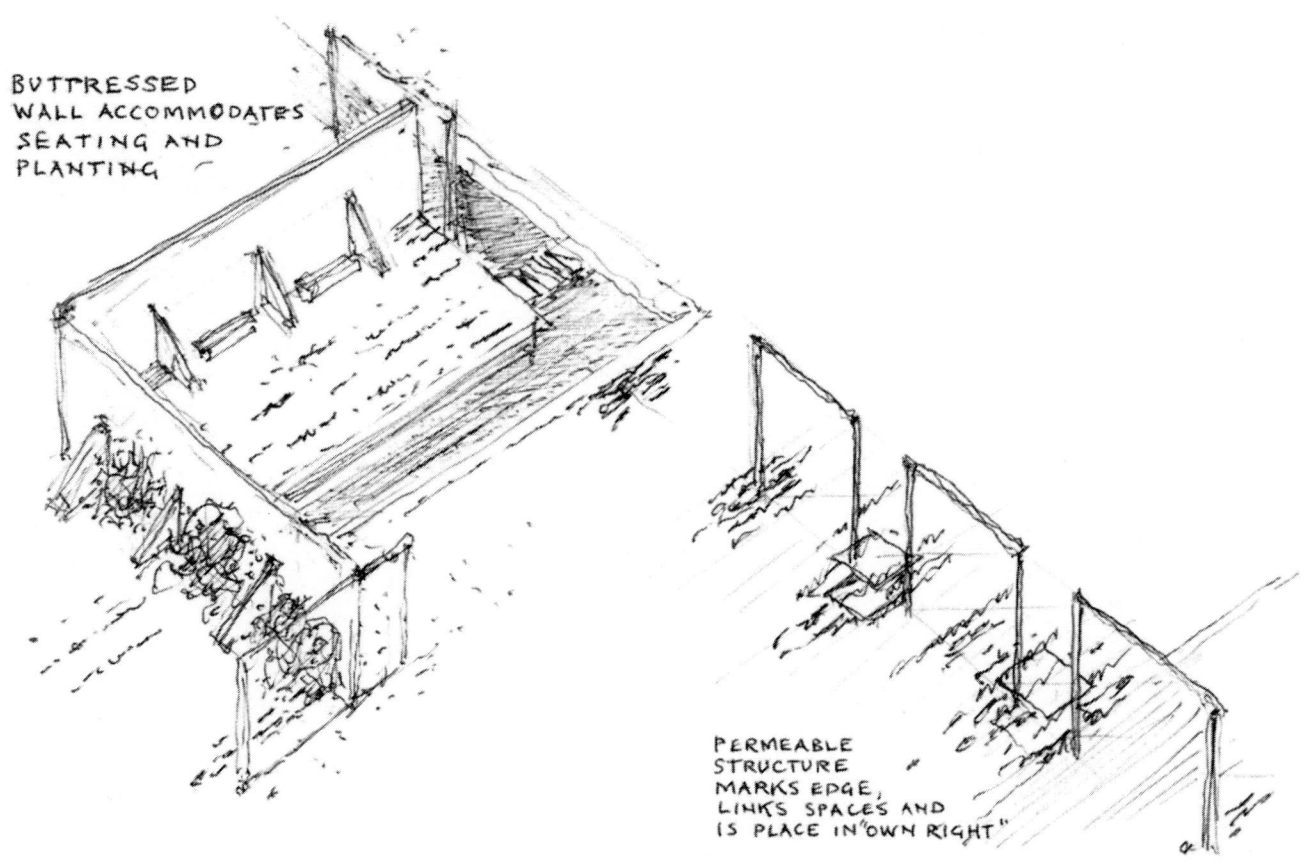

BUTTRESSED
WALL ACCOMMODATES
SEATING AND
PLANTING

PERMEABLE
STRUCTURE
MARKS EDGE,
LINKS SPACES AND
IS PLACE IN "OWN RIGHT"

Walls – buttressed and indented

Buttressed and indented walls provide sitting niches for social activity along their edge. They also provide niches for planting, sculpture or water. Wall structures of this form are inherently very stable and often give the appearance of great permanence regardless of age.

Permeable structures

Built structures such as open fences, railing or trellis forms are appropriate where visual permeability between one space and another is required without physical access. Many permeable structure designs are 'light' and integrating as they mesh together the landscape on either side (see also Spaces/Built, p. 73).

Water's edge

The place where land meets water is an important edge that attracts diverse and intense use, which the designer facilitates.

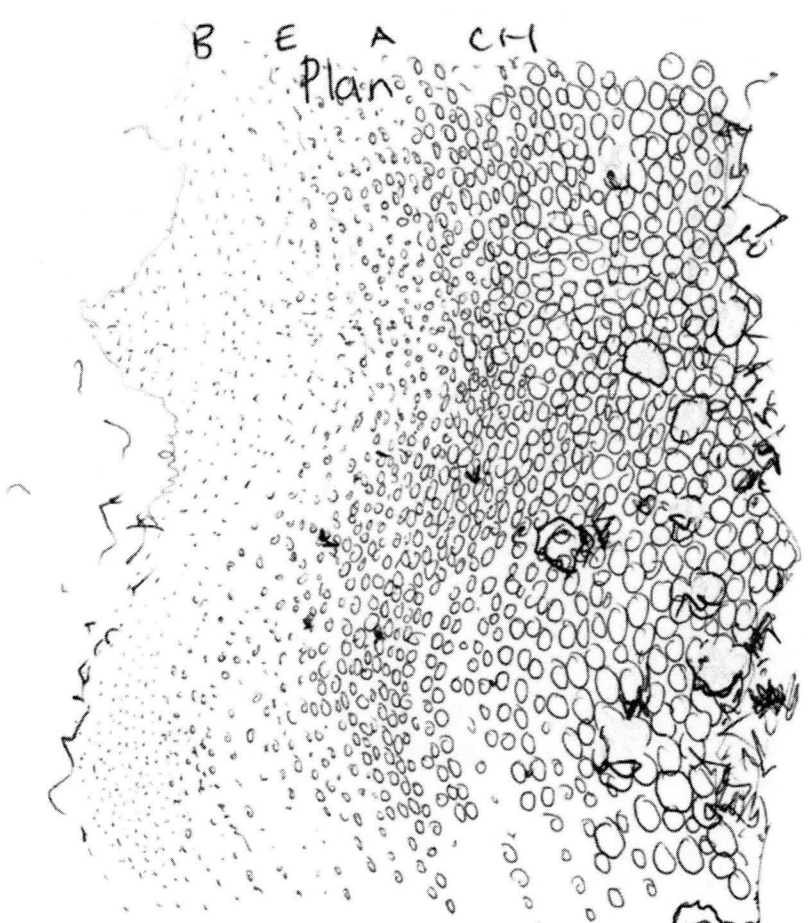

Beaches

Natural and artificial beaches are edges which provide people with recreational space and direct access to water. The shallow gradients of beaches draw people towards the water's edge. Beaches are also gentle topographic and 'textural' gradients with subtle visual transitions between land and water. Sandy beaches provide important recreational places, particularly for children.

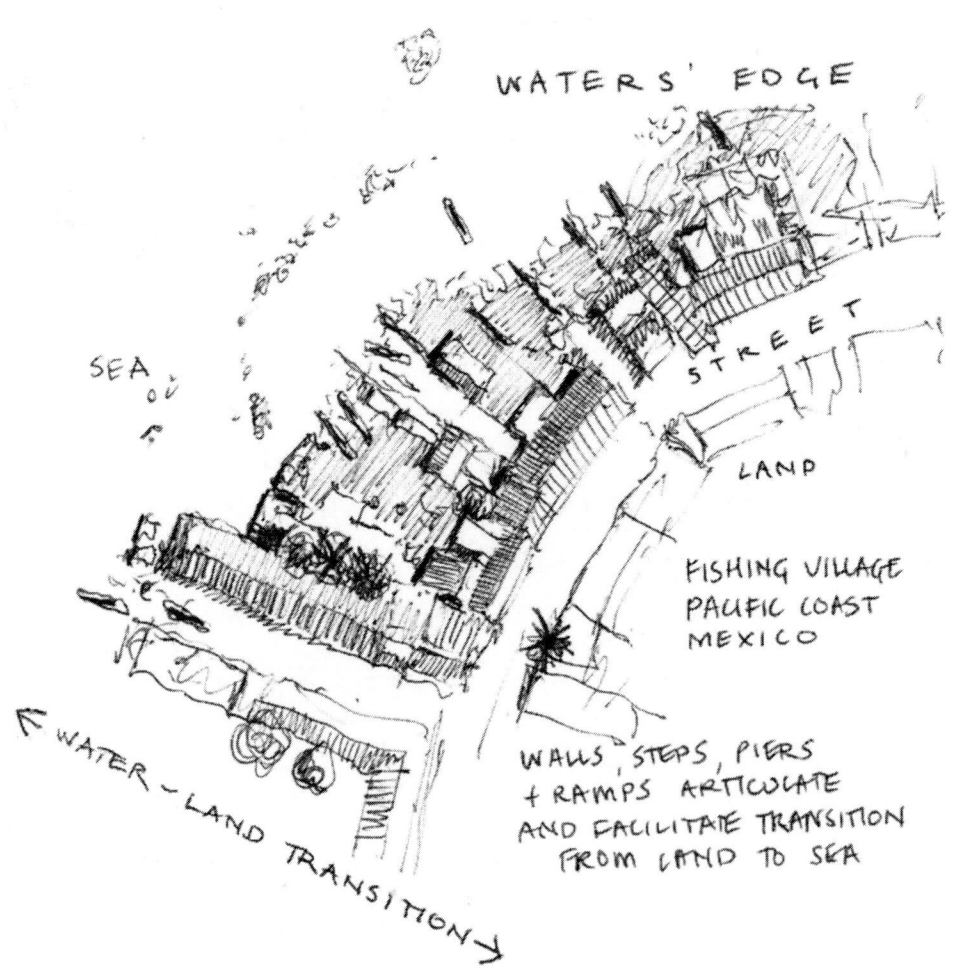

WATERS' EDGE

STREET

SEA

LAND

FISHING VILLAGE
PACIFIC COAST
MEXICO

WALLS, STEPS, PIERS
+ RAMPS ARTICULATE
AND FACILITATE TRANSITION
FROM LAND TO SEA

← WATER ~ LAND TRANSITION →

Platforms, boardwalks and piers

Platforms, boardwalks and piers on waterfronts cater for people's strong desire to access and walk along water edges or out over water. Structures associated with water's edge support activities on water and access to water.

141

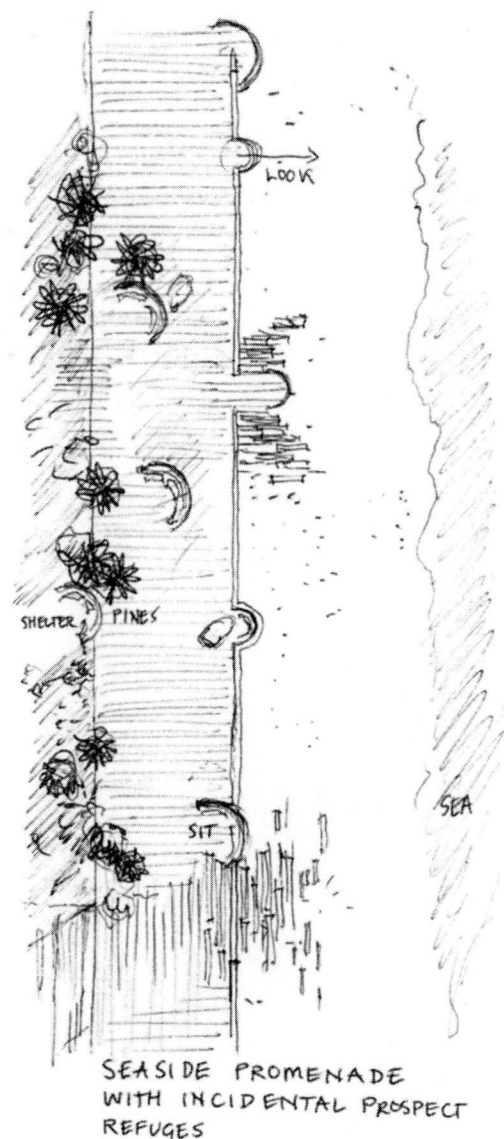

SEASIDE PROMENADE
WITH INCIDENTAL PROSPECT
REFUGES

Promenades

Promenades are both waterside (particularly seaside) paths and edge spaces. Promenade describes a long broad edge for recreation and social activity; walking, talking, skating, exercising, taking in views of the sea and sky, and beach recreation. The design of seaside promenades is strongly constrained by local climate.

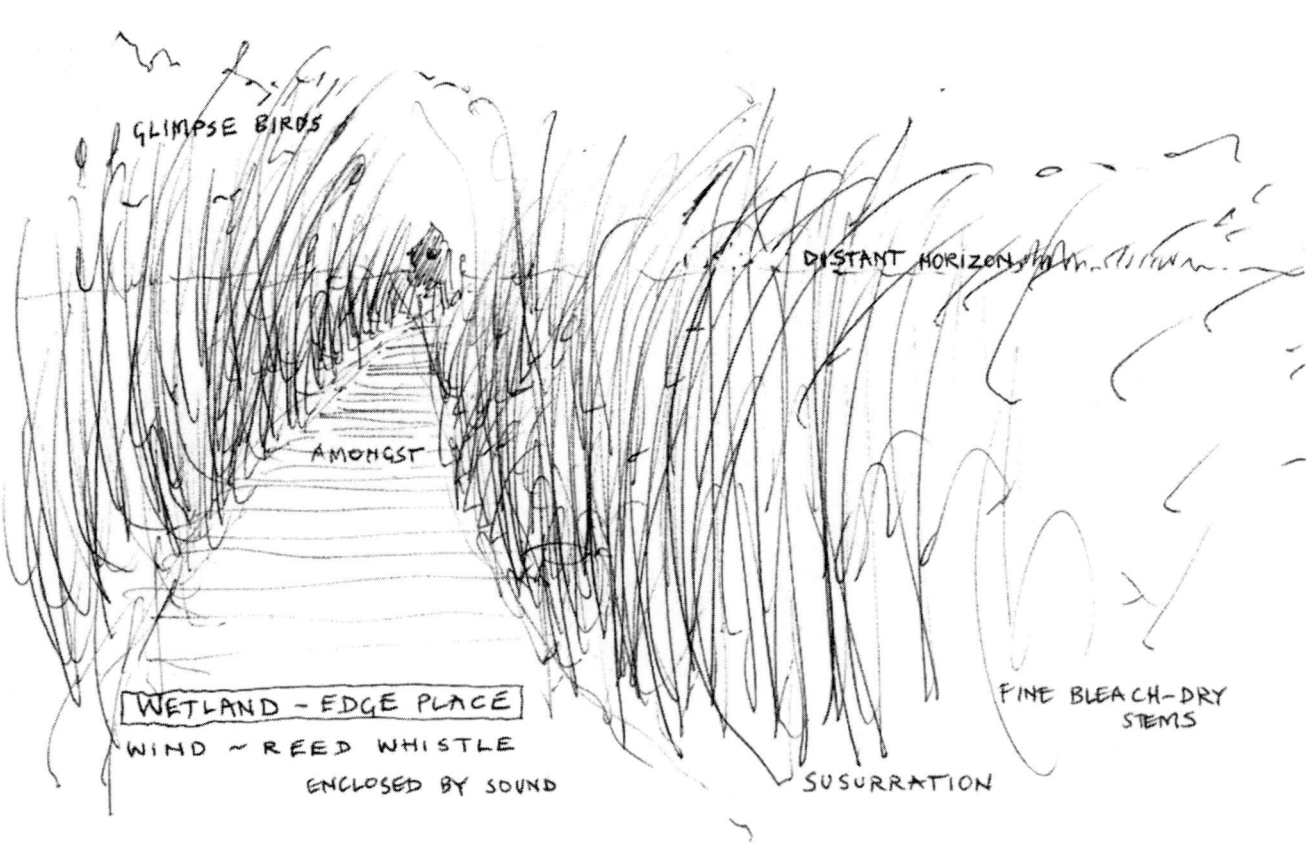

GLIMPSE BIRDS

DISTANT HORIZON

AMONGST

FINE BLEACH-DRY STEMS

WETLAND ~ EDGE PLACE
WIND ~ REED WHISTLE
ENCLOSED BY SOUND

SUSURRATION

Wetlands and marginal water places

Wetlands on the edges of lakes and rivers provide important habitats for plants and wildlife. They are often recreational places because of this and because of their visually distinct 'in between-ness'. Natural marginal water's edges need protection and careful management of access by visitors.

143

5 Foci

In this context 'foci' is a collective term used to describe focal forms and places in the landscape. The definition here includes landmarks but is not limited to referring to these. Foci describes both forms and places in the landscape that attract people or are visually dominant and distinctive – differentiated from their context.

They are given attention in this section as important components of landscape design that affect the use and experience of landscapes. They have important relationships to spaces and paths in particular. A framework for understanding the role of foci is given and examples of the use of topography, vegetation, structures and water to form foci are illustrated.

"NUCLEAR SAIL" IAN HAMILTON FINLAY (WITH JOHN ANDREW) 1973 SLATE 5FT
AT STONYPATH, SCOTLAND

Definitions

A focus can be defined as:

- a form or centralised group of forms (often vertical) that contrast(s) with the surrounding landscape
- a landscape form which assists orientation

- a form that marks a place of spiritual, cultural or social significance attracting people and becoming a destination and gathering point
- an 'event' in the landscape.

145

WOODLAND CEMETERY, STOCKHOLM
ARCHITECT: GUNNAR ASPLUND WITH
S. LEWERENTZ

FOCI OF CROSS + MOUNT WITH TREES DRAW
THE EYE AND CONTRAST WITH LIGHT OF SKY,
SMOOTH GRASS + DARK WOODLAND BEYOND.

People's use and experience of foci

Foci play a significant role in human use and experience of landscape. As the definitions of the term suggest, foci mark places of cultural significance, help people to orient themselves and attract people as places of differentiation.

Foci may be natural forms 'adopted' by people, or they may be specifically created for any of the functions described above.

IGA STUTTGART - 1993 - DESIGNED HANS LUZ + PARTNERS
AXIAL PATH ENDS IN DRAMATIC SPHERICAL FOCUS
FOCUS CHANGES CHARACTER WITH LIGHT, WATER, WEATHER....

Foci, destination places and paths

Much recreational activity in the landscape involves travelling to foci, dwelling and returning. Foci are 'natural' stopping places. They have a very strong relationship with paths (especially axial paths) as goals. At a distance, foci draw the eye and inspire movement towards them. Natural foci such as single large statuesque old trees or rocky tors can take on cultural and spiritual significance and become places of pilgrimage, celebration and ceremony. Paths are then constructed to enable journeys to these foci. Foci may be created as destinations formed at the end of a path but also as sequential markers along a path.

TREE AS FOCAL
GATHERING
PLACE

DETAIL AFTER "THE HARVESTERS" PIETER BRUEGEL
1565 METROPOLITAN MUSEUM OF ART NEW YORK

Places to gather

Foci are forms around which people 'naturally' gather.
They are often artworks or artefacts and therefore places
for cultural and social events. Memorial sites and forms
are also gathering places, as are places or forms considered to have spiritual significance.

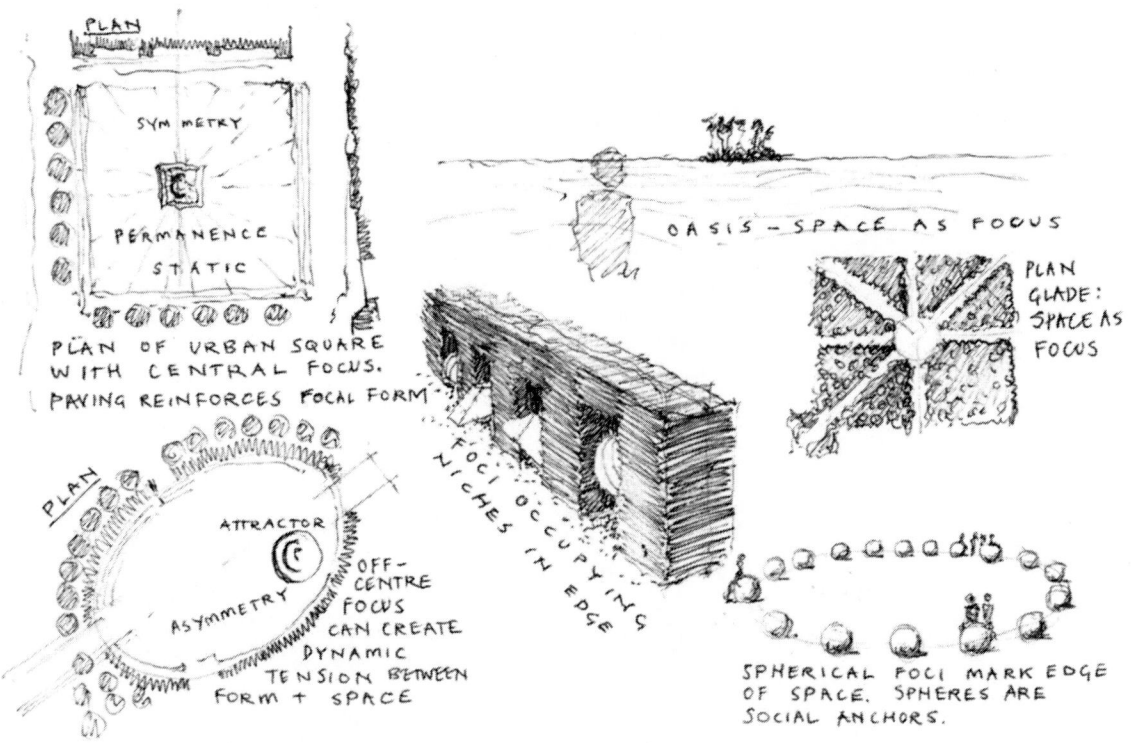

PLAN

SYMMETRY

PERMANENCE

STATIC

PLAN OF URBAN SQUARE
WITH CENTRAL FOCUS.
PAVING REINFORCES FOCAL FORM

OASIS - SPACE AS FOCUS

PLAN
GLADE:
SPACE AS
FOCUS

PLAN

ATTRACTOR

OFF-
CENTRE
FOCUS
CAN CREATE
DYNAMIC
TENSION BETWEEN
FORM + SPACE

ASYMMETRY

FOCI OCCUPYING NICHES IN EDGE

SPHERICAL POCI MARK EDGE
OF SPACE. SPHERES ARE
SOCIAL ANCHORS.

Foci and spaces

Focal forms often occupy the centre of a space. Centrality is an important theme in landscape architecture and can either be used or questioned. Centrality can suggest unity, self or hierarchy, symmetry and stasis. Off-centre focal forms contribute to a different spatial sense, less hierarchical and more dynamic. Focal forms within spaces draw people into those spaces, but also provide objects on which to rest one's gaze from the edge of a space.

Focal spaces

If providing some distinctive or differentiated form or experience, spaces can act as foci in the landscape. Examples of focal spaces are oases, glades or plateaus.

Foci and edges

Focal forms can be located singly or in groups along edges. For example, light marble sculptures are foci in dark green hedge niches and can be grouped into rhythmic sequences. As single forms on an edge, foci can be places to stop and sit, or may mark a gateway or threshold through to another space. Focal forms such as posts may be arranged to form a permeable edge and may also function as informal seating or waiting places (anchors).

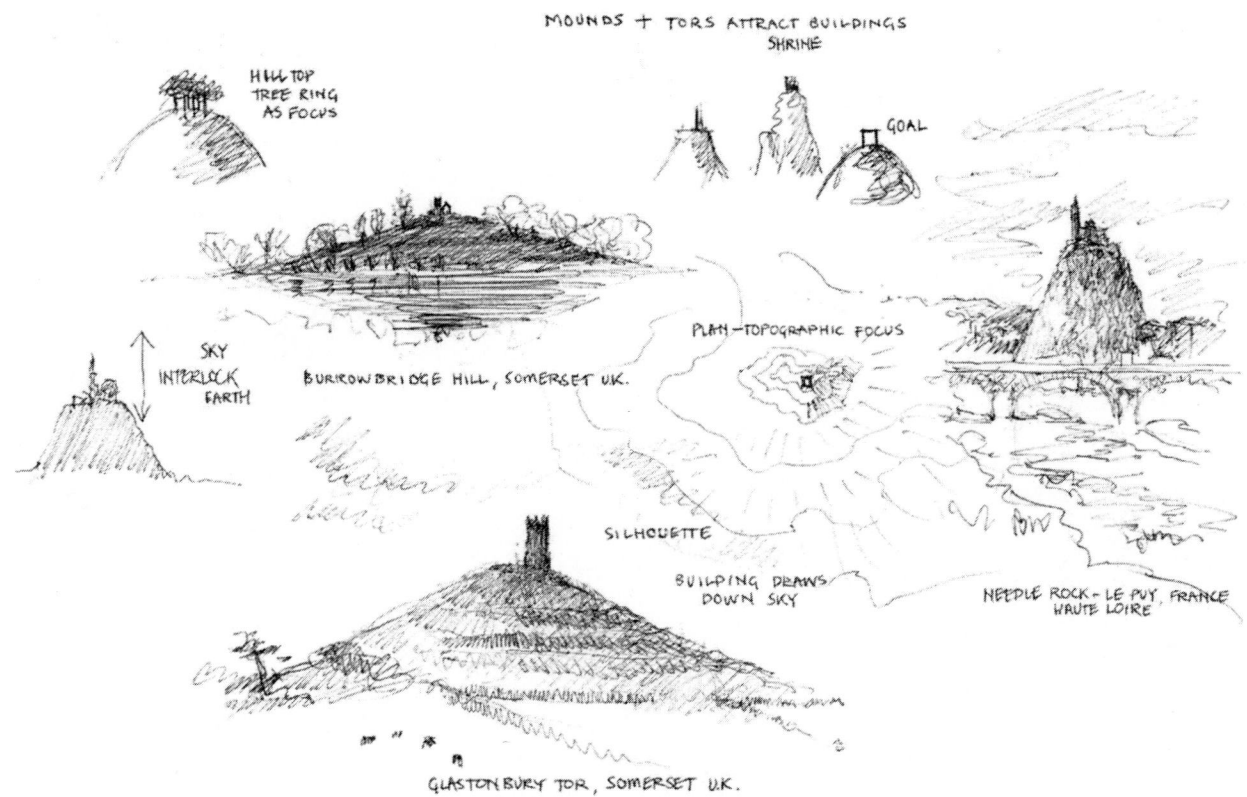

MOUNDS + TORS ATTRACT BUILDINGS
SHRINE

HILL TOP
TREE RING
AS FOCUS

GOAL

SKY
INTERLOCK
EARTH

BURROW BRIDGE HILL, SOMERSET UK.

PLAN - TOPOGRAPHIC FOCUS

NEEDLE ROCK - LE PUY, FRANCE
HAUTE LOIRE

SILHOUETTE

BUILDING DRAWS
DOWN SKY

GLASTONBURY TOR, SOMERSET U.K.

Public sculpture

Public sculpture frequently plays a focal role in the land-scape. In addition to its cultural and aesthetic intentions, sculpture may also provide orientation functions. As sculptures create places of 'differentiation' in the land-scape they are also often – as suggested previously – places to gather.

Buildings as foci

Buildings play a central role as foci and landmarks in the landscape, especially if they are single isolated structures in natural, rural or predominantly vegetated environments.

Landmarks for orientation

As travellers we use landmarks to help orientate ourselves. Landmarks aid people in distinguishing their spatial location because of their 'differentiation' in form from their context. They therefore play important roles in helping people to find their way about and in the creation of mental maps of places. Lynch's work on landmarks (1960) developed this theory. Foci also help people to better judge distance.

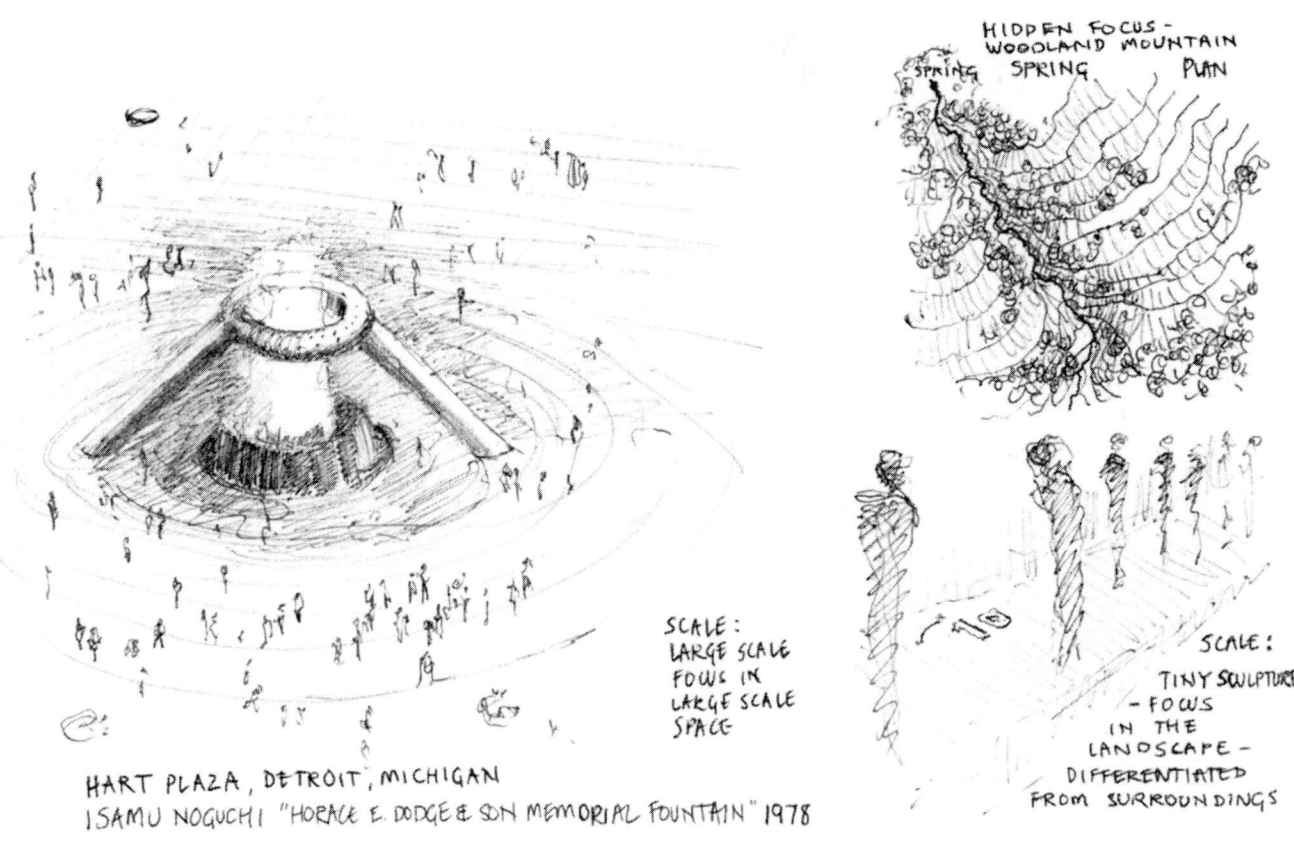

SCALE:
LARGE SCALE
FOCUS IN
LARGE SCALE
SPACE

HART PLAZA, DETROIT, MICHIGAN
ISAMU NOGUCHI "HORACE E. DODGE & SON MEMORIAL FOUNTAIN" 1978

HIDDEN FOCUS -
WOODLAND MOUNTAIN
SPRING   SPRING   PLAN

SCALE:
TINY SCULPTURE
- FOCUS
IN THE
LANDSCAPE -
DIFFERENTIATED
FROM SURROUNDINGS

Scale of foci

A focus can either be very small – for example, a brass plate in the pavement – or it can be a visually dominant monumental form. An important design task is to consider the scale of a focus in relation to its context and function.

Hidden foci

Foci are not often hidden; indeed, lack of visibility would seem to contradict the definitions given at the beginning of this section and the functions ascribed to foci. However, there are contexts in which a landscape form might exert a powerful attraction for people but be relatively inconspicuous. Examples of hidden foci include springs, hollows and subterranean tombs.

DRAWING AFTER PHOTOGRAPH "A WELSH GARDEN"
BILL BRANDT c.1940
ECCENTRIC FOCI CONTRAST IN FORM, TEXTURE
+ LIGHT/DARK

Contrast

It is primarily through contrast with its surroundings that a focus is apparent as a distinct form in the landscape. In design, the creation and use of foci may often be as a counterpoint to dominant space characteristics. In this way a flat smooth space may contain a contrasting strongly vertical focus with coarse texture. Alternatively, a smooth, light-coloured 'shelf' becomes a focus on a dark rugged steep hillside. Smooth in rough places; rough in smooth; dark and light; bright and dull; warm and cool – these are all potential contrasting qualities between foci and their context.

Verticality of form

Foci are often strongly vertical forms, which enables them to function as visually dominant landmarks. Vertical forms contrast with the prevailing and relative horizontal nature of many landscapes. Islands are focal as relatively vertical forms within the flat plane of the sea, as are mounds and mounts in flat places (see Foci – Topographic, p. 155). In strongly vertical landscapes such as mountainous places, foci may contrast with forms of flatness or horizontality, or forms of even greater verticality.

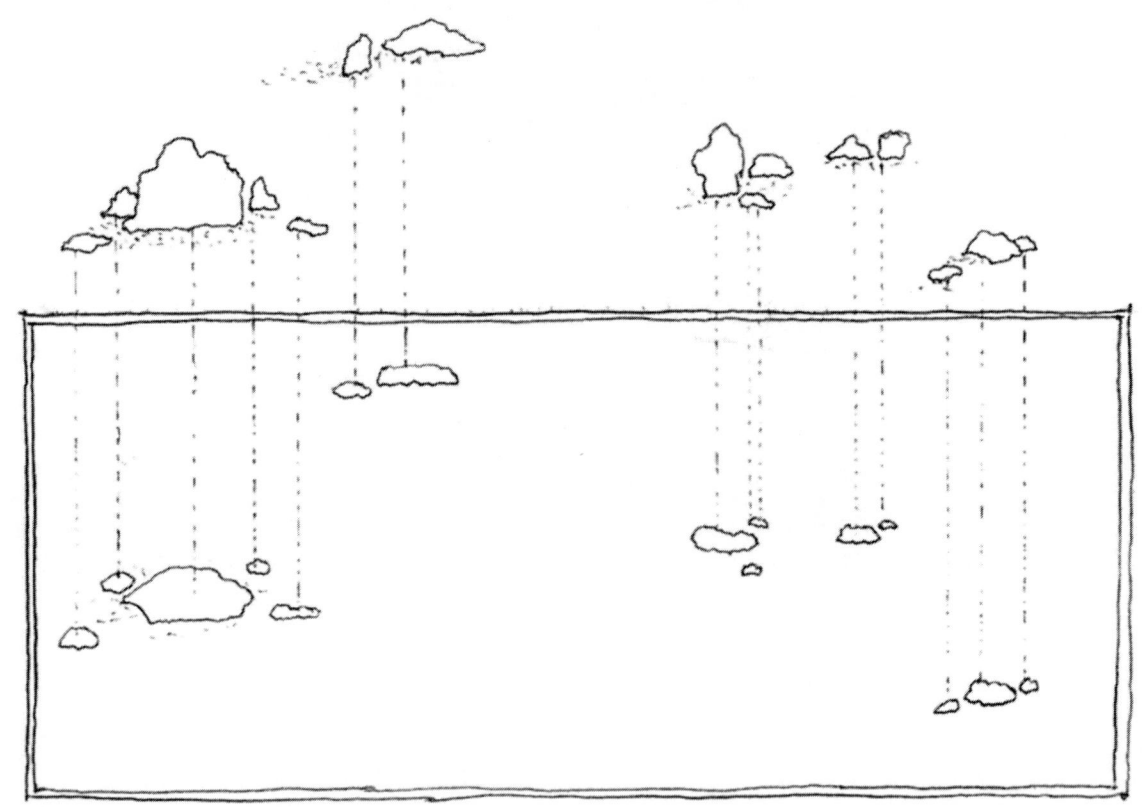

PLAN AND ELEVATIONS OF ROCKS IN ZEN GARDEN OF CONTEMPLATION
RYOAN-JI, DAIJU-IN MONASTERY, KYOTO
ISOLATED ROCKS FORM FOCAL GROUPS - COUNTERPOINT TO RAKED
GRAVEL FLOOR

Centrality and isolation of form

Forms placed centrally in spaces often take on the status of foci whether this is intended by the designer or not. Equally, a form isolated from other forms can take on the visual and experiential functions of a focus.

Singularity of form

Distinctive, unexpected and rare (singular) forms in landscapes also assume the status of foci because they draw our attention and often take on, or are intended to have, cultural significance.

Topographic foci

Topographic foci are illustrated over the following pages.

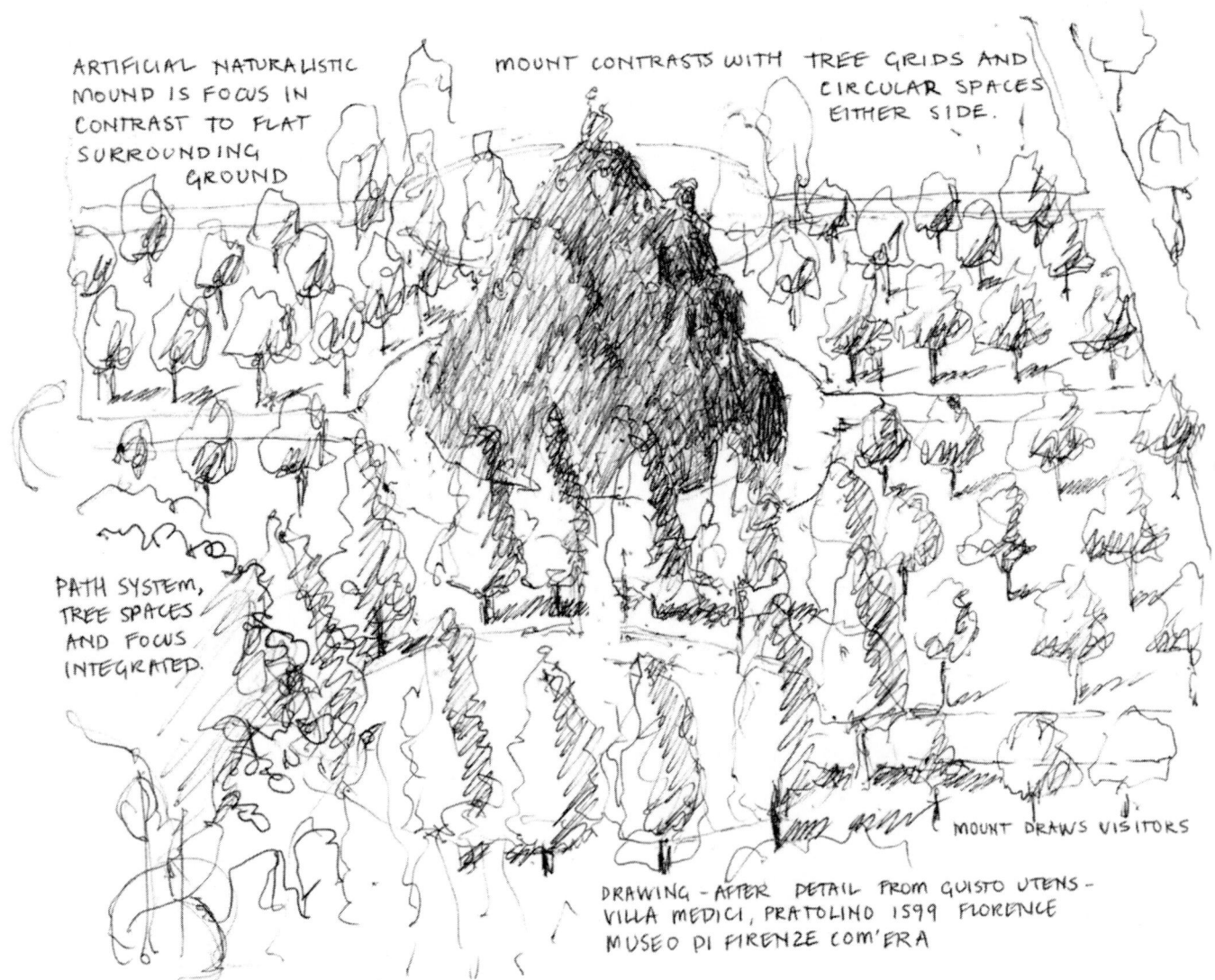

ARTIFICIAL NATURALISTIC MOUND IS FOCUS IN CONTRAST TO FLAT SURROUNDING GROUND

MOUNT CONTRASTS WITH TREE GRIDS AND CIRCULAR SPACES EITHER SIDE.

PATH SYSTEM, TREE SPACES AND FOCUS INTEGRATED.

MOUNT DRAWS VISITORS

DRAWING - AFTER DETAIL FROM GUISTO UTENS - VILLA MEDICI, PRATOLINO 1599 FLORENCE MUSEO DI FIRENZE COM'ERA

Mounts, tors and mountains

Natural isolated high landforms such as mountains or tors, together with constructed mounds and mounts, act as foci in landscape. The eye is drawn by their contrast with lower-lying topography and vertical emphasis. They can be used in design to attract users to a place. They can be endpoints to journeys, central points or places to climb and overlook landscape and its activities. Mounts can also play a significant role in children's play (see Spaces/Mounds and Mounts, p. 58, and Paths/Topographic/Zig-zag, p. 97).

155

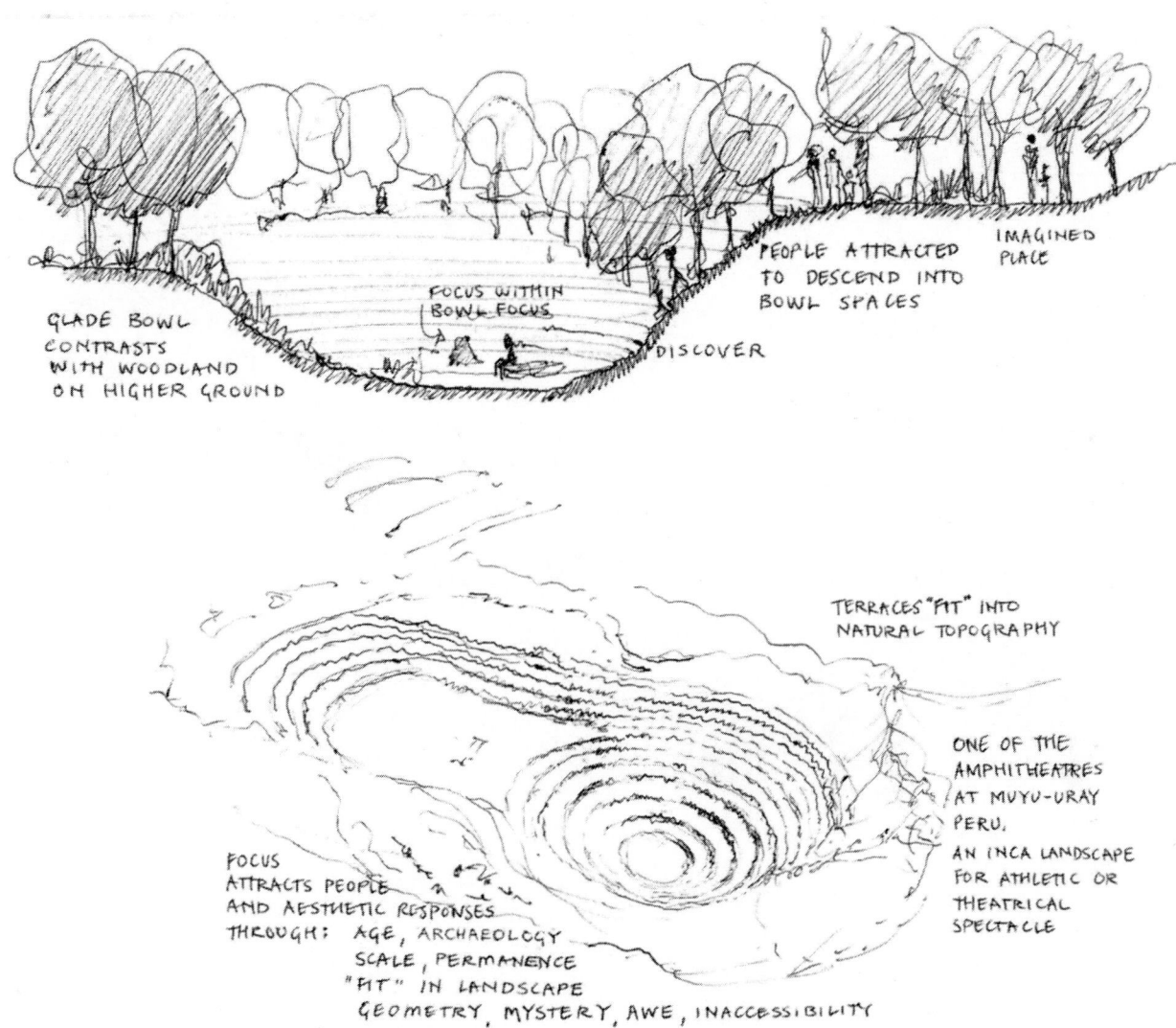

GLADE BOWL
CONTRASTS
WITH WOODLAND
ON HIGHER GROUND

FOCUS WITHIN
BOWL FOCUS

DISCOVER

PEOPLE ATTRACTED
TO DESCEND INTO
BOWL SPACES

IMAGINED
PLACE

TERRACES "FIT" INTO
NATURAL TOPOGRAPHY

ONE OF THE
AMPHITHEATRES
AT MUYU-URAY
PERU.
AN INCA LANDSCAPE
FOR ATHLETIC OR
THEATRICAL
SPECTACLE

FOCUS
ATTRACTS PEOPLE
AND AESTHETIC RESPONSES
THROUGH: AGE, ARCHAEOLOGY
SCALE, PERMANENCE
"FIT" IN LANDSCAPE
GEOMETRY, MYSTERY, AWE, INACCESSIBILITY

Bowls and craters

Artificial and natural depressions in topography can act as foci, attracting people to sheltered or hidden ground. Bowls or craters provide distinctive microclimate and form in contrast to surrounding land. Natural topographic depressions may be modified for focal cultural functions such as theatre or the siting of sculpture. Artificially created bowls in public places often need clear purposes and gentle sides to avoid 'pit-like' characteristics. See also Spaces/Bowls and hollows (p. 57) and Foci/Hidden foci (p. 151).

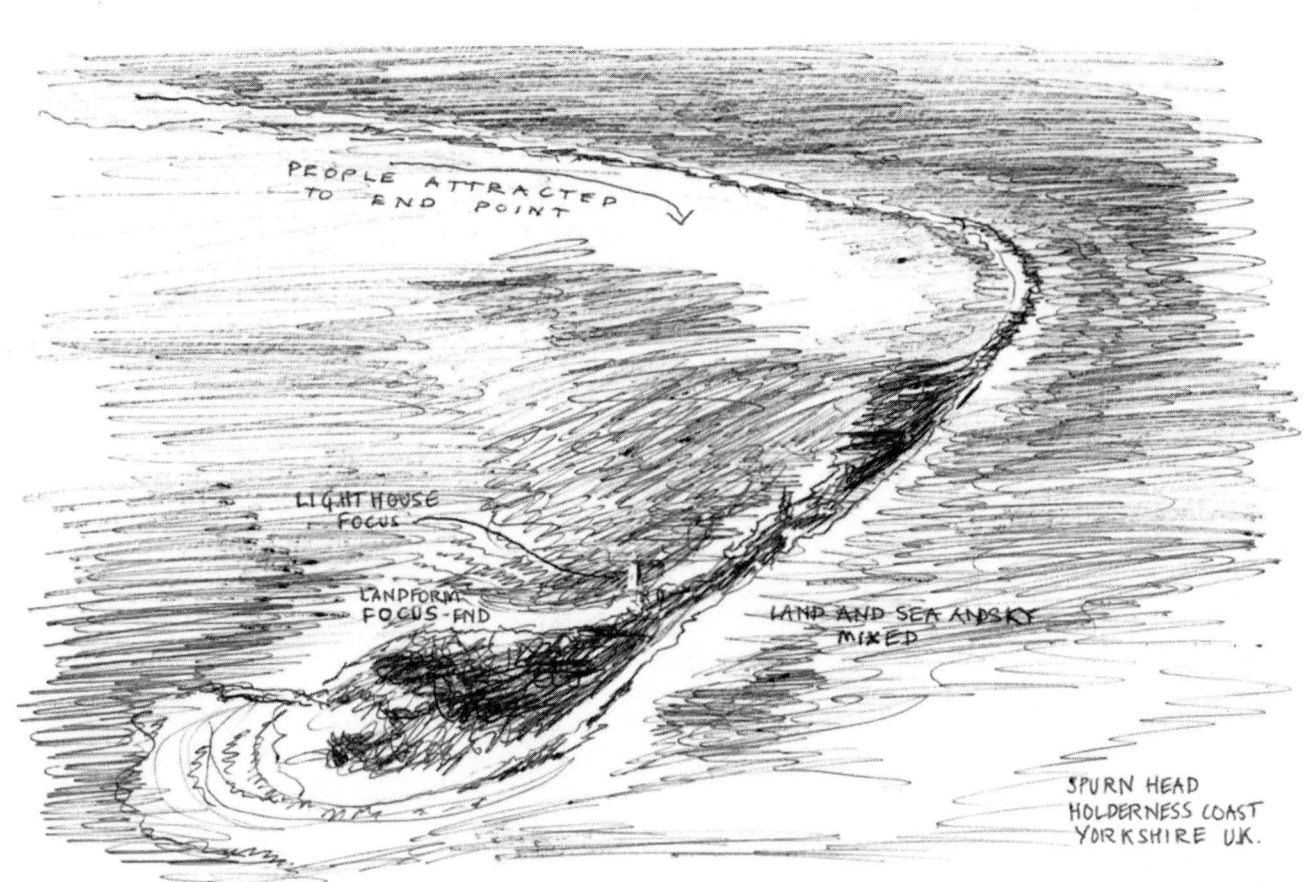

Labels within image: PEOPLE ATTRACTED TO END POINT; LIGHTHOUSE FOCUS; LANDFORM FOCUS-END; LAND AND SEA AND SKY MIXED; SPURN HEAD HOLDERNESS COAST YORKSHIRE U.K.

Points and spurs

Spurs or spits of land attract people to journey out along their length to an endpoint. They can be constructed in places to provide walks and prospect over landscape and to form edges while providing distinctive focal endpoints in the form of buildings, spaces or sculptures. Natural spurs are forms of inspiration for design.

157

Vegetation foci

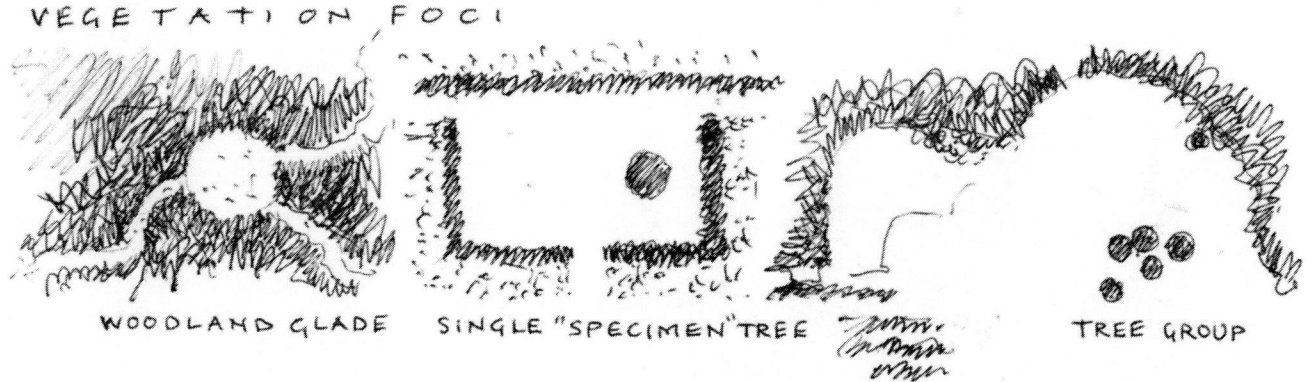

VEGETATION FOCI

WOODLAND GLADE   SINGLE "SPECIMEN" TREE   TREE GROUP

In relatively open spaces, single or grouped trees become focal forms as they provide a vertical counterpoint to the relatively horizontal ground plane. Glades contrast with the surrounding forest canopy and are also focal because they attract people. In contrast to the massing of plants as structural enclosing elements, focal vegetation treats plants as individual specimens.

TOPOGRAPHY ENABLES SILHOUETTE OF
GROUP TREES - DRAWS WALKER AS DESTINATION

SINGLE FOCAL TREE
AT END OF PATH
DRAWS EYE AND WALKER

DRAWING OF "HILL AND PLOUGHED FIELD NEAR DRESDEN" BY
CASPAR DAVID FRIEDRICH C1824 OIL ON CANVAS
KUNSTHALLE, HAMBURG

OFF-CENTRE SPECIMEN
TREE AS SPACE FOCUS

CENTRAL TREE AS FOCUS

Single trees

Focal trees can be used as endpoints to paths and as forms which punctuate open areas. Specimen trees are selected for their intrinsic aesthetic qualities to be viewed in isolation or from a distance. Focal trees 'attract' seating.

Single trees conserved from rural landscapes, very old trees and distinctive urban trees can have tremendous presence. People often develop strong attachments to trees of age and they therefore become or continue to be focal forms.

Group of trees

In large-scale spaces, grouped trees of the same species may form focal masses. They can be used to dramatise and accentuate high ground as silhouettes forming dark patterns against the sky. Tree rings become focal spaces enticing people to enter. In hot open spaces, tree groups are focal shady oases.

EYE IS DRAWN ACROSS
LANDSCAPE AS IT LINKS
SIMILAR FORMS

FOCAL FORMS PATTERN
AND FORM COUNTERPOINT
TO HORIZONTAL FLOOR PLANE.

WESTBURY COURT, GLOUCESTERSHIRE UK.

LATE C17 GARDEN

Topiary forms

Topiary treats plants as dense sculptural masses enabling them to be solid and static forms which convey permanence and age. Topiary forms may be contrasted with the texture and colour of other plants. Topiary depicting other forms (birds, vessels) may attract because the care involved in clipping over time encapsulated in the form is appealing. Topiary forms on parterres punctuate the floor plane and draw the eye across it.

Built foci

Different types of built foci are illustrated on the following pages.

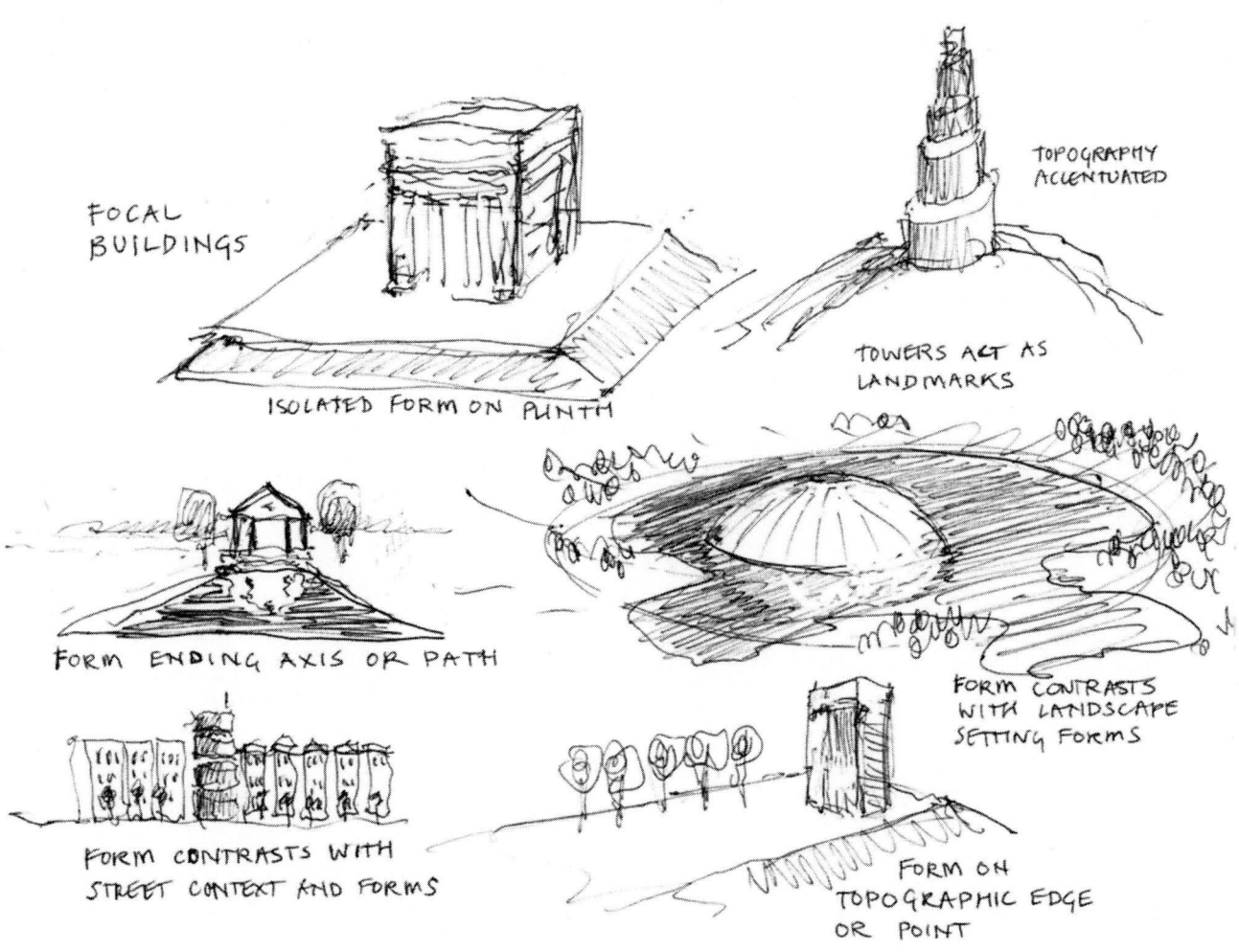

FOCAL
BUILDINGS

ISOLATED FORM ON PLINTH

TOPOGRAPHY
ACCENTUATED

TOWERS ACT AS
LANDMARKS

FORM ENDING AXIS OR PATH

FORM CONTRASTS
WITH LANDSCAPE
SETTING FORMS

FORM CONTRASTS WITH
STREET CONTEXT AND FORMS

FORM ON
TOPOGRAPHIC EDGE
OR POINT

Buildings

Buildings can be sited and designed as landmarks in places. They can contrast with or accentuate topography and can also dominate high places. They are commonly endpoints to axes of paths, water, vegetation, or terraces.

In form they can be a counterpoint to a landscape's character and forms. Landscape and architecture can suffer when buildings are created as focal forms in inappropriate contexts.

WINDMILL FOLLY, 1647 CHESTERTON WARWICKSHIRE UK

Follies, theatrical structures and remnants

Closely related to both sculpture and focal buildings, the concept of follies in the landscape remains appealing. 'Folly' comes from the old French for 'mad', and the theatrical and joyful potential of unusual, strange, ambiguous or mysterious structures in landscape is often desirable in recreational landscapes. However, follies also often require functions beyond the purely visual.

'Remnant' structures incorporated into new landscapes provide resonance of the past, at the same time as accruing new meanings in the changed landscape. Structures should often be preserved or adapted if new uses can be found for them for reasons of continuity and sustainability (see Landscape fabric/Recycling versus *tabula rasa*, p. 15).

163

PEOPLE ARE DRAWN
TO TOUCH STONES

REMNANTS AND
REMINDERS

ARRANGEMENT AND ISOLATION
ATTRACTS PEOPLE

EVEN IN MORE
CONTEMPORARY
DESIGN STANDING
STONES SUGGEST
AGE AND PERMANENCE

STONE CIRCLE AT CASTLERIGG
KESWICK, CUMBRIA U.K.

Rocks and standing stones

Rocks and large standing stones become foci if they protrude or are set significantly above the ground plane or if they were set by ancient peoples. The weight, mass and texture and 'permanent' characteristics of rock provide distinctive qualities in design. Boulders and roughly hewn stones are 'of the earth' and can be used to evoke primeval or 'timeless' qualities in design. Conversely, they can be amorphous forms placed without care in the mistaken belief they make places 'natural'.

164

ANTHONY GORMLEY'S "ANGEL OF THE NORTH" - GATESHEAD TYNE + WEAR UK.
WELDED WEATHERING STEEL
AS A SCULPTURE THE WORK HAS MANY MEANINGS AND INTERPRETATIONS.
AS A FOCUS IN THE LANDSCAPE IT IS SYMBOLIC; A GATEWAY,
A PLACE TO VISIT; A LANDMARK FOR ORIENTATION. IMAGE, FABRICATION
FORM AND MATERIAL CONNECT TO PLACE - GEOGRAPHY -
SHIP BUILDING AND INDUSTRIAL FABRICATION OF TYNE AND WEAR.

Sculpture

Sculpture often plays a focal role in the landscape. Art attracts visitors so that any kind of sculpture becomes focal. Sculpture can also be sited at places that are already focal. Land and environmental art can make spaces or places that become focal. Focal sculptures may be permanent and built, or they may be temporary or dynamic using, for example, lighting technology or landscape elements of water, vegetation or climate.

165

Water foci

Water in landscapes attracts people in general but here water foci has specific meanings. It refers to a water element 'concentrated' in one location that attracts people through verticality, sound, texture, light, movement or coolness and which contrasts with its setting or context.

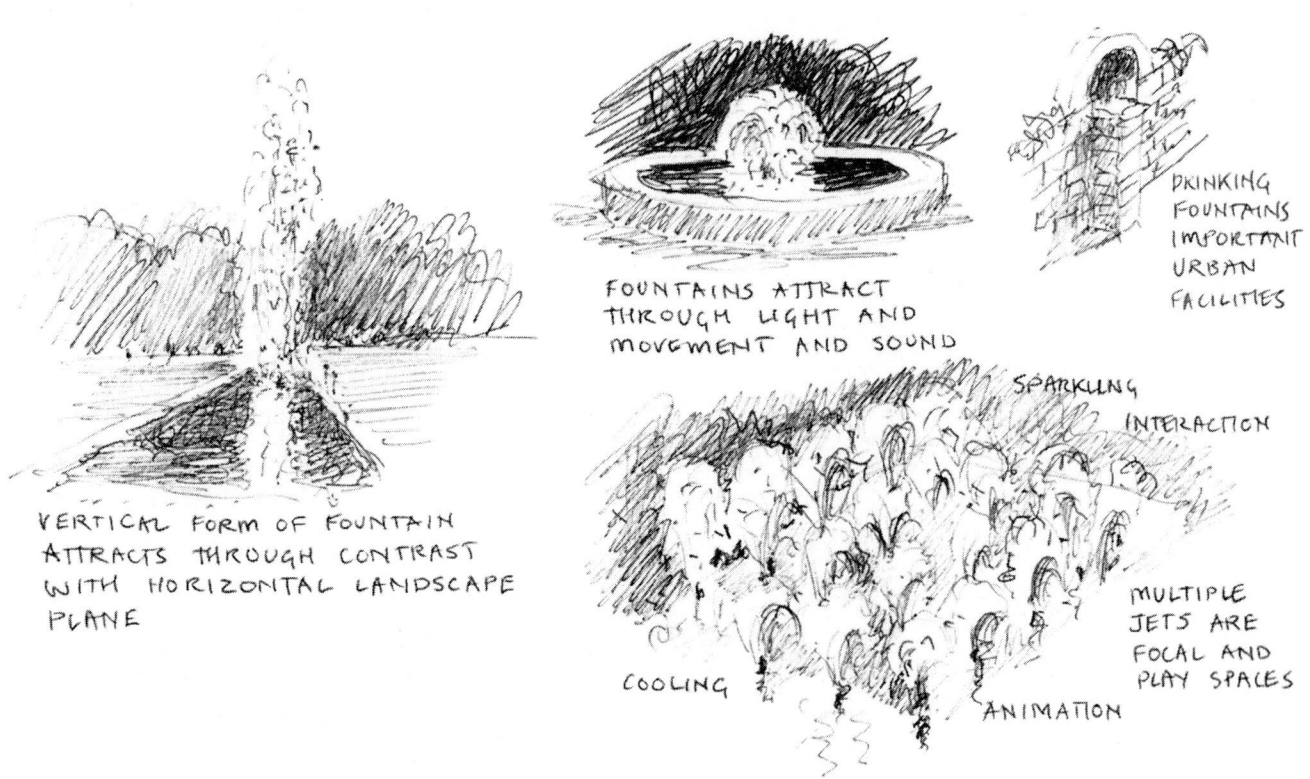

VERTICAL FORM OF FOUNTAIN
ATTRACTS THROUGH CONTRAST
WITH HORIZONTAL LANDSCAPE
PLANE

FOUNTAINS ATTRACT
THROUGH LIGHT AND
MOVEMENT AND SOUND

DRINKING
FOUNTAINS
IMPORTANT
URBAN
FACILITIES

SPARKLING
INTERACTION
MULTIPLE
JETS ARE
FOCAL AND
PLAY SPACES
COOLING
ANIMATION

Fountains

Fountains celebrate water as a life-giving resource and their exuberance draws people to interact and play. Fountains can also express power and wealth and control over natural environments. In contemporary urban environments, it is often inappropriate to create fountains that cannot be interacted with. In urban contexts their sound and the cooling properties of water can improve local microclimate, and thus attract people.

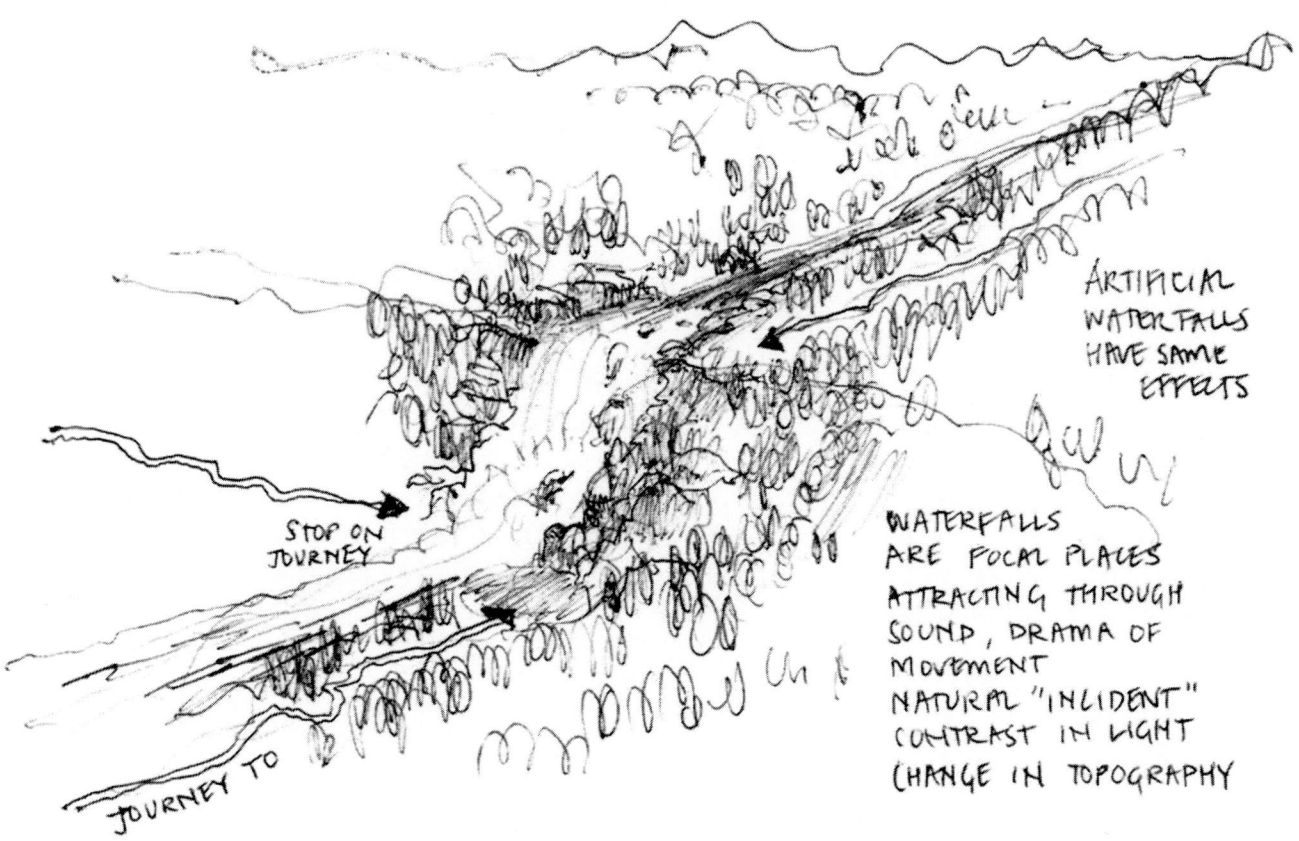

ARTIFICIAL
WATERFALLS
HAVE SAME
EFFECTS

STOP ON
JOURNEY

WATERFALLS
ARE FOCAL PLACES
ATTRACTING THROUGH
SOUND, DRAMA OF
MOVEMENT
NATURAL "INCIDENT"
CONTRAST IN LIGHT
CHANGE IN TOPOGRAPHY

JOURNEY TO

Waterfalls

The drama and power of waterfalls also strongly attract people to their location in natural and urban environments. Waterfalls are gathering places to stop, enjoy and picnic. See also Spaces/Water (p. 79).

Springs, fonts and wells

Relatively small and hidden water foci such as springs and wells attract people because of historic or cultural significance, or if water can be drunk from them. Drinking water in focal places is a rare but desirable experience.

168

6 Thresholds

Thresholds are spatial components of the landscape which provide for integrated, subtle and complex transitions through the landscape. Thresholds are relatively small spaces which 'sit' between larger spaces or between buildings and landscape. Like edges, thresholds 'knit' the fabric of landscape together, but unlike edges they are 'centred' rather than linear spaces.

Thresholds are included in this book because, like edges, their potential and necessity in design are often overlooked.

In this section, the concept of thresholds is defined and illustrated examples are given of the use of topography, vegetation, structures and water in their formation.

THE "TING" (BUILDING) IS BUILT ON/AS <u>THRESHOLD</u> BETWEEN LAND AND WATER
MEDIATING EXPERIENCE OF LAND + WATER   - AN ARCHITECTURAL EXAMPLE
DRAWING AFTER : HANDSCROLL BY QIAN XUAN (1235-1300)

Definitions

A threshold can be defined as:

- a small transitional space between larger spaces or paths
- an 'in between' place
- a space on an edge
- a landscape form that visually links one place with another
- an entrance place or gateway
- a place of ending or beginning, rest and anticipation.

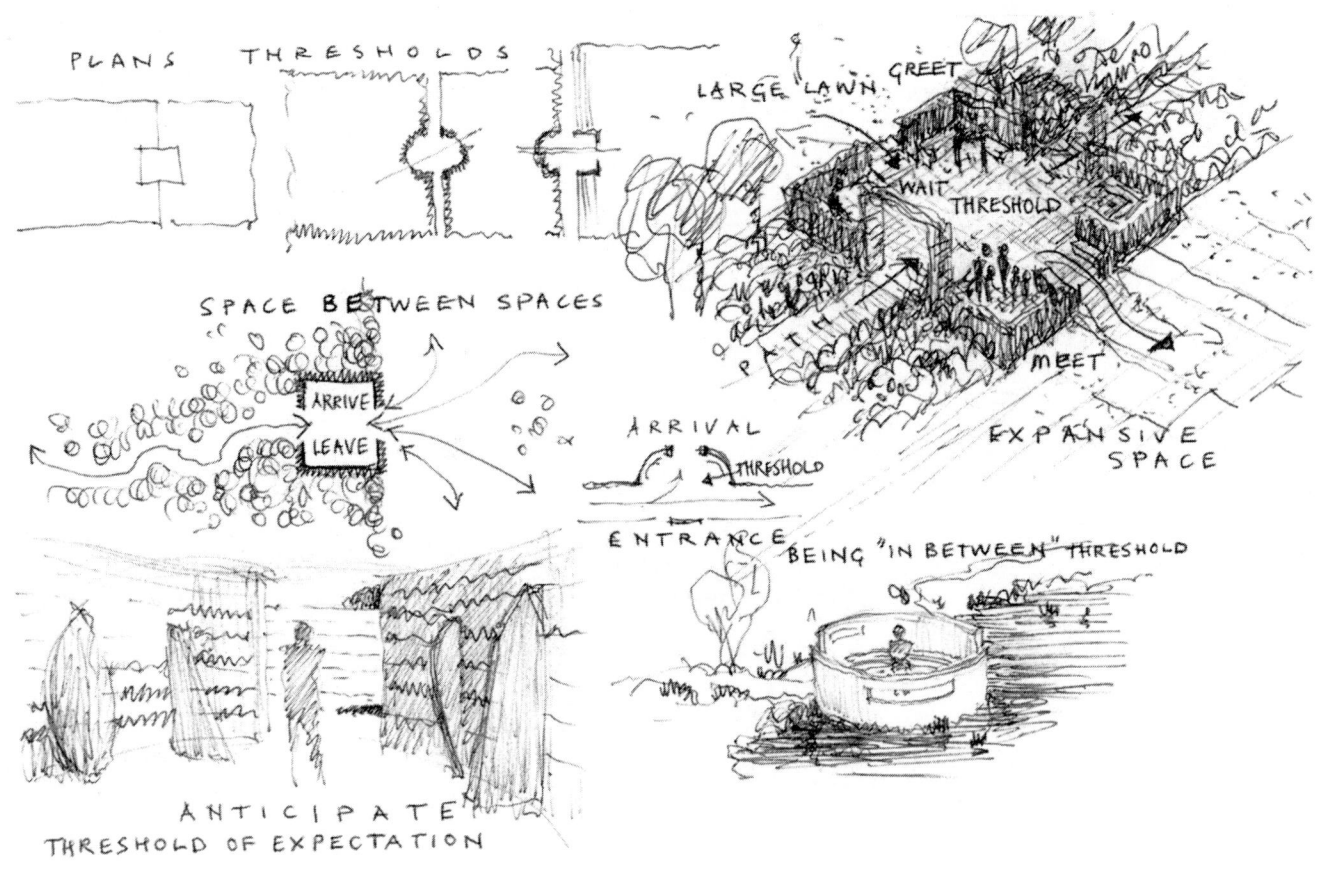

People's use and experience of thresholds

Thresholds are places of transition and, if well designed, places that help to integrate the physical landscape and the experience of it. Thresholds give spatial configuration to people's need to adjust from one situation or experience to another. They are places in which people wait, rest, anticipate, arrive and leave, greet, contemplate, change – they are places in which to acclimatise or prepare. A threshold can often provide visual and physical integration of the landscape if it possesses qualities of both the spaces it connects – the environment that is being left behind as well as the place being entered.

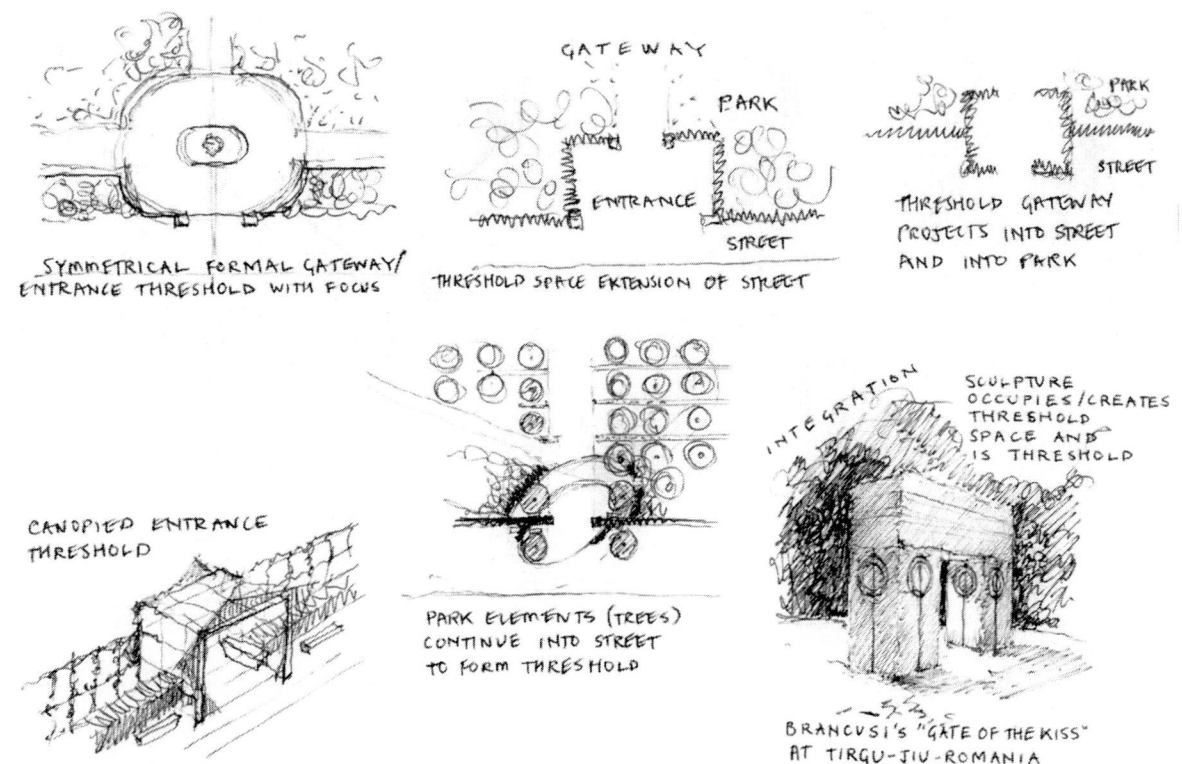

SYMMETRICAL FORMAL GATEWAY/
ENTRANCE THRESHOLD WITH FOCUS

THRESHOLD SPACE EXTENSION OF STREET

THRESHOLD GATEWAY
PROJECTS INTO STREET
AND INTO PARK

CANOPIED ENTRANCE
THRESHOLD

PARK ELEMENTS (TREES)
CONTINUE INTO STREET
TO FORM THRESHOLD

SCULPTURE
OCCUPIES/CREATES
THRESHOLD
SPACE AND
IS THRESHOLD

BRANCUSI'S "GATE OF THE KISS"
AT TIRGU-JIU-ROMANIA

Entry spaces – outdoor anterooms

Just as buildings have spaces (for example, halls or porches) specifically devoted to arrival and the social, cultural and practical activities associated with this; so entrance areas or 'outdoor anterooms' are important spaces in the urban landscape, affecting the transition between one environment and context and another. Entrance thresholds are usually relatively small spaces that enable people to carry out activities associated with transition or simply give 'breathing space' between one experience and another. Activities in entrance places (particularly to parks) include waiting, meeting, sitting, resting, watching, selling/buying refreshments, posing for photographs, using toilets and washing facilities and parking bikes.

Gateways

Gateways refers to threshold structures commonly associated with entry spaces. Gateways may be actual (gated) or symbolic and mark the transition from one type of landscape or space to another. They signal arrival and, for this reason, can become focal places, particularly if the gateway structure has popular cultural meanings. Gateway structures may be architectural (buildings), sculptural, topographic or formed on a smaller scale with vegetation.

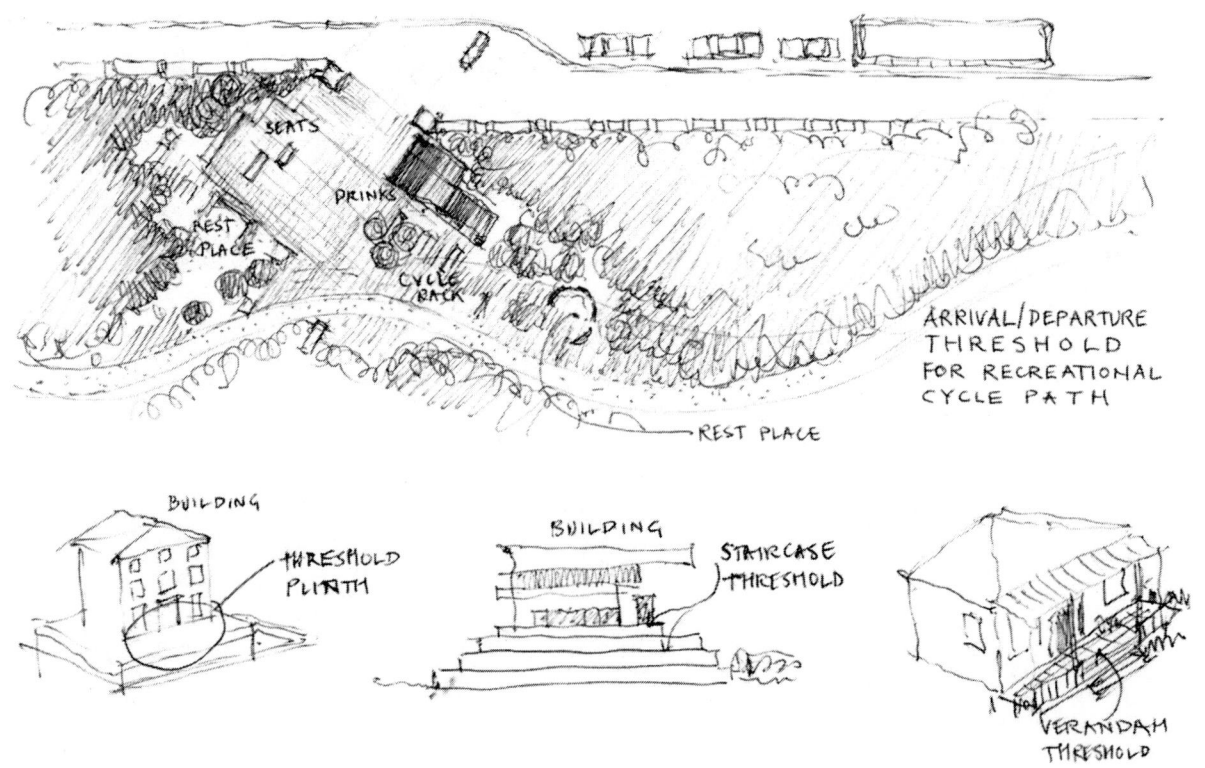

Building entrance places

Threshold is used here to refer to the immediate outdoor setting of a building's entrance(s) and its associated frontage and not to (perhaps confusingly) the threshold one crosses to enter a building. These important spaces are often neglected by both architect and landscape architect, and are commonly either too small or too large and fail to cater for activities associated with arriving and leaving public or private buildings. If well designed, building entrance places can be important social environments. They also play a significant role in integrating interior with exterior. Plinths, staircases, ramp structures, verandas, colonnade spaces are (like edges) hybrid architecture and landscape spaces, and should be designed in integrated ways to accommodate social and practical activity as well as cultural expression.

Places of arrival, setting out and rest

Spaces from which journeys start or in which journeys end are threshold places of transition, waiting and social activity. From the tiny space associated with bus or tram stops to major exterior spaces associated with railway stations, these threshold places require consideration of all the social and practical functions associated with travel. Journey thresholds are places to rest, wait, shelter, eat, to greet or say goodbye, to talk or read.

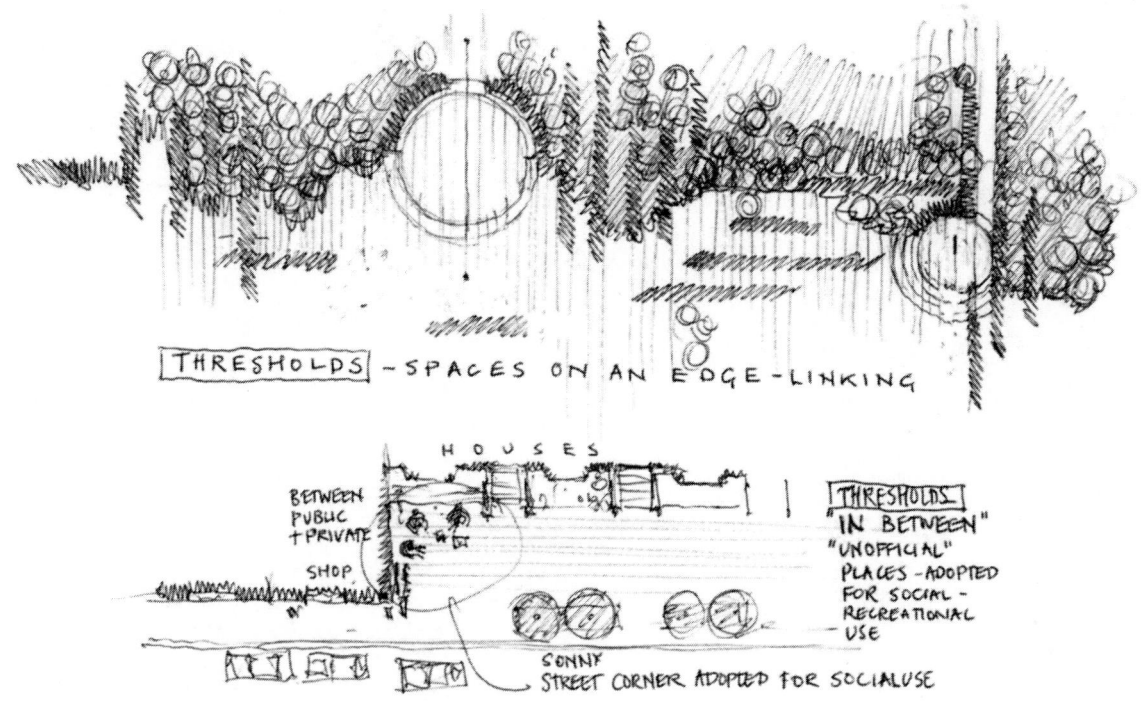

'In between'

A small space that contrasts with its setting or neighbouring spaces can be described as a threshold as it allows different experience and use than the dominant landscape of larger spaces. Small 'in-between' spaces are often places of calm – they are havens that allow 'breathing space' between dominant 'realities'. This 'half in half out' experience is particularly important in design of spaces between land and water and between building and landscape.

'Unofficial' places

Thresholds can also be used to describe 'unofficial' unmanaged 'in between' places that are adopted by people for specific recreational or social uses. These places are of great importance in the education of designers

– they should be studied and understood because they meet people's needs or, more often, because they could meet these needs more effectively. Children are particularly important users of small incidental spaces.

A small space linking larger spaces across an edge

In design, threshold spaces are often integrated with edges to enable movement across or through the edge to connect spaces on either side. Niches (described in Edges/Sub-spaces, p. 127) with access on either side can be considered thresholds, but may also have the social functions of niches.

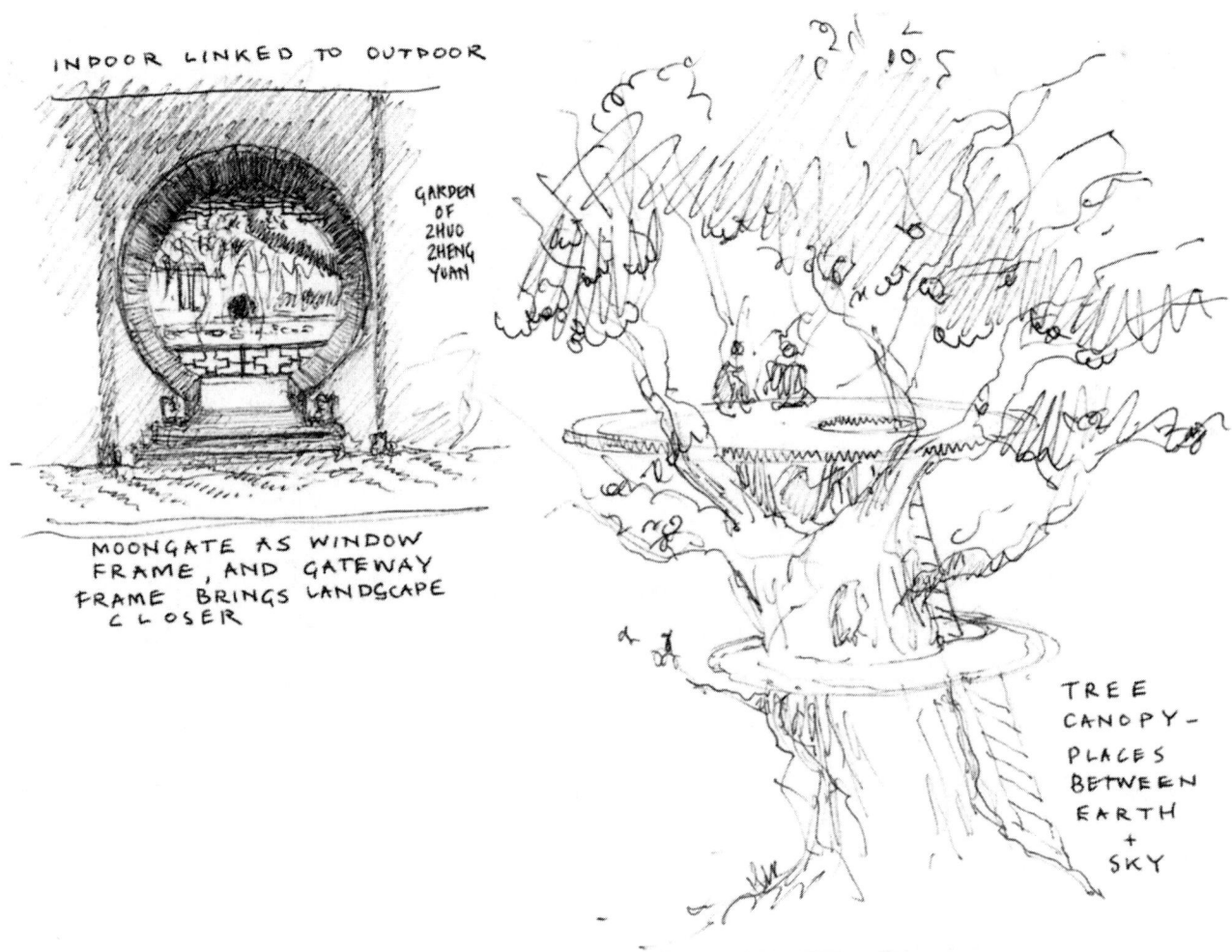

INDOOR LINKED TO OUTDOOR

GARDEN OF ZHUO ZHENG YUAN

MOONGATE AS WINDOW FRAME, AND GATEWAY FRAME BRINGS LANDSCAPE CLOSER

TREE CANOPY - PLACES BETWEEN EARTH + SKY

Windows and frames

In the landscape, window and frame forms act as visual rather than spatial thresholds. They visually link one environment with another by connecting the frame with the framed. Windows and frames mediate the experience of landscape in providing 'prospect–refuge' experiences and also a landscape sequence and narrative associated with movement through the landscape.

Places between earth and sky

Like horizons (see Edges/Horizons, p. 122), threshold spaces between earth and sky hold strong attractions. As 'in-between' spaces they can be places of rest, calm and refuge. Earth and sky thresholds may be hilltop or mountain-top spaces, built platform spaces or tree top places.

Topographic thresholds

As a space-forming element topography can be manipulated to create thresholds between two spaces or to provide for hilltop earth–sky thresholds. Passing between landforms or walking up and over topography and resting at the top or bottom creates a sense of arrival and separateness. Topography can obscure places beyond and thus create a feeling of anticipation.

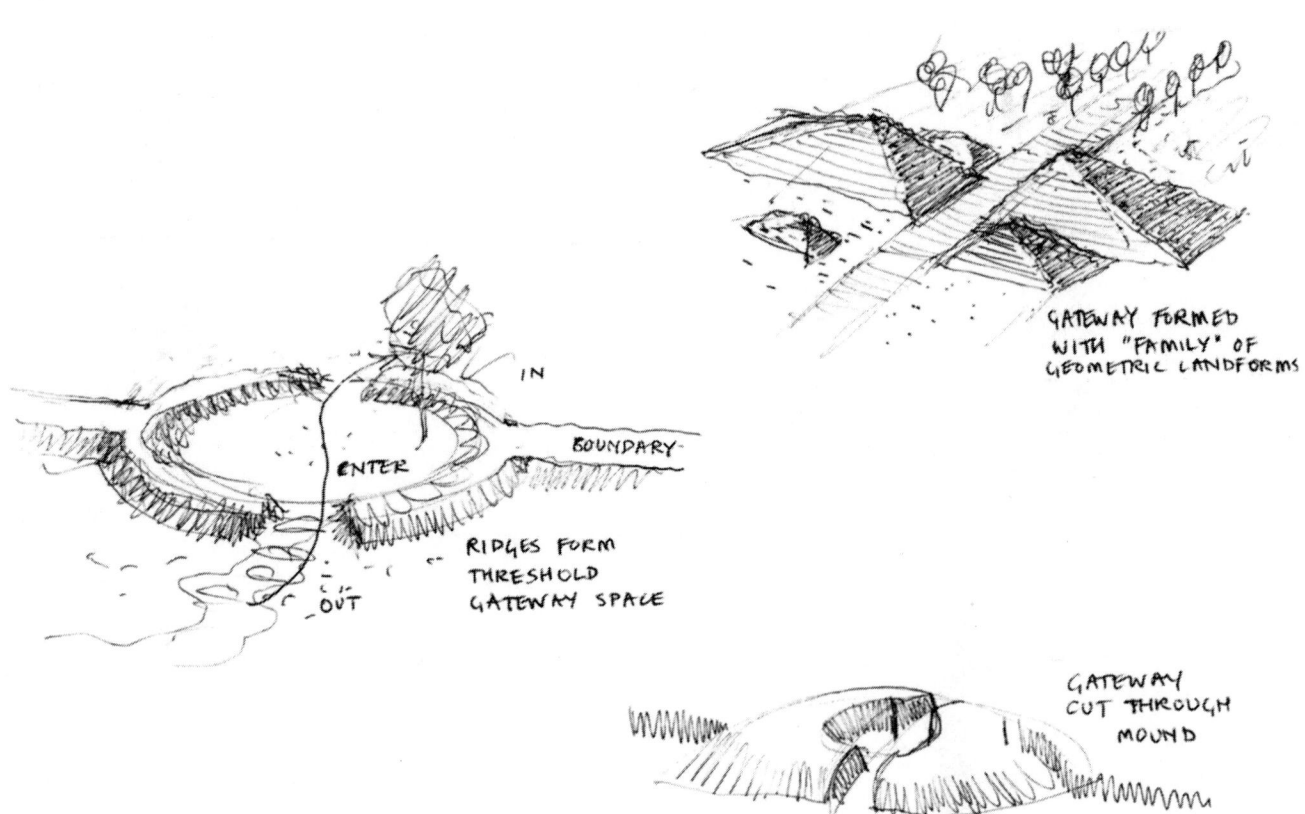

GATEWAY FORMED
WITH "FAMILY" OF
GEOMETRIC LANDFORMS

IN

ENTER

BOUNDARY

OUT

RIDGES FORM
THRESHOLD
GATEWAY SPACE

GATEWAY
CUT THROUGH
MOUND

Topographic gateways

On a monumental or intermediate scale, topography can be formed to create gateways. Landform can be manipulated naturalistically or geometrically to signal arrival and entry. Landform gateways may also be symbolic, conveying something of the place they mark the entry to.

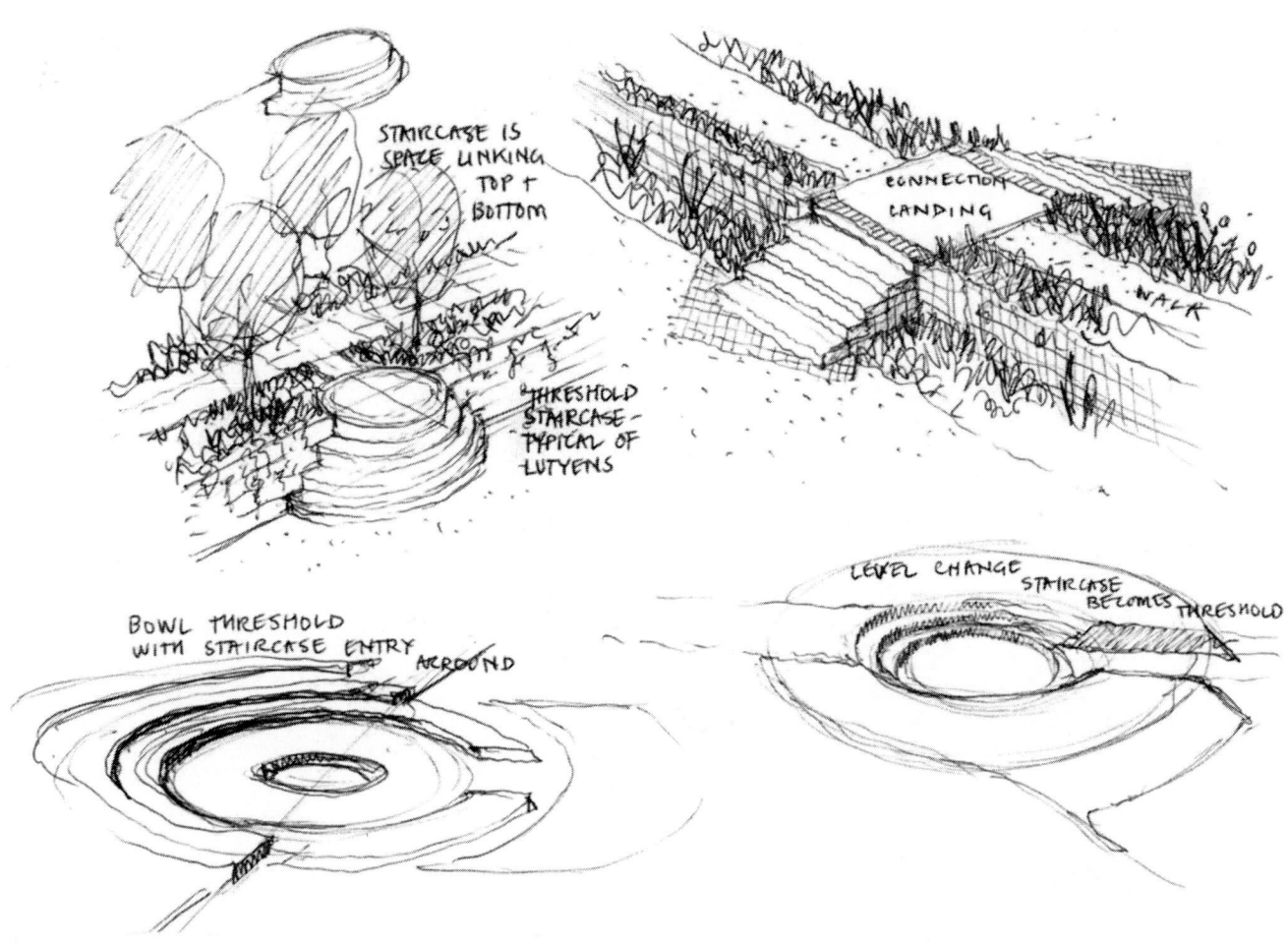

Landings and staircases

Staircases form integrating thresholds between one place and another, particularly if they project into the spaces they connect. As threshold spaces they should be generously proportioned to enable stopping, sitting and resting. Landings act as more spacious places within staircases and as thresholds in their own right with similar purposes.

Hollows

Hollowed thresholds can be created between larger, higher and lower space, particularly where a staircase splits and encloses the threshold space. Thresholds like these can be ornamented with water, vegetation and sculpture and therefore also become focal places.

Vegetation thresholds

Trees, shrubs and herbaceous plants can be used to shape and form thresholds. Vegetation can play important structural roles at entrance places for example with symmetrical arrangements or enclosure by hedge forms. Scented plants may be exploited at gateways. Vegetation also plays important sensory roles in places of rest or calm.

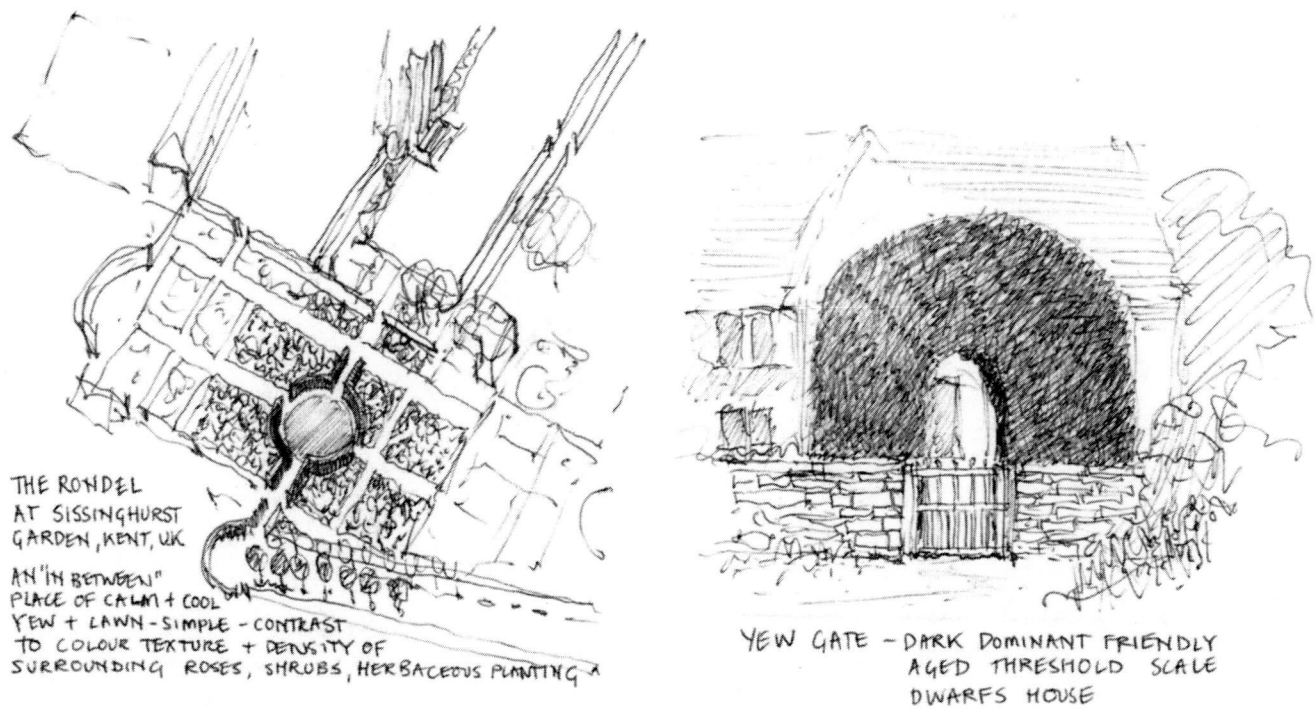

THE RONDEL
AT SISSINGHURST
GARDEN, KENT, UK.

AN "IN BETWEEN"
PLACE OF CALM + COOL
YEW + LAWN - SIMPLE - CONTRAST
TO COLOUR TEXTURE + DENSITY OF
SURROUNDING ROSES, SHRUBS, HERBACEOUS PLANTING A

YEW GATE - DARK DOMINANT FRIENDLY
AGED THRESHOLD SCALE
DWARFS HOUSE

Green threshold 'rooms'

Vegetation can be used in small threshold spaces to contrast with the character of adjoining large spaces or paths, thus creating a distinct or transitional space. Vegetation may be simple and cooling in transitional spaces to contrast with the brightness, complexity, built character and business of adjoining spaces. Or vegetation may make a threshold rich in comparison with its adjoining spaces. Vegetation may be used to 'signal' what is beyond in entrance places.

Green gateways

Passing under and between vegetation provides an immediate sensory contact with plants. Plants are therefore frequently cultivated and trained to form gateways, arches and entrance pergolas. Green gateways herald the transition from street or square to garden or park or mark the transition between one garden space and another.

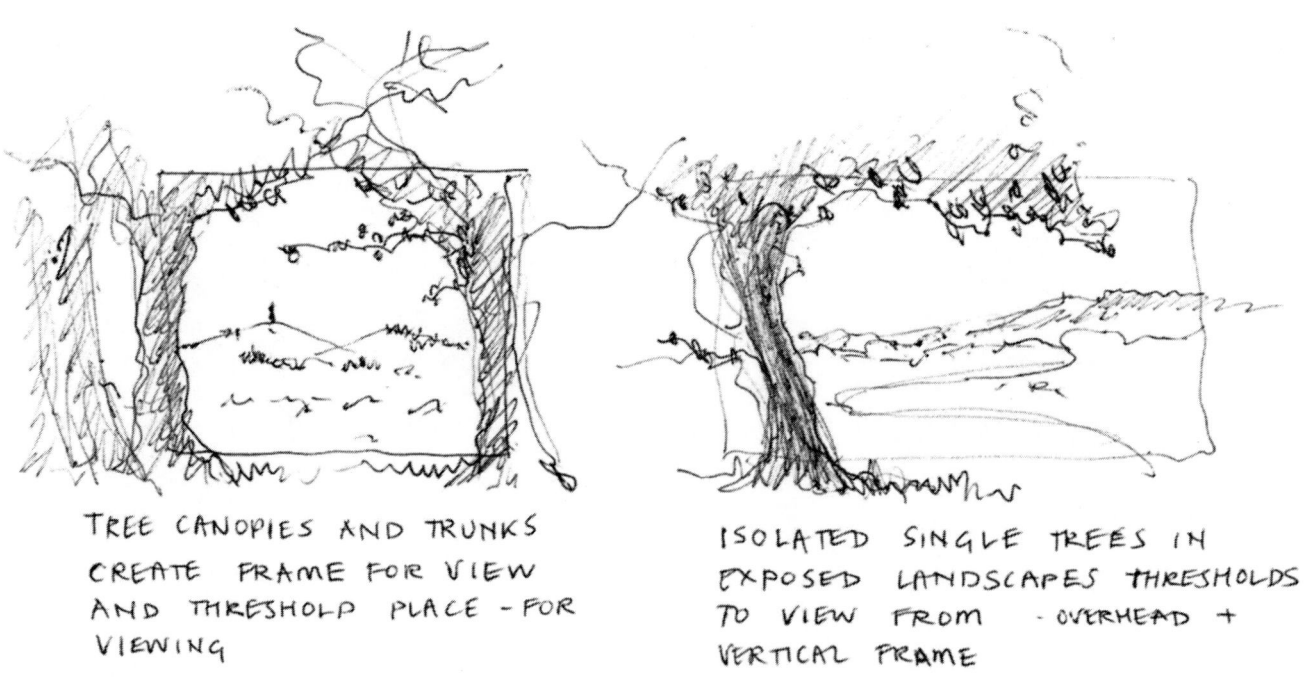

TREE CANOPIES AND TRUNKS
CREATE FRAME FOR VIEW
AND THRESHOLD PLACE - FOR
VIEWING

ISOLATED SINGLE TREES IN
EXPOSED LANDSCAPES THRESHOLDS
TO VIEW FROM · OVERHEAD +
VERTICAL FRAME

Windows and frames

Vegetation can be arranged to frame views of more distant landscapes or landscape components, particularly foci. Tree canopies or vegetation trained on pergolas form overhead or complete frames. The complex and soft texture of foliage and branches 'locks' sky and distance into the immediate 'space' of the viewer, thus bringing them closer, mediating and giving scale to distant forms.

Tree canopies

Staircases and platforms in or among trees provide the opportunity for people to be close to the leaves, branches and wildlife of trees and give a sense of being in between land and sky. Structures within trees are constrained by the need to protect the trees' roots, bark and canopy for healthy growth (see p. 175).

Built thresholds

Some common uses of built structures as thresholds are illustrated over the following pages.

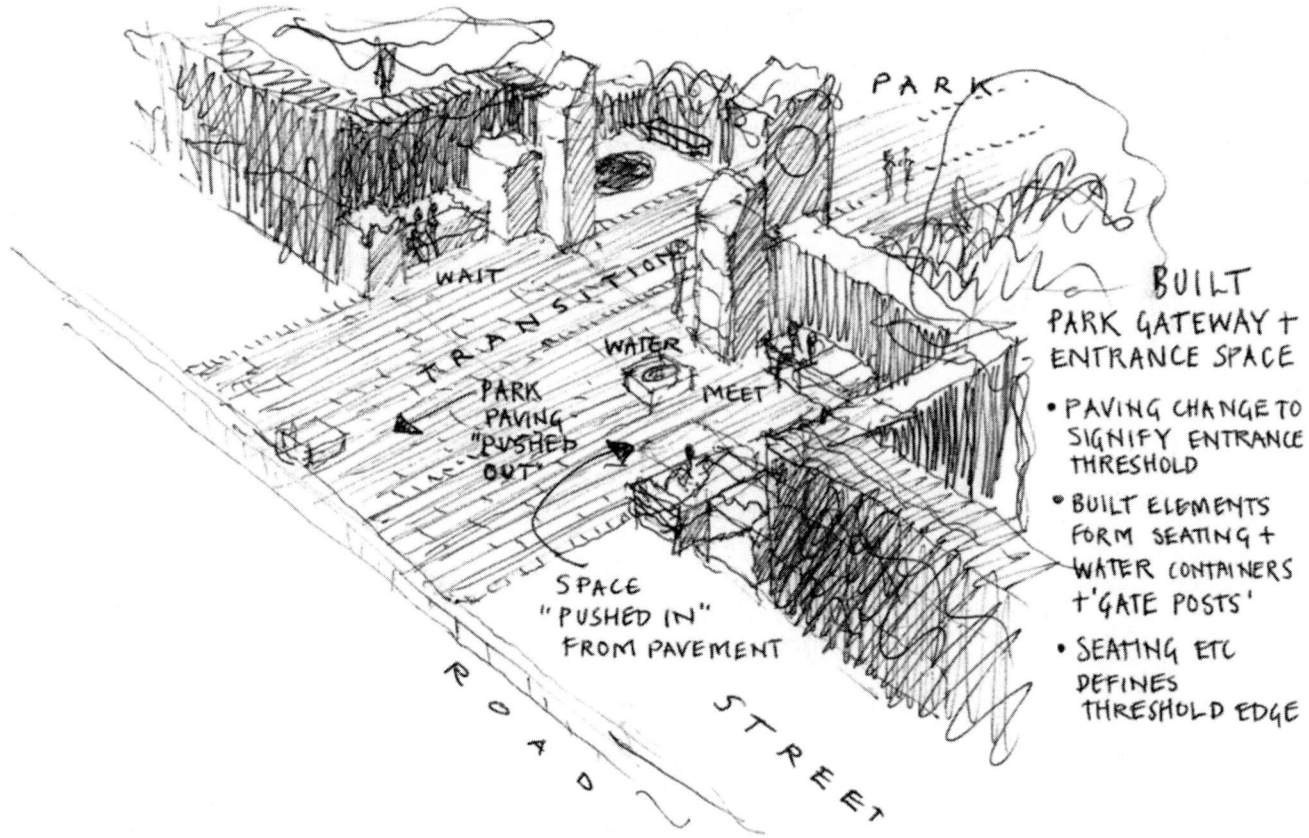

Built gateways

Structures (whether buildings, sculpture or actual gated or arched constructions) are most commonly used to mark gateway thresholds. Design considerations for the form of built gateways include purpose, appropriate scale, context and materials.

Built outdoor 'rooms'

In linking two landscape experiences or public places, built outdoor 'rooms' can provide distinct and intimate colour, textural, sound and light experiences between places. Materials and forms may be used to calm between or anticipate landscapes beyond.

Pavement

A change in paving can mark a threshold by defining a transitional space. In particular, paving changes in streets can signal building entrance thresholds. Surface materials within a building can be extended into the landscape at entrance places and vice versa.

TERRACE LINKS
HOUSE TO GARDEN
-TRANSITIONAL
BUILT SPACE
BRINGS GARDEN
"INTO" HOUSE

Terraces

Terraced thresholds can be extensions of buildings by connecting architecture to the landscape by extending floor planes into the landscape for distinct topographic relationships and recreational purposes. Terrace spaces can bring inside out and outside in.

184

Water thresholds

Water thresholds are places of, or over, water that provide connections between land and water. They provide the opportunity to be simultaneously half on land and half on water. The desire to have prospect out over water or to recreate next to water is very strong, and water threshold spaces are therefore important in providing settings for human activities.

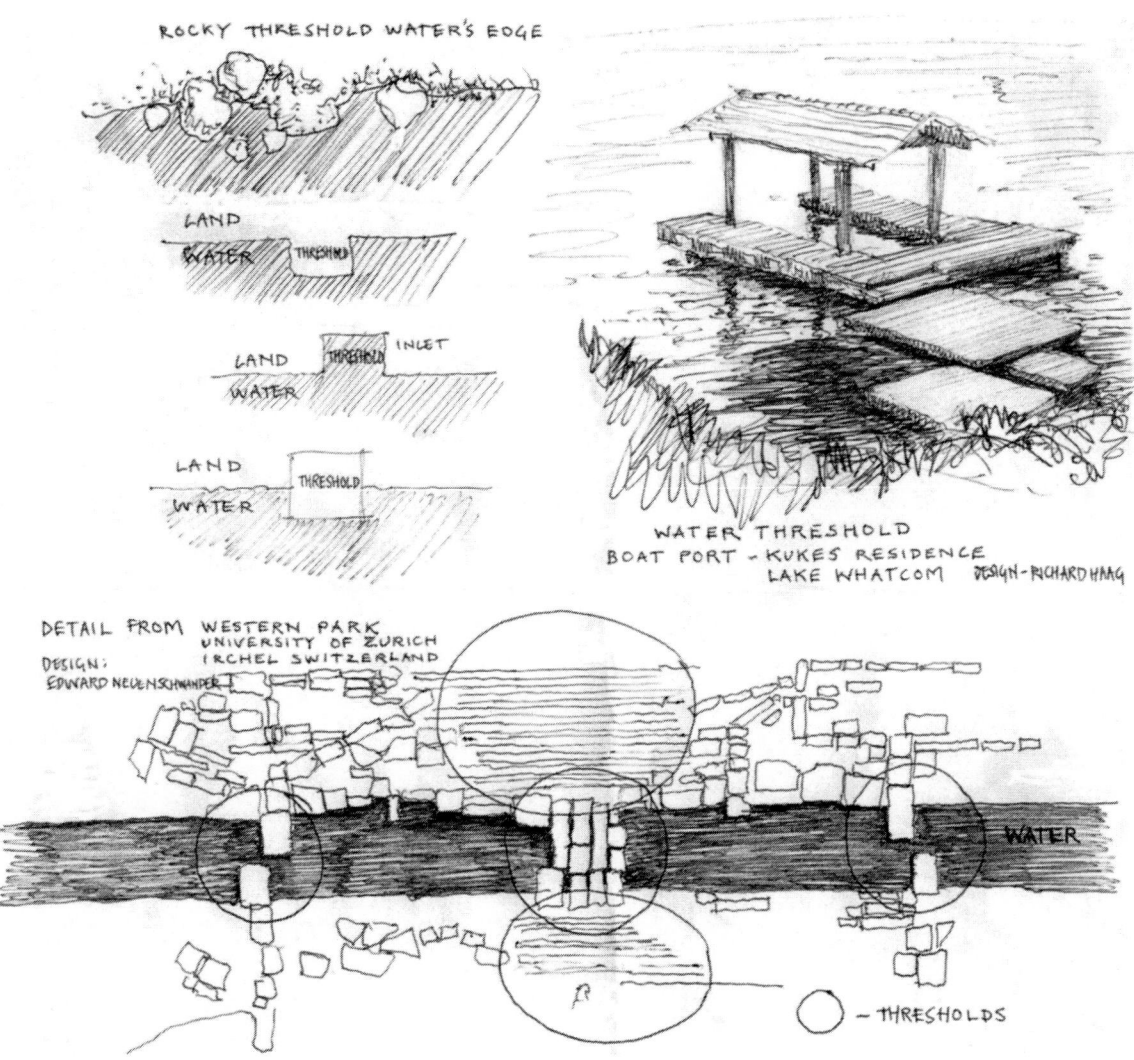

ROCKY THRESHOLD WATER'S EDGE

LAND
WATER   THRESHOLD

LAND   THRESHOLD   INLET
WATER

LAND
WATER   THRESHOLD

WATER THRESHOLD
BOAT PORT - KUKES RESIDENCE
LAKE WHATCOM   DESIGN - RICHARD HAAG

DETAIL FROM WESTERN PARK
UNIVERSITY OF ZURICH
DESIGN: IRCHEL SWITZERLAND
EDWARD NEUENSCHWANDER

WATER

○ - THRESHOLDS

Inlets and harbours

Natural or artificial inlets from larger waterbodies are natural stopping and bridging points and are therefore places of threshold. On a large scale, harbours provide threshold spaces between sea and land.

Decks and platforms

Decks and platforms out over water provide people with intimate contact with water short of bathing or paddling. Decks allow people to fish, to occupy space among wildlife and water's edge vegetation, or be surrounded by the intense light that waterbodies reflect and the sound of water lapping against structure, beach or rock.

WATER IN ENTRANCE PLACES:
- ANIMATES - RELAXES -
- WELCOMES - COOLS -
- ATTRACTS - CALMS

Water in rest and entrance places

Small waterbodies have many qualities that are desirable in threshold environments particularly in entrance and rest places. Water can simultaneously calm and animate. It can suggest the promise of larger waterbodies beyond the threshold or be associated with symbolic or actual cleansing. It can make a place very light, or alternatively damp and cool in contrast to adjoining places, or provide drinking water. Crossing over a waterbody to enter a place marks a transition.

7 Detail

This section is devoted to the physical fabric of landscape at a 'close-up' or 'immediate' scale. It explores the potential in design to provide distinct experiences through attention to detail. While previous sections have explored form and fabric at a larger or intermediate scale, this one considers surfaces, textures, light, ornament, furniture and colour at a small scale.

'Immediate' sensory experience of landscapes may often be the conceptual starting point for the design of a landscape. Therefore 'detail' does not refer to 'detailing' as a final stage in the design process, or to something added after structure and space have been created, but as an integral and fundamental consideration throughout the development of spaces, paths, edges, foci and thresholds.

This section is therefore not concerned with detailing in the sense of the design of landscape to implementation level. The purpose here is to inspire ways of thinking about the detailed 'close-up' qualities of landscapes by considering and evoking – through text and images – the diversity of sensory experiences afforded through abstract elements (colour, texture, pattern) and topography, vegetation, structures and water.

The text of this section is often 'loose' (unpunctuated). The aim is to evoke the sensory characteristics of landscape.

Definitions

Detail refers to:

- elements providing 'immediate' or 'close-up' sensory experience of landscape
- small-scale (smaller than people) structural components of landscape
- surface texture, pattern, colour and light
- furniture.

FLORA'S FEET – DRAWING OF DETAIL OF "PRIMAVERA" SANDRO BOTTICELLI
CLOSE CONTACT WITH LANDSCAPE

People's use and experience of landscape detail

Close-up experience of landscape is very different from a more distant experience of places. As we get closer to landscape elements they create different impressions, and our appreciation of them changes. Being able to touch, manipulate and interact with the landscape at an immediate scale is a very important part of landscape experience and appreciation. Touching earth, sand or grass; smelling plants; paddling in water; enables people to 'feel part of' a place. Children have a particularly close physical relationship with landscape surfaces and elements, not only because they are closer to the ground but because they investigate and learn about environments by touching and tasting.

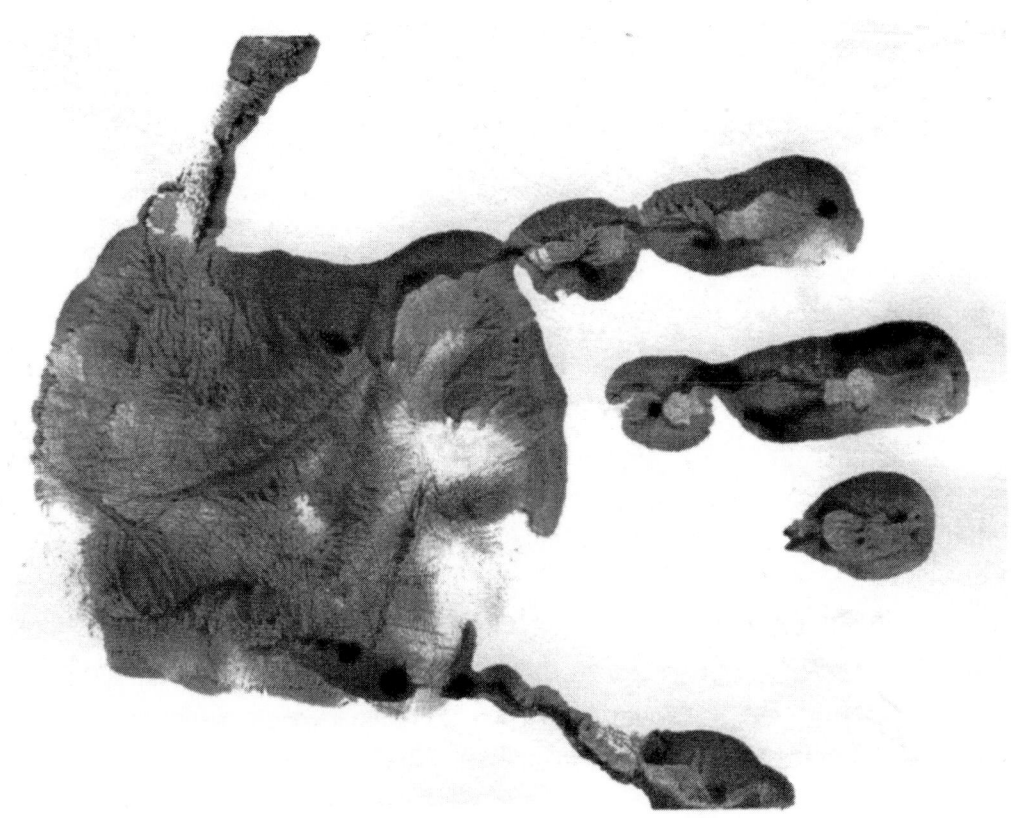

Detailed design and the senses

Design thinking at a detailed level can be enhanced by considering all the sensory experiences: sound, smell, touch and taste, as well as sight. Sight is dominant in design thinking and we tend to underestimate the strength of influence of other senses on our experience of landscape. Scents, tastes, sounds and tactile experiences all strongly influence how we feel about and use places. In particular, taste and touch provide very direct physical contact and 'join' people to environments. The non-visual senses are also dominant in evoking memories and associations, whether pleasurable or otherwise. The senses together enable us to 'make sense' of places. Stimulation of different senses also affects social activity in public places.

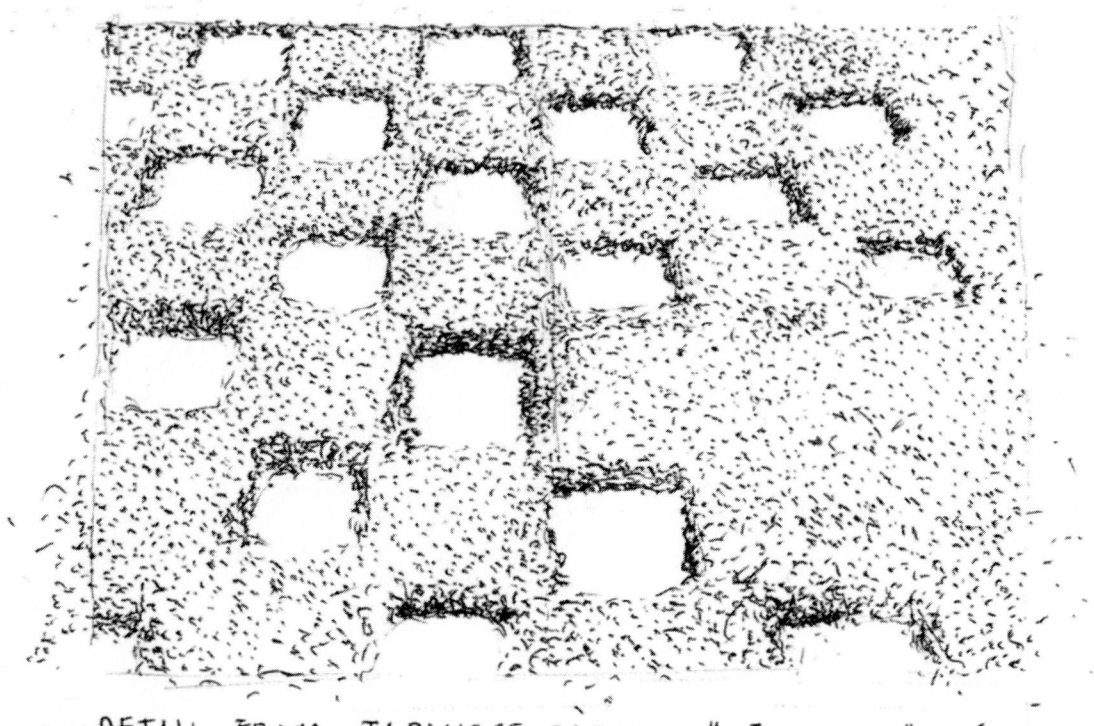

DETAIL FROM JAPANESE GARDEN -"TŌFUKU-JI" BY
SHIGEMORI MIREI (1939), IN KYOTO
PATTERN - REGULAR WITH IRREGULARITIES -
SQUARE GRANITE SLABS AMONGST MOSS.

Surface texture, pattern, colour and light

The detail of pattern, colour, texture and light are not only important in providing richness, diversity and complexity to animate landscape experience, but also in providing simplicity and coherence to unify experience. Pattern, texture, colour and light can be considered as primary abstract elements of design. Learning to manipulate and integrate these elements or qualities is an important part of design. On the following pages each of the elements is defined and some of their potential in design is summarised and illustrated.

Pattern

Pattern can refer to surface ornament such as the arrangement of paving, or to repetition of forms or types of form over an extended area. People have a 'natural' positive response to pattern as well as a desire to make patterns. Patterns enable people to identify or create order. They are visually rewarding in simultaneously possessing diversity and unity. Design generation of patterns in landscape architecture is influenced by geometry, natural forms and processes, together with patterns of use (for example, agricultural patterns or social patterns of use).

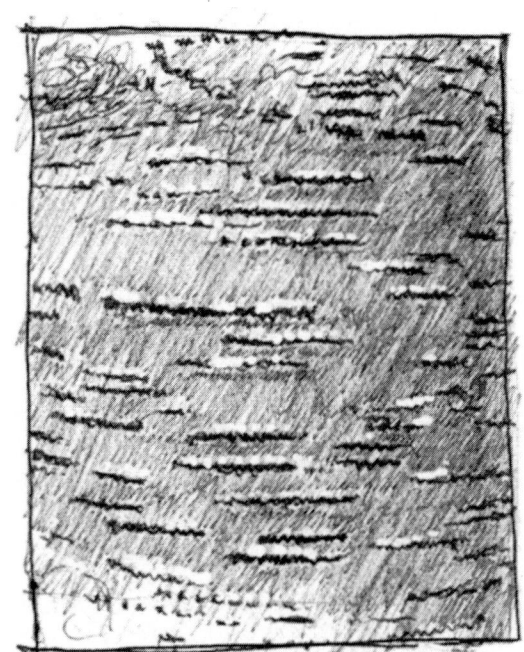

TEXTURE IN LANDSCAPE
DRAWING FROM FEININGER'S
PHOTOGRAPH "TRUNK OF
GREY BIRCH" 1964

Texture

Texture animates landscapes and enables people to connect what they see with their sense of touch. As with pattern, texture provides unity and diversity in the surface of forms. Texture can be manipulated in scale from coarse to fine and be used in juxtaposition or in gradients from rough to smooth. Texture is intimately related to light and changes in light.

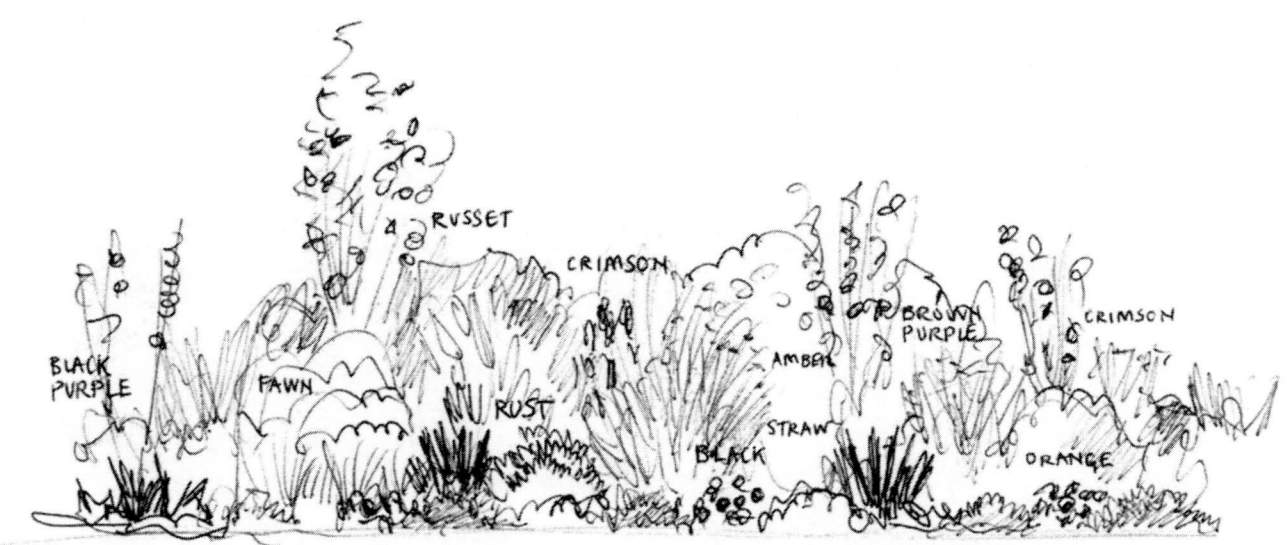

Colour

Like texture, colour is also intimately related to light and
alters significantly as light changes. Climatic considerations are essential when designing with colour. The
designer considers palettes, how many different sorts of
green there are, seasonal colour, strong and muted
tones, drabness, garishness. The designer manipulates
colour relationships.

QUALITIES OF LIGHT + TEXTURE
DRAWING AFTER PHOTOGRAPH BY W. H. FOX TALBOT
"THE STRAW STACK" c. 1840

Light

Landscape architects mostly 'design with' or within the natural 'climatic' light of the sun, cloud, mist and rain. At night, inventive lighting can enliven places. During the day, climate and its effects on light should be studied, particularly when design forms are transposed from different parts of the world with different climates.

195

Furniture

The design and siting of landscape furniture is a complex part of landscape architecture. Furniture such as seating, bollards, lighting and litter bins can either clutter or unify designed places. Designing furniture specific to a site or context is desirable in providing distinct identity to places but is expensive. Prefabricated furniture is less expensive but often fails to 'fit' or reinforce a sense of place.

Seating

Most public places lack sufficient or appropriate seating. Seating should be provided everywhere in the landscape that people wait, meet, stay or socialise. One aim of seating design, particularly in public squares, is often to integrate it with other elements to avoid the forlorn appearance of many empty seats when not in use. Sitting in the landscape enables more intimate contact with a place, especially through touch, because it provides the opportunity to pause and rest.

Earth and rock detail

RIPPLES IN SAND

Earth and rock – sight

The colour, texture and patterning of rock and earth surfaces provide distinctive landscape experiences. Muted colours and texture in particular are paradoxically soft and hard because of the way light falls on them. The surface of rocks illustrates their formation process, for example, as seen in the sedimentary layers of sandstone. Rock therefore gives an intriguing sense of both permanence and change.

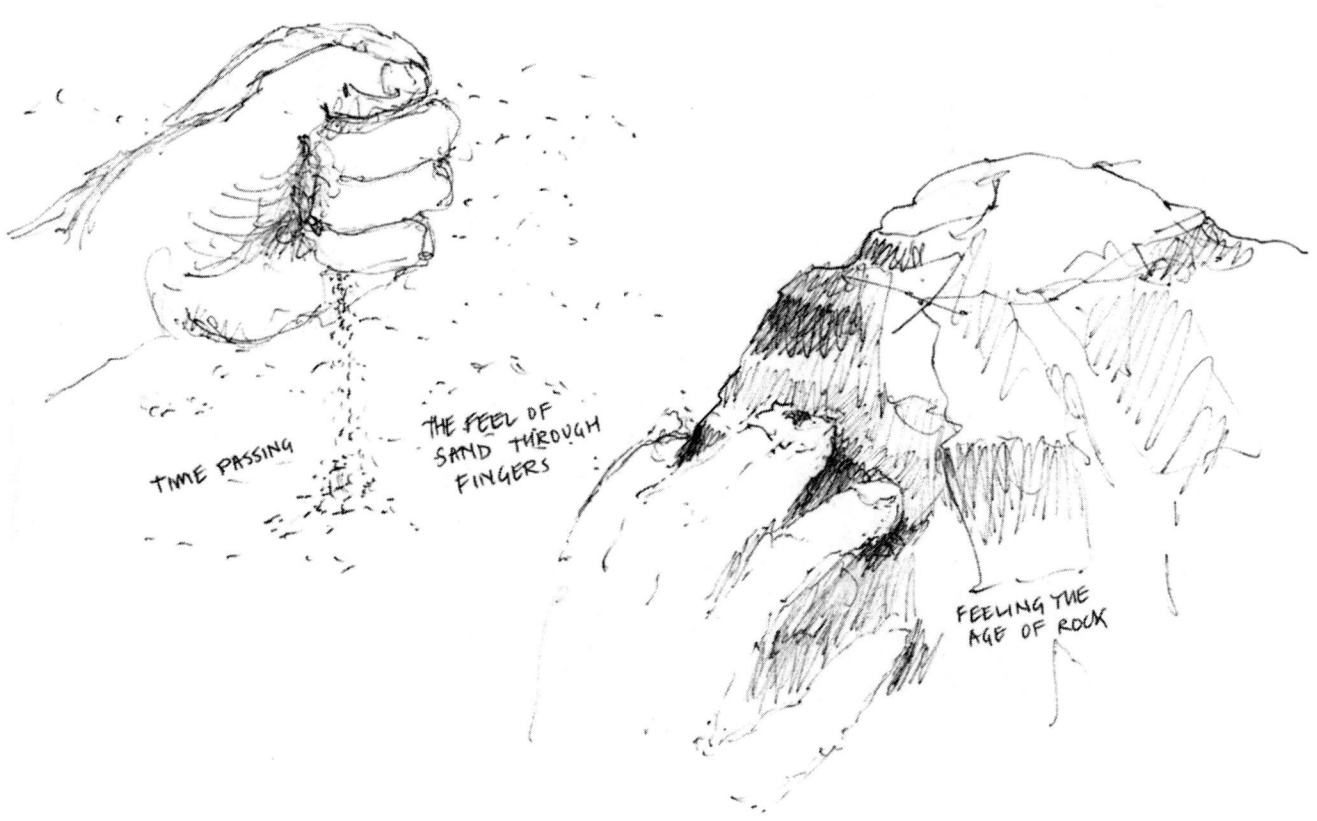

TIME PASSING

THE FEEL OF SAND THROUGH FINGERS

FEELING THE AGE OF ROCK

Earth and rock – touch

Touching silky shale or rough limestone reminds us of process and rock compostion. Feeling rock is like touching the bones of the earth. Running sand through fingers makes us acutely aware of time and process, or it can just feel pleasant. Rock is hard underfoot. Sand and earth are giving.

Earth and rock – sound

A dominance of rock surfaces in a landscape creates echo. Earth muffles sound. Stone surfaces clatter with hard-soled boots and hoofs. Stone and earth are sound barriers.

Earth and rock – smell

Rock and earth smell when damp, but not so much when dry unless dust is raised. Earth smells are very distinctive and rely on close contact with ground. Humus-rich soils have sweet rich scents. The smell of damp stone can be either attractive or unattractive.

Vegetation detail

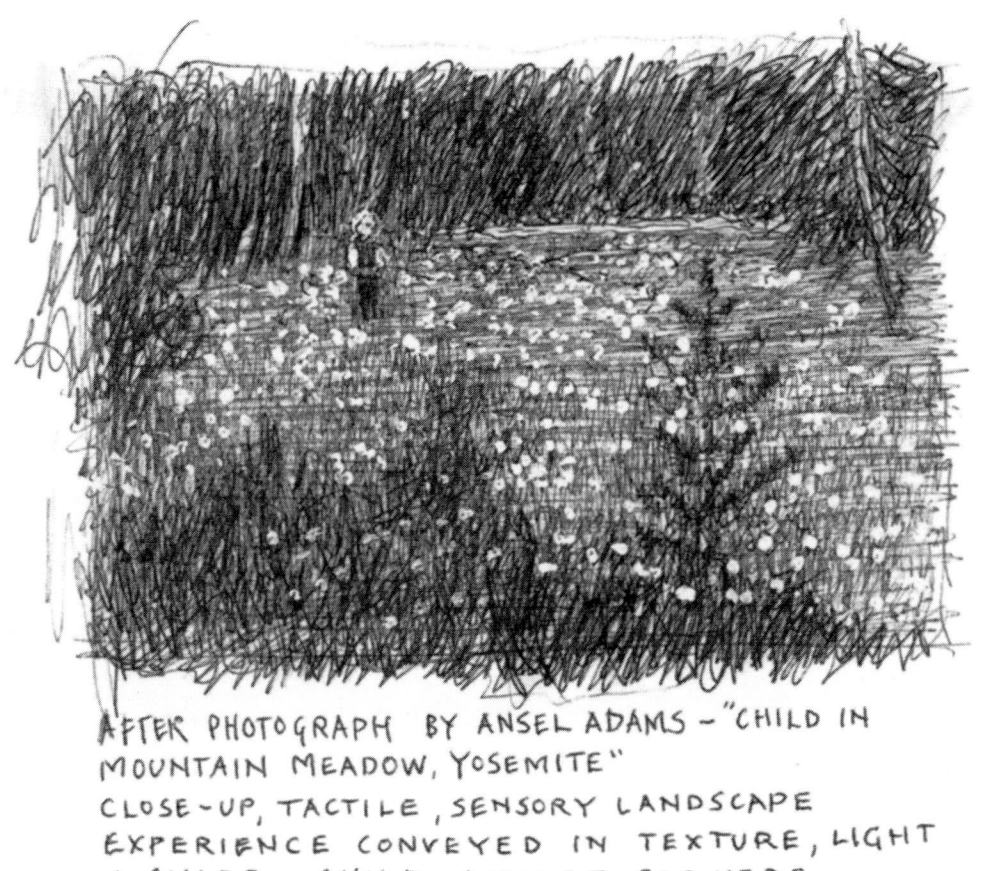

AFTER PHOTOGRAPH BY ANSEL ADAMS - "CHILD IN
MOUNTAIN MEADOW, YOSEMITE"
CLOSE-UP, TACTILE, SENSORY LANDSCAPE
EXPERIENCE CONVEYED IN TEXTURE, LIGHT
+ SHADE - CHILD AMIDST FLOWERS.

Vegetation – change and time

A very important dimension in considering the detail of
vegetation in design is the effect of linear and cyclic time.
Plants change in habit, texture and form over time as they
grow and change according to season in temperate
climates. Plants are also dynamic in character as they
move in the wind.

Vegetation – sight

The diverse and dynamic habit, colour, texture, pattern
and tone of plants make them versatile and complex
materials for design. Plants are exploited for their particular visual qualities, dense twiggy form, arching slender
growth, scarlet stems or icy blossom.

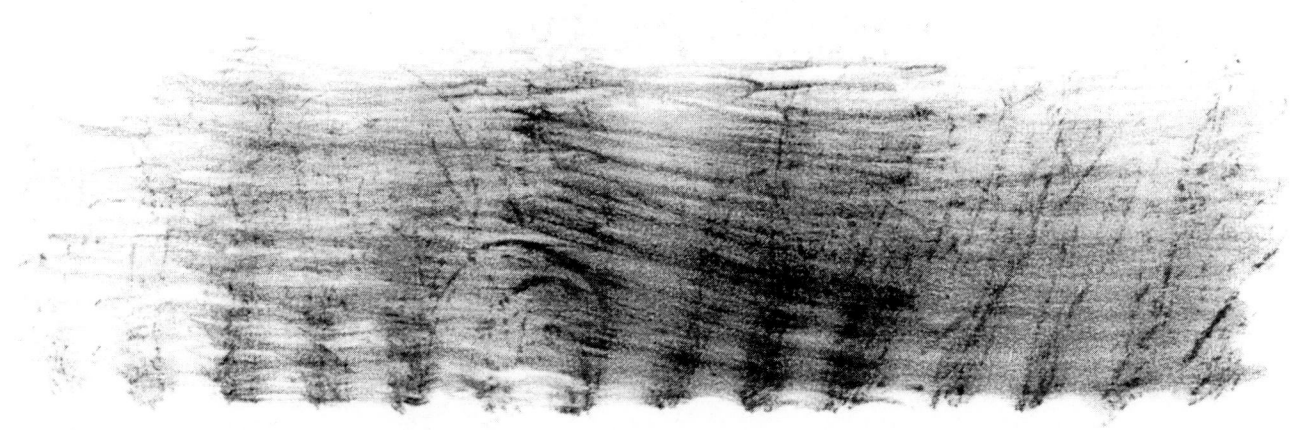

WIND IN MAIZE FIELD

Vegetation – touch

The texture of plants draws people to touch them, to experience their downy leaves or fissured bark. Robust landscapes regenerate easily when people are allowed to pick plants. Designers should play with touch, creating thorny, spiky, feathered, sappy, glossy, waxy combinations.

Vegetation – sound

Plants move in wind or when touched and therefore often create sound – the easeful susurration of reeds, grasses, corn fields and trees, the rhythm of rain beating on broad leaves. Sounds are heightened through closed eyes. Birds and cicadas sing from trees.

Vegetation – smell

The scent of plants delights. All parts of a plant smell. We are keenly tuned to this in an evolutionary way. Plant scents vary, acrid to sweet, sickly, fruity, musky. People touch plants to emit their scent more strongly.

Vegetation – taste

Landscapes produce food but food plants are rare in public landscapes: why? To prevent the unintentional vandalism of plants or because maintenance requirements are too onerous? And then there's the difficult question of food ownership. The enormous pleasure of eating from and in the landscape means that edible plants should always be a consideration in design.

Built detail

DETAIL FROM THE RINSHUN PAVILION
TIMBER POST INTERLOCKS WITH
STONE BASE

Built detail – sight

The texture, colour, pattern and tone of structures
make people love or hate them.

Built detail – touch

Encourage touching to extend appreciation and connectedness to place. Exploit the tactile properties of materials. The 'warmth' of timber comforts while the extreme cool or heat of metals can repel. Concrete is unforgiving to the touch. Stone is less so (although perhaps only through association). Glass is cool, slippery, shiny. Stainless steels are icy.

Built detail – sound

Structures can resonate through movement in wind or from objects projected against them. Structures reflect people's sound, and people make sounds from structures in landscape, rattling, tapping, drumming, chinking.

Built detail – smell

Many structures have little scent. Smells are dispersed in landscape. New timber and certain woods can scent the air. Tar and bitumen, hot pavements and rusting metal have distinctive redolence.

206

Water detail

DRAWING AFTER DETAIL FROM "A BIGGER SPLASH" DAVID HOCKNEY 1967

Water detail – sight

Like vegetation, water is varied and dynamic in appearance. Extremes of dark and light can be manipulated. Textural extremes of movement and stillness dramatise. Rhythm, ripple and the flash of dragonflies animate. Light-sparkle smoothness. Still water is a mirror to sky, plants, people and birds.

Water detail – sound

Quiet and subtle sound of water; lapping, tinkling, babbling, relax but need ambient silence. The roar and splash of fast-moving water exhilarates and masks other sounds in cities. Bird sounds echo over water surfaces. People love to make sound with water. Ice reverberates to stones skimmed on frozen lakes or crackles underfoot in glassy puddles.

HAND IN FAST-MOVING WATER

Water detail – touch

Water cools on touch. Assume that people will want to touch with hands and bare feet or bathe. Allow for wading against the drag of rushing water or being drenched by fountains. Rain on the face need not be unpleasant. Allow for dangling feet, sliding on slippery green stones and drying feet in sun on rocks.

TASTE
DEW

Water detail – taste and smell

Water vapour and water carry with them scents and
tastes. The salt of sea air, stagnancy or freshness. Mist
and rain make landscape smell very different to sunny
weather. Water changes the taste of air. Being able to
drink from water in landscapes is too rare a pleasure.

Bibliography, further reading and sources for illustrations

Form and Fabric in Landscape Architecture has been informed by a wide range of literature which it is not possible to list in total. The bibliography below lists only literature cited. The further reading list below is comprised of books which have most informed *Form and Fabric in Landscape Architecture* but are not specifically referenced in the bibliography.

Bibliography

Appleton, J. *The Experience of Landscape*, 2nd edition, Chichester, John Wiley, 1996.

Bentley, I. *et al. Responsive Environments*, London, Architectural Press, 1984.

Greenbie, B. *Spaces: Dimensions of the Human Landscape*, New Haven, Yale University Press, 1981.

Kaplan, R. and Kaplan, S. *The Experience of Nature: A Psychological Perspective*, New York, Cambridge University Press, 1989.

Lynch, K. *The Image of the City*, Cambridge Mass., MIT Press, 1960.

Further reading

Alexander, C., Ishikawa, S. and Silverstein, M. *A Pattern Language*, New York, Oxford University Press, 1977.

Bourassa, S.C. *The Aesthetics of Landscape*, London, Belhaven Press, 1991.

Gehl, J. *Life Between Buildings: Using Public Space*, 3rd edition, Copenhagen, Arkitektens Forlag, 1996.

Rutledge, A.J. *A Visual Approach to Park Design*, New York, John Wiley, 1985.

Whiston Spirn, A. *The Language of Landscape*, New Haven, Yale University Press, 1998.

Sources for illustrations

All drawings in the book have been made by the author. The following list indicates the sources and authors of photographs and plans on which drawings have been based. The authors of paintings and other artworks on which drawings have been based are indicated in the hand-written captions for the illustrations.

Page

6   Bas-relief from the Centre National d'Art et de Culture Georges Pompidou, reproduced in J. Dethier, *Down to Earth: Mud Architecture*, London, Thames and Hudson, 1982, p. 24.

7   Cover photograph from D.C. Money, *Climate and Environmental Systems*, London, Unwin Hyman, 1998.

8   Money, D.C. *Climate and Environmental Systems*, London, Unwin Hyman, 1998, p. 104.

18   Photograph by Ishimoto Yasuhiro in Teiji Itoh, *The Gardens of Japan*, 2nd edition, Tokyo and London, Kodansha International, 1998.

20   Photograph by Maki Naomi in Teiji Itoh, *The Gardens of Japan*, 2nd edition, Tokyo and London, Kodansha International, 1998.

22, 23, 24, 25
     Photographs by Art on File, Kurt Rader, Mary Randlett and Richard Haag Associates; plan by Richard Haag Associates, in Francisco Asensio-Cerver, 'Civil Engineering (Nature Conservation and Land Reclamation)', *World of Environmental Design*, 1994.

26, 27
     Plan in Francisco Asensio-Cerver, 'Urban Spaces I, Streets and Squares', *World of Environmental Design*, 1994.

28, 29
     Plan by Michel Courajoud; photographs by Gerard Dufresne in Francisco Asensio-Cerver, 'Peripheral Parks' *World of Environmental Design*, 1994.

30   Photograph by Monika Nikolic in Michael Lancaster, *The New European Landscape*, Oxford, Butterworth Architecture, 1994, p. 30.

31   Photograph from G. Jellicoe and S. Jellicoe, *Landscape of Man*, London, Thames and Hudson, 1987, p. 242; plan from K. Woodbridge, *The Stourhead Landscape*, The National Trust, 1991, p. 44.

33   Claudia Lazarro, *The Italian Renaissance Garden*, New Haven and London, Yale University Press, 1990, p. 165.

40   Photograph by Ishimoto Yasuhiro in Teiji Itoh, *The Gardens of Japan*, 2nd edition, Tokyo and London, Kodansha International, 1998.

51   'Villa Medici' in G. Jellicoe and S. Jellicoe, *Landscape of Man*, London, Thames and Hudson, 1987, p. 157.

53   Photograph from R. Fedden and R. Joekes, *The National Trust Guide*, London, Book Club Associates/Jonathan Cape, 1977, p. 243; plan from *Hidcote Manor Garden*, The National Trust, 1988, pp. 18–19.

54   Photograph by Rudolph Burckhardt, Isamu Noguchi Foundation Inc., in M. Treib (ed.), *Modern Landscape Architecture: A Critical Review*, Cambridge, Massachusetts, and London, MIT Press, 1993, p. 52.

55   Jellicoe, G. and Jellicoe, S. *Landscape of Man*, London, Thames and Hudson, 1987, p. 103 and p. 298.

58   'Parc de la Villeneuve' in Francisco Asensio-Cerver, 'Peripheral Parks', *World of Environmental Design,* 1994; 'Barrows' in P. Coones and J. Patten, *The Penguin Guide to the Landscape of England and Wales,* Penguin, 1986, p. 77.

60   Jellicoe, G. and Jellicoe, S. *Landscape of Man,* London, Thames and Hudson, 1987, p. 160.

61   Woodbridge, K. *The Stourhead Landscape,* The National Trust, 1991, p. 48.

70   Moughtin, C. *Urban Design: Street and Square,* 2nd edition, Oxford, Architectural Press, 1999, p. 110.

72   Jellicoe, G. and Jellicoe, S. *Landscape of Man,* London, Thames and Hudson, 1987, pp. 168–9.

74   Robinson, B. W. *Persian Drawings from the 14th through the 19th Century,* Boston and Toronto, Victoria and Albert Museum and Little, Brown and Company, 1965, p. 102.

75   'Pracas', Plate 11 in A. Cabrera, M. Nuñes and H. Ruas, *Olhar o Chao,* Industrias Lever Portuguesa Lda. Imprensa Nacional-Casa Moeda.

76   Wylson, A. *Aquatecture: Architecture and Water,* London, Architectural Press, 1986, p. 180.

77   Plan of 'Otake Rika' based on 'Sakutei-kihisho' by Hisatsune Shuji, published by Seibundo Shiakosha, 1979 and reproduced in Teiji Itoh, *The Gardens of Japan,* 2nd edition, Tokyo and London, Kodansha International, 1998.

78   Photograph of the work of Luis Barragán by Susan Seidman, in S. Wrede and H.W. Adams, *Denatured Visions: Landscape and Culture in the Twentieth Century,* New York, The Museum of Modern Art, 1991, p. 50.

79   'Auditorium Plaza' photograph by Angela Danadijieva in A. Wylson, *Aquatecture: Architecture and Water,* London, Architectural Press, 1986, p. 181.

82   Cooper, G. and Taylor, G. *Paradise Transformed: The Private Garden for the Twenty-first Century,* New York, Monacelli Press, 1996, p. 53.

95   Photograph by Alain Provost in Francisco Asensio-Cerver, 'Urban Spaces I, Streets and Squares', *World of Environmental Design,* 1994.

98   Photograph by Ralph Lieberman in Lazarro, Claudia, *The Italian Renaissance Garden,* New Haven and London, Yale University Press, 1990.

100   Crowe, Sylvia and Mitchell, M. *The Pattern of Landscape,* Chichester, Packard (Applied Ecology, Landscape and Natural Resource Management Series), 1988.

102   Photograph from The Harry Smith Horticultural Photographic Collection in M. Balston, *The Well-Furnished Garden,* London, Mitchell Beazley, 1990, p. 156.

106   Jacobs, A. *Great Streets,* Cambridge, Massachussetts, and London, MIT Press, 1993.

108   *Elements and Total Concept of Urban Pavement Design,* Graphic-sha Publishing Co., 1990, p. 202.

116   Lazarro, Claudia, *The Italian Renaissance Garden,* New Haven and London, Yale University Press, 1990.

122   *The Real Thing : An Anthology of British Photographs 1840–1950,* Arts Council of Great Britain, 1975, p. 42.

124   'Comb of the Wind' in M. Lancaster, *The New European Landscape,* Oxford, Butterworth Architecture, 1994, p. 86.

137   Rudofsky, Bernard. *Architecture without Architects,* Garden City, New York, Doubleday and Company, 1964, p. 5.

145   Photograph by Dave Paterson in J. Beardsley, *Earthworks and Beyond: Contemporary Art in the Landscape,* New York, Abbeville Press, 1989, p. 73.

146 Jellicoe, G. and Jellicoe, S. *Landscape of Man*, London, Thames and Hudson, 1987, p. 293.

147 Photograph by IGA Stuttgart, in M. Lancaster, *The New European Landscape*, Oxford, Butterworth Architecture, 1994, p. 39.

151 Photograph of Hart Plaza by Balthazar Korab, in J. Beardsley, *Earthworks and Beyond: Contemporary Art in the Landscape*, New York, Abbeville Press, 1989, p. 132.

152 *The Real Thing: An Anthology of British Photographs 1840–1950*, Arts Council of Great Britain, 1975, p. 107.

153 Jellicoe, G. and Jellicoe, S. *Landscape of Man*, London, Thames and Hudson, 1987, p. 96.

155 Lazarro, Claudia, *The Italian Renaissance Garden*, New Haven and London, Yale University Press, 1990.

156 Muyu-Uray Theatres in Bernard Rudofsky, *Architecture without Architects*, Garden City, New York, Doubleday and Company, 1964, p. 8.

160 Lennox-Boyd, A. and Perry, C. *Traditional English Gardens*, Weidenfeld & Nicolson, 1987, p. 152.

163 Jellicoe, G. and Jellicoe, S. *Landscape of Man*, London, Thames and Hudson, 1987, p. 232.

164 Burl, A. *The Stone Circles of Britain*, London, Yale University Press, 1976, p. 39.

186 'Richard Haag Jetty' in G. Cooper and G. Taylor, *Paradise Transformed: The Private Garden for the Twenty-first Century*, New York, Monacelli Press, 1996, p. 41; 'Western Park' in M. Lancaster, *The New European Landscape*, Oxford, Butterworth Architecture, 1994, p. 32–3.

189 Centre Culturel du Marais, Exhibition Catalogue, *Claude Monet at the Time of Giverny*, 1983.

192 Photograph by Matsumura Yoshihara in Teiji Itoh, *The Gardens of Japan*, 2nd edition, Tokyo and London, Kodansha International, 1998.

193 Hattersley, R. *Andreas Feininger*, Morgan and Morgan, 1973, p. 51.

195 *The Real Thing: An Anthology of British Photographs 1840–1950*, Arts Council of Great Britain, 1975, p. 38.

201 Adams, Ansel and Newhall, Nancy. *This is the American Earth*, San Francisco, Sierra Club, 1960, p. 102.

205 Photograph by Norman F. Carver Jnr., in J. Ormsbee-Simonds, *Landscape Architecture*, New York, F.W. Dodge Corporation, 1961, p. 38.